DATE DUE

MAR 23 '90			

DEMCO 38-297

SOCIAL ENGINEERING IN FAMILY MATTERS

Burton Mindick

PRAEGER

PRAEGER SPECIAL STUDIES • PRAEGER SCIENTIFIC

New York • Philadelphia • Eastbourne, UK
Toronto • Hong Kong • Tokyo • Sydney

Library of Congress Cataloging-in-Publication Data

Mindick, Burton.
    Social engineering in family matters.

    Bibliography: p.
    Includes index.
    1. Family policy—United States.   2. Family
social work—New York (State)—Syracuse—Case
studies.   I. Title.
HV699.M52   1985   362.8′ 25′ 0973   85-6595
ISBN 0-03-001477-8 (alk. paper)

Published in 1986 by Praeger Publishers
CBS Educational and Professional Publishing, a Division of CBS Inc.
521 Fifth Avenue, New York, NY 10175 USA

© 1986 by Praeger Publishers

6789 052 987654321

Printed in the United States of America on acid-free paper

INTERNATIONAL OFFICES

Orders from outside the United States should be sent to the appropriate address listed below. Orders from areas not listed below should be placed through CBS International Publishing, 383 Madison Ave., New York, NY 10175 USA

Australia, New Zealand
Holt Saunders, Pty. Ltd., 9 Waltham St., Artarmon, N.S.W. 2064, Sydney, Australia

Canada
Holt, Rinehart & Winston of Canada, 55 Horner Ave., Toronto, Ontario, Canada M8Z 4X6

Europe, the Middle East, & Africa
Holt Saunders, Ltd., 1 St. Anne's Road, Eastbourne, East Sussex, England BN21 3UN

Japan
Holt Saunders, Ltd., Ichibancho Central Building, 22-1 Ichibancho, 3rd Floor, Chiyodaku, Tokyo, Japan

Hong Kong, Southeast Asia
Holt Saunders Asia, Ltd., 10 Fl, Intercontinental Plaza, 94 Granville Road, Tsim Sha Tsui East, Kowloon, Hong Kong

Manuscript submissions should be sent to the Editorial Director, Praeger Publishers, 521 Fifth Avenue, New York, NY 10175 USA

For Ruth
My research assistant, confidante, friend, and wife
who brings such joy to my own family matters
For Joey and Susie,
my own beloved children
and
For all our mothers, fathers, and children who deserve
the best of our caring, concern, knowledge, and resources as
they grow together.

ACKNOWLEDGMENTS

Most grateful acknowledgement is made to the Carnegie Corporation of New York for research support to the author and to co-investigators William Cross, Jr., Moncrieff Cochran, and Urie Bronfenbrenner. Special thanks are due our project officer and corporation vice-president, Mrs. Barbara Finberg, for her patience, vision, and steadfast encouragement of the research effort over many years. The views expressed here, however, are those of the author alone, and not necessarily those of the Carnegie Corporation.

Also to be acknowledged with thanks is Human Sciences Press for permission to reprint portions of a research paper written by the present author and Eulas Boyd in sections of Chapter Four of this volume. The original paper is entitled, "A Multi-Level, Bipolar View of the Urban Residential Environment: Local Community vs. Mass Societal Forces," and appears in *Population and Environment: Behavioral and Social Issues,* 5(4), 221-41.

The author is indebted to Urie Bronfenbrenner, Moncrieff Cochran, William Cross, Nancy Gilgosch, Ken Hodges, Edward Kain, Ralph Taylor, and several anonymous reviewers for helpful comments on a prior draft of portions of this manuscript. I am particularly grateful to process analyst Gloria Cox who read and commented knowledgeably upon the entire manuscript. I learned much from the above commentators, but any errors must be laid at my doorstep.

Much of what was achieved in this research project was the result of the intelligent, creative, and careful work of process analysts Eulas Boyd, Gloria Cox, and Jane Serkland. Also to be acknowledged with gratitude are the efforts of Ann Brinton, Valerie Caracelli, Marian Grabowitz, Steven Hall, Maxine Heffron, and Anne Pierce. Special thanks go to Mary Larner for her bibliographic assistance and knowledgeable perspectives on early childhood intervention programs.

A profound debt of gratitude is owed to members of the Family Matters Program staff and its director, Frank Woolever. I want to express similar feelings of thanks to liaison staffer Bebe Cook and particularly for the valuable contribution to our efforts by Mary Maples as well as to members of the outcome research and analysis teams led by Nancy Burston and Charles Henderson, and especially to analysis team member Liz Kiely. I would also like to recognize the substantive and moral support of various Cornell staff members beginning with Gerri Jones and Kay Stickane through and including Ray Rist, my earliest mentor in the study of process; the immediate past chair of the Department of Human Development and Family Studies, Phillip Schoggen; and College of Human Ecology dean, Jerome Ziegler. I would like to thank the staff and directors of the Cornell Institute for Social and Economic Research and its directors, Bob McGinnis and Tim Mount, and especially Jean Pearson. All of the above persons have been supportive of the research and have been highly cooperative, giving me the benefit of their thinking and project-related experience. I am especially thankful to my colleagues Urie Bronfenbrenner, Mon Cochran, and Bill Cross for their patience in allowing me to look over their shoulders as designers and movers of the Family Matters Program while they carried out their work.

A special vote of gratitude must be registered for John Lemley, the administrative manager of the Ecology of Human Development project, for his attention to technical details in making the operation run on a day-to-day basis.

Thanks also go to Praeger editor George Zimmer for his patience and help, especially when unforeseen problems of considerable magnitude threatened the completion of the manuscript.

My deepest thanks, however, must be reserved for my wife and research assistant, Ruth Mindick, who typed and indexed the manuscript, collected, coded, and analyzed a fair portion of the data, and did bibliographic research with a degree of accuracy and intelligence that would delight most any boss, and who not only excused me from family recreation and responsibility so that I could work on this manuscript but also gave of what would normally be her own family and leisure time so that we could almost meet our originally scheduled publishing deadline.

Thank you and bless you all.

CONTENTS

1

THE PASSION FOR PROGRESS

From the earliest annals of our species to present day headlines, there is abundant evidence of a human striving to better life's circumstances for oneself, for one's fellows, or for some abstract world condition. This fixation to fix can be seen in circumstances as mundane as those that prevail in the average U.S. household when a paterfamilias decides to challenge personally his home's leaky plumbing (rather than engaging the services of a professional), and time, family, dinner, and social engagements are all forgotten in a kind of manic attempt to mend. We might include under the heading of a passion for betterment such examples of human behavior as: reaching for greater financial security, efforts at nest feathering of various kinds, and self-improvement endeavors ranging from training in the use of personal computers to aerobic exercise.

SOCIAL BETTERMENT

Perhaps even more interesting than those enterprises aimed at bettering one's own circumstances are those that seem intended to help others. Charitable efforts, evangelistic endeavors, attempts to promote world peace, the pursuit of scientific truth, interventions into the social order (especially those designed to ameliorate the lot of economically disadvantaged persons) — in short, the drive to promote what we construe to be *progress* has been with us for millenia. Ofttimes the emotions of those who advocate and/or carry out such efforts at social betterment run strongly and deeply. Lally (1982), for example, has confessed with unusual candor the intensity of his feelings about his "Family Development Research Program" carried out in Syracuse, New York. Using the phrase of Tolstoy, he says that the program was for him, for most of its staff, and for many of its families "a passionate affection."

While the sentiments of others who strive for progress may not be quite as strong, we will have occasion to note later in this chapter that both the conative and the affective components which underlie our ameliorative efforts are forces very much to be reckoned with. Some of the elements of this striving for human betterment are contained in a delightful tale recounted as factual by Kertzer (1976, pp. 110-12). But whether wholly factual or not, a content analysis of the story's key elements is most instructive.

PLOTTING FOR PLOTS' SAKE

According to Kertzer's account, in the mid-1920s a religious group that had recently acquired land for use as a cemetery found itself confronted by a reluctance on the part of its members to allow their deceased relatives to become the first to be buried in newly established "hallowed ground." To eliminate the problem of "lone-liness" in the new cemetery, the congregational board decided to break the ice by *contriving* the first burial. A home for the aged in a nearby community was contacted and a set of incentives was offered to any resident who met the following qualifications: (1) the person was to have no living relatives; (2) have little in the way of financial resources; and most important of all, (3) be in poor physical health.

An indigent 78-year-old, completely alone in the world and having a variety of ailments, any one of which might be considered terminal, was found, and the congregational board offered him an attractive package of benefits. The old man was to receive the sum of 25 dollars a week for the rest of his life and would be accorded free burial, if he agreed to sign a document authorizing his burial to take place in the congregation's new cemetery. The sickly senior citizen is said to have signed the document unhesitatingly, feeling that he had struck an excellent bargain. The congregational committee left the home for the elderly satisfied, believing that they had not only solved their cemetery problem at what they calculated to be a very modest cost (surely, the old man would not live more than a month), but they could also take satisfaction in having benefited someone eminently worthy of their largesse.

After several months passed, however, when the committee had received no request for the burial of the old gentleman and with the financial outlays continuing, they inquired at the old-age home where they had found the object of their charity, only to learn that he had moved out just the day before and had taken his own apartment. Several months later, the congregational board found out that using their weekly stipend, the former indigent had made a down-payment on a grocery store in a nearby state. By year's end, the abashed committee found that one whom they had seen virtually at death's door had recently taken a wife, and the two were managing their thriving grocery store. Kertzer provides no more details about the fate of the congregational cemetery or, more important, about the former pauper. But interestingly, he speculates at the end of the account that, "Conceivably, his grocery store was absorbed by a giant conglomerate, and he is now one of its vice-presidents" (p. 112).

THE ELEMENTS OF OUR
EXPECTATIONS FOR PROGRESS

As mentioned above, there are elements present in this story that are worthy of our consideration because they appear to be present in many of the attempts at human betterment throughout the ages, not excluding those of our own day. In bare-bones outline and expressed in terms of latter day social engineering, the story of the old age home resident might run as follows. An elderly, lonely, indigent in ill health received from the private sector a relatively modest transfer payment (although 25 dollars in the mid-1920s was by no means a pittance), and within a very short period of time, he achieved financial independence, considerably improved health, was gainfully employed, and won the companionship of a wife who also became gainfully employed and financially secure. Interestingly enough, even this multifaceted miracle is insufficient for Kertzer in his vicarious aspirations for his hero. Kertzer speculates that perhaps the old man is still alive today (by my calculations he would have to be nearly 130), and a giant of commerce sitting on the executive board of a conglomerate.

The elements present in this story that are of interest to us in this context are: (1) a relatively modest intervention results in (2) a change in the fortunes of a disadvantaged member of society in ways that are profound and manifold, (3) over a very brief period of time, (4) with little apparent effort on the part of the beneficiary, and (5) the outcome is one of unalloyed happiness, except, perhaps, for the congregational board still trying unsuccessfully to peddle its unsold cemetery plots. From their perspective, their intervention turned out to produce, like many another in history, effects opposite to those intended.

THE ELEMENTS OF ACHIEVEMENT MOTIVATION

What is of most concern to us in the present analysis, however, is the elderly hero of Kertzer's narrative, with whom most of our sympathies are likely to lie, and the five elements distinguished above. It seems appropriate to contrast the major components in the account of his achievements with those in stories typifying achievement motivation in recognized research. The work of Mc-Clelland and his associates (1953) provides an excellent contrast in the major components that have been found to characterize stories of achievement produced under various conditions of external stimulation. McClelland et al. (1953) conceptualize accounts of achievement motivation in terms of three or sometimes four elements: (1) the person seeking to achieve, (2) any obstacles to that achievement, (3) the goal to be attained, and (4) any person who may or may not be present who sympathizes with the would-be achiever and hence provides "nurturant press." Within this framework, which is in effect a story outline, McClelland et al. distinguish three processes that must be present in the stories composed under thematic apperception test (TAT) stimulation if optimal levels of achievement motivation are to be inferred. There must be "success in competition with some standard of excellence, unique accomplishment, and long-term involvement."

ASPIRATIONS FOR SOCIAL PROGRESS
VERSUS ACHIEVEMENT MOTIVATION

Analyzing our story of the erstwhile old-age home resident turned entrepreneur in terms of these processes, we find little in the way of information about competition with some standard of excellence in McClelland's sense. No instrumental acts in attainment of the goal are described — e.g., "the old man and his wife worked very hard," or "for long hours," or "they provided high quality merchandise or services." The success achieved, especially as Kertzer (1976) projectively embellishes the tale with the old man attaining conglomerate board membership, is quite disproportionate to the effort expended. It seems to be all a matter of luck.

As for "unique achievement" in McClelland's terms, success in business activity generally would not by itself be considered unique, certainly not on a par with the usual examples of artistic creation, scientific invention, or other "extraordinary accomplishments" (1953, p. 113). It is only the age and infirmity of the hero (by no means trivial disadvantages) that make the achievement remarkable.

Finally, the third criterion process for achievement motivation, long-term involvement, is totally lacking. The stipend is provided, and within a few months the old gentleman has moved out of the institution. Soon he is in his own apartment and in business. By the end of the year he is married and the grocery store is thriving. A favorite U.S. theme, "get rich quick," in this tale is accompanied by "get well soon," and "get hitched quick," forming a medley of happy motifs of almost instant gratification.

Referring to other elements that are considered important in any narrative that is supposed to embody achievement motivation, the obstacles seem nonexistent. Not only is marketplace competition easily overcome, but mastered also are old age, illness, and loneliness. All of this, of course, comes about because of a heavy dose of "nurturant press," i.e., the 25 dollar-a-week stipend.

HOW READY ARE WE TO BETTER SUCCESSFULLY?

We must concede, of course, that this example is of our own choosing and that Kertzer's account (1976) was not composed in response to TAT stimulation. But the last is irrelevant, since Mc-Clelland has demonstrated the presence of achievement motivation themes in children's books from several disparate cultures in terms similar to those used for analyzing the results of formalized projective testing (McClelland, 1961). As for the former objection, the question of whether our aspirations for social betterment are somehow typified by the Kertzer tale (1976), this volume will attempt to probe the question of whether one of the key elements in the nonsuccess of so many of our contemporary social programs is our passion for progress, our fixation to fix without an awareness of just what is involved in such an achievement.

Our assumptions seem to have been that basic human nature and underlying social structure are inherently and almost unequivocally positive and amenable to change — a set of premises that is probably grounded in the environmental determinism that is so much a part of U.S. culture (anyone can do anything, given a chance), and the very strong predilection for "nurture" over "nature" in U.S. social science. Zigler (1979) has referred to this bias as "the environmental mystique," that ". . . held essentially, that young children are so malleable that rather minimal intervention in the early years will have major and lasting impact" (Ibid. p. 501).

Unhappily, our expectations seem to have been that with just a bit of tinkering, massive social problems will be loosened from their strangling grip upon us and perhaps even disappear. Or, to use the kind of martial metaphor that was so popular a few decades ago, as a result of this unfortunate underestimate of the strength "of the enemy," we have gone into battle prepared for too short a campaign, very much underequipped and underweaponed, at the very least (cf. Pilisuk and Pilisuk, *How We Lost the War on Poverty*, 1973). It has also been suggested that possibly some of our social ills are just plain intractable, or if remediable, only at costs too great to be borne, not only in financial terms but in terms of the side effects of the remedy.

THE RECORD OF SOCIAL PROGRAMS
OF THE PAST THREE DECADES

Consequently, our political leaders have vacillated between ardent advocacy of social engineering and trenchant criticism and despair (cf. Moynihan, *Maximum Feasible Misunderstanding*, 1969 and Moynihan, *The Politics of a Guaranteed Income*, 1973). But clearly, whatever political leaders may say or do, scholarly assessments of many of the programs designed to better our society during the 1950s and the 1960s are overwhelmingly negative (Weiss 1972). Findings of no effect or dubious effect are the norm. Or, as Berman and McLaughlin (1978, p. 209) have put it, "If one word can describe the experience of social reformers during the past decade, it is frustration." Perhaps Elmore (1978) has stated the case most poignantly. "The big ideas that have shaped social policy — maximum feasible participation, equality of opportunity, self-sufficiency, compensatory treatment . . . seem to have become caricatures of themselves the moment they ceased to be ideas and began to be translated into action" (p. 186).

Despite these abundant nonfindings, some advocates of betterment efforts, and among them social scientists, have attempted to justify certain interventions on the grounds that if they do no good, they also do no harm, and are the kind of thing that society ought to be doing for its own moral well-being (cf. Stember, 1968). Lerman (1968), for example, has concluded that although certain treatment programs for delinquents have no appreciable effect on future recidivism, such programs ought to be continued because they are more humane than other alternatives.

By contrast, however, there is today a heightened awareness of the potential for negative side effects produced by social programs. This awareness has "fanned the embers of a neo-Spencerian revolt against government intervention of any sort" (Sieber, 1981, p. 11). Proponents of programs of the kind launched during the Great Society era see the negative fallout of such efforts as far smaller than the magnitude of the benefits they conferred. Levitan and Taggart (1976, p. 9), for example, argue that "the negative spillover of social welfare efforts were too frequently overstated and were usually unavoidable concomitants of the desired changes." But not only is the cost-benefit ratio of many programs still at issue, the even thornier question of reverse effects has been raised. For example, Forrester (1971) has presented convincing evidence that many of the urban redevelopment programs of the 1950s and 1960s, though ostensibly designed to provide low-income housing and generally to help the poor, have had the opposite effect. Forrester (1971) argues that such projects have often increased crowding and *reduced* the amount of available housing, attracted a greater number of economically disadvantaged persons to the cities, displaced central city businesses; and in the absence of adequate mass transit, they have thus *increased poverty*, since the working poor can no longer reach the jobs that have migrated to the urban periphery or the suburbs.

More recently, there have also been allegations that some social programs, for example our welfare system, *create* and *maintain* poverty rather than diminish it (Grace, 1984). More generally, Sieber (1981) has catalogued an impressive array of interventions attempted by both liberal and conservative ideologues that have had outcomes opposite those intended. Sieber has characterized these as "fatal remedies." Sieber also points out that while advocates of certain interventions may be willing to accept some bad along with what they regard as the greater good produced by their pet programs, it is far harder to justify efforts that boomerang, i.e., that produce harm precisely in the areas where they seek to help.

Auerbach (1974) has sounded similar notes of alarm. Interpreting Burkean political conservatism in the *International Encyclopedia of the Social Sciences*, Auerbach has cautioned, "If we insist on imposing the simple perfection of a logical ideal on an imperfect, complex reality, we shall only succeed in destroying both the amount of good that already exists and the limited improvements that are feasible" (p. 222). But whether the social programs of the past several decades have been regressive or just plain ineffective, the predominant scholarly view of such interventions has been far from encouraging.

This disappointment has not been confined to university scholars nor has it been limited in the breadth of its implications. Indeed Sieber (1981) points to a "plague of pessimism" about the idea of progress among Western intellectuals and a large segment of the public. Writing in the same vein, Henshel warns, "The sense of progress is dead among the intelligentsia . . ." and "Having long ago lost their faith in God, they are losing their faith in themselves and in human action" (1976, p. 50). Sieber quotes Nisbet's view that our literature, art, philosophy, theology, and science show that "disbelief, doubt and disillusionment have taken over" (1980, p. 318). Banfield's (1974, p. ix) work is adduced to the effect that the nature of man and society preclude solution of our serious problems by rational management. "Indeed by trying we are certain to make things worse" (Ibid.).

WHY DIDN'T BETTERMENT WORK?

In response to the "bad news" evaluations of our efforts at social change and the generalized pessimism about programs, proponents have responded in a number of ways. One of the more common arguments is that our interventions have been good both in concept and in execution. The failing has been in their intensity, scope, and duration. Implicitly, this argument claims that if only more effort, resources, money, and/or authoritative approval for social programs were present, then success would surely be achieved (cf. Levitan and Taggart's 1976 volume *The Promise of Greatness.*)

For example, Harrington (1974), responding to Moynihan's criticism of federal programs of the previous decade as being too intrusive, has argued that such pervasive government intervention *"never took place"* (italics in original), because sufficient funds were not allocated for such purposes — this despite the fact that between 1965 and 1970 the percentage of federal civilian expenditures as a proportion of GNP *nearly doubled*. Such an argument is hard to contradict, and indeed there can be little question that in the best of all possible worlds, if one could spend enough money and exert enough effort over a sufficiently wide area, and over a long enough time period, better outcomes might be expected in at least some instances. This, however, would not be true for Sieber's (1981) and Auerbach's (1974) regressive programs, where perseverance and greater intensity would only make matters worse. The remedies would cause still more fatalities.

In addition, society's priorities do not always permit unlimited allocations of resources to increasingly smaller problem areas. As Rossi (1966) pointed out long ago, the most easily remediable areas of many social problems have already been treated effectively by many broad-gauge relatively inexpensive interventions in our society and the "soft sides" of these problems have already yielded to ameliorative efforts. Thus, earlier in this century universal education, prenatal care, and public-health standards for sanitation produced an extremely high standard of living in the western world relative to other parts of the globe in areas such as literacy, infant mortality, and longevity. As Rossi keenly notes, the easiest parts of these problems have been solved. It is the more obdurate aspects of social ills that remain. Just possibly, it is only highly intensive, or individualized (and thus highly costly) efforts that can cure the remainder of the more intractable ills.

Such efforts may be costly not only in financial terms, but also in human resource allocation, in the size and intrusiveness of government, as well as in the side effects of any decision to take a specific course of action. This last element, the fact that any action decision in human behavior involves both risks and benefits is one that is only recently reemerging in our awareness of the consequences of social policy making, having been forgotten for some time in our passion for progress. It has become increasingly clear that we can sometimes choose which risks we prefer to trade off against the benefits we seek. What we apparently can never do is to provide a set of advantages that are totally detached from risks that we would rather do without (cf. Levitan and Taggart, 1976).

Such arguments as the above that are related to the soundness of both program conceptualizations *and* their implementation are sometimes supplemented by contentions that the unproven efficacy of social change efforts lies not in the ideation and in the execution but in the measurement of outcomes. Thus Guba (1969) has faulted modern educational *evaluation* rather than recent educational innovations themselves, a perspective reflected more recently and more broadly by Fetterman (1982). If only we had a proper way to measure outcomes, then the efficacy of the intervention would be readily apparent.

In a similar vein, the original negative assessment of Headstart by the Westinghouse Report has been challenged on methodological grounds by many scholars, and a recent Consortium report (Lazar and Darlington, 1982) has attempted to vindicate this long-standing and highly favored early childhood intervention. Similarly, challenges to public education programs (as opposed to those of private parochial schools) by Coleman (Coleman et al., 1981; 1982) have been the subject of not only scholarly argument, but rather immoderate ad hominem attacks and counterattacks as well. Thus Cain and Goldberger (1983) have called the "statistical and 'implied policy analysis' [of Coleman et al.] . . . comical . . . and sad" in their study of public and private schools, also stating that the work falls ". . . below the *minimum standards* [italics mine] for social scientific research" (p. 217). Coleman and Hoffer (1983) accuse their rival academic colleagues of similar inferior workmanship and of lacking "responsibility." When our passion for progress and its outcomes are questioned, emotions run extremely high. As stated earlier, the conative and affective components of aspiration for social betterment are not to be trifled with. For ardent social reformers, it is not only that we haven't done enough positively in our betterment efforts. It is also a matter of our not having fairly evaluated the progress that has already been made.

SOCIAL PROGRAMS: CONCEPTUALIZATIONS OF THEIR IMPLEMENTATION

One last response to the question of why social programs as instruments of progress have had such doubtful effectiveness has been that the problem of efficacy lies not with the ideation behind such efforts but in their implementation — i.e., ". . . the translation of project plans and proposals into practice (Berman and McLaughlin, 1978, p. 215). In recent years, there have been a number of important attempts in various programmatic areas designed to show that interventions might well have succeeded had they been carried out properly. Evaluations have turned from an emphasis on *effects* to the description and assessment of *process*.

One of the more ambitious of these studies of program processes is Pressman and Wildavsky's (1979) volume, *Implementation: How Great Expectations in Washington are Dashed in Oakland; Or, Why It's Amazing that Federal Programs Work at All, This Being the Saga of the Economic Development Administration as Told by Two Sympathetic Observers Who Seek to Build Morals on a Foundation of Ruined Hopes*. The book's full title is presented here to give the flavor of this and some other examples of implementation research. As the Candide-style title suggests, Pressman and Wildavsky's basic argument is that despite good intention and high expectation, federal programs should not be expected to be effective, given the way that they are administered. In the case history Pressman and Wildavsky present, if there had been a reduction in the number of decision points in the transmission of program ideas from federal planners to local authorities carrying out those ideas, delays would have been eliminated and implementation generally would have been more coherent. The whole economic development program and others like it might well have succeeded in producing the intended job opportunities.

In an even more dramatic illustration of implementation failure, Cook (1979) has lamented the degree of realization of "the constructive potential of desegregation efforts." He says, "That only a fraction of this potential has been realized is a tragic consequence of *the manner in which* [italics mine] school desegregation has all too often been carried out." Cook was one of four social psychologists who in 1954 drafted the "Social Science Statement" to the Supreme Court which is credited with influencing the Court's historic decision on school desegregation. Yet, such desegregation rarely meets the conditions established by Cook et al. for friendlier race relations. These conditions are: (1) equivalence of activities and opportunities; (2) consistent official endorsement of desegregation; (3) absence of interracial competition; and (4) interracial contacts among students as *individuals*. In the absence of such circumstances of implementation Cook (1979) states that "It's surprising that outcomes have been favorable as often as they have."

Concerns about implementation or "slippage" between intentions and program outcomes have multiplied in recent years. The Pressman and Wildavsky volume mentioned above is by no means an isolated phenomenon. Indeed, studies of implementation have led to a veritable reconceptualization of interventions and innovations and the manner in which they ought to be carried out. Thus, the Rand study, *Federal Programs Supporting Educational Change* (Rand, 1975) put forward the idea that program implementation needs to be *bilateral*, embodying processes of *mutual adaptation* involving both those who carry out the program as well as those who are to be its beneficiaries (cf. also S. Kaplan, 1976; Farrar, DeSanctis, and Cohen, 1980).

In a related view, several "implementationologists" have suggested that an *evolution* of program strategies needs to take place. Some program designers have built in such evolution, for example, in the Head Start Planned Variation Program. Despite some recent argument to the contrary, there has been some movement away from the strict experimental tradition in social science that requires rigorous specification of a "treatment" that is followed unswervingly for all subjects to its successful or unsuccessful outcome as shown in "dependent variable measurement" (Majone and Wildavsky, 1978; Farrar, DeSanctis, and Cohen, 1980). Indeed Maccoby (1983), speaking to the issue of the manner in which interventions designed to enhance human development are carried out and evaluated, has even gone so far as to say that perhaps the time has come to remove from our heads "the 30-year-old wiring of learning theory" and experimental psychology.

THE PRESENT STUDY AND ITS ARGUMENT

The impetus for the research that is reported here was provided by this new emphasis on program *evolution* and the wave of concern by social scientists about the manner in which social programs are carried out rather than an exclusive preoccupation with their results. Thus, this book constitutes a contribution to the literature of "implementationology," although, as will become apparent in subsequent pages, we do not see the indifferent success of recent social interventions as being strictly a matter of their implementation. The case study of program processes to be described below and our reading of the evaluation literature more broadly gives rise to a different and more complex set of conclusions. We can adumbrate those conclusions and the fundamental argument of this volume in the following three statements:

(1) Social programs confront problems deeply rooted within interlocking human and physical environmental systems. The solutions to these problems are not at all obvious; and even where effective betterment strategies can be found, there is invariably a risk-benefit tradeoff that must be accepted.

(2) Most social programs are not well equipped with informational, financial, organizational, and other pragmatic resources to deal adequately with the problems they seek to remedy.

(3) Therefore, it is of little surprise that despite (a) benevolent intention; (b) creative, intelligent, and at least somewhat knowledgeable program design; (c) charismatic leadership; and (d) what appears to be genuine need by those served, action programs are, at best, only moderately or inconsistently successful.

THE SCOPE OF THE PRESENT STUDY — CASE STUDY AND COMPARISON

To document and illustrate these three assertions, we will in the following pages of this volume describe and analyze the implementation of the "Family Matters" Program, the intervention component of the Comparative Ecology of Human Development Project, a five-nation study of young families. The analysis of the program will be placed in two successively broader perspectives — that of the urban context where the program was carried out, and that of other interventions, especially those aimed at early childhood and family life generally. Thus, what follows is both an extended case study, one that has been carried out in more than customary depth, and a comparative analysis of social programs, with Family Matters used as a detailed illustration of much of what is positive and negative in our attempts to better our society.

Following the view of Rist (1981), we believe that such a case study is not itself "social engineering" but can provide "social enlightenment," through "long-term and intensive familiarity" with one of the more important intervention attempts of our day. Rist (1981) favorably contrasts the longitudinal, in-depth methodology of this kind of ethnographic research with the "prefabricated or furtive . . . hit and run encounters with society" often provided by social or educational research that puts all of its eggs in two baskets, pretest and posttest. Furthermore, Elmore (1978, p. 226) has observed ". . . that the evidence on social program implementation is skimpy . . ." and there is, ". . . a great need for descriptive studies of social program implementation" (Ibid., p. 227). Thus, we believe that the case history to be described below can make a valuable contribution to the empirical literature, to the advance of theory, and to implementation of future interventions as well.

It may of course be argued that the intervention was not necessarily totally representative of all social programs. In some respects, e.g., its knowledge base, the sincerity of its intentions, its leadership, the worthiness of its aims, and the genuine need for its offerings among a good number of its participants, it might have been expected to be superior to many other programs. In other respects, e.g., intervention knowhow and organizational management, it might have been expected to be less adequate. But in those respects that we see as being typically problematic in many contemporary and innovative social programs vis-à-vis the circumstances they seek to alter, Family Matters serves as an example of considerable heuristic value. It is also an example that we hope will drive home the lessons to be imparted in a way that a simple enunciation of principles cannot. The case history material is emphasized to help lessen the vagueness and superficiality that might result from either an a priori statement of principles or an alleged review of social programs in general.

Yet we must acknowledge that the case study, no matter how intensively investigated, has its limitations (cf. Fienberg, 1977). Indeed, we recognize and will have more to say later about the inadequacy of research methodologies generally ". . . for the study of the impact of public policy as an aid to future policy" (Coleman, 1972; Rist, 1981). Thus, although we have eschewed the approach of simply culling snippets of description from various interventions and making broad generalizations based on such selection, comparative material about other programs *is* included in this volume to enhance the generalizability of the conclusions drawn from the case study.

Also, it must be pointed out if Family Matters was "not average" in all respects, its aspirations and historic origins were part and parcel of the same Great Society programs that sought social progress that are now so very much at issue. Indeed, as we will observe in Chapter 8, it was the demonstrated lack of efficacy of traditional "top-down" models of management (cf. Elmore, 1978) that prompted Family Matters and similar interventions to adopt an organizational model for themselves that contrasted sharply with more hierarchical management strategies, with results that will be described below. Also, as we shall see later, Family Matters like its older relative, Head Start, both in its implementation strategy and its aspirations tried to be different from previous institutionalized efforts. Both were radical programs — not radical in the political sense, but in the simple denotative meaning of dealing with *root causes* of social inequalities. Thus, our treatment will emphasize the innovative social programs of the past two decades, but where appropriate, we will also consider the relevance of the book's argument and to older and more institutionalized programs.

We believe that this exercise is made all the more salient by the recent Grace Commission finding (Grace, 1984, p. 66) that there are probably as many as "963 social programs" sponsored by the federal government as well as disturbing allegations of the fraud, waste, mismanagement, inefficiency, and just plain uselessness in and of such programs (Grace, 1984; Lambro, 1980). The Grace (1984a; b) and the Lambro (1980) books bear the titles: *War on Waste*; *Burning Money*; and *Fat City*, respectively. They represent a 20-year cumulation of public concerns about social programs that are expressed in part by mass market publications that deal with such issues as health care, welfare, education, criminal justice, drug control, and government agencies generally. These trade and more scholarly publications bear provocative and often negative titles, such as: *Death at an Early Age* (Kozol, 1967); *Regulating the Poor* (Piven and Cloward, 1971); *Kind and Usual Punishment* (Mitford, 1974); *Medical Nemesis* (Ilich, 1976); *Power, Inc.* (Mintz and Cohen, 1976); *Agency of Fear* (Epstein, 1977); *The Urban School: Factory of Failure* (Rist, 1978); and the important and stimulating Sieber (1982) volume about reverse effects cited earlier, *Fatal Remedies*. The criticism expressed in such volumes, the very real public concern, and the vast proportion of our national resources, efforts, and aspirations invested in our collective efforts aimed at social progress lend heightened significance to inquiries such as this one that seeks to answer the questions, how do our attempts at social engineering work, and where they don't work, why don't they?

2

BETTERING CHILD DEVELOPMENT

Among the noblest and best motivated of human attempts to better the lot of their fellows and to improve society at large have been efforts to improve the life circumstances and enrich the growth experience of children. Good intention abounds in this endeavor. The passion for progress finds here the worthiest of causes for its expression. Our hope appears to be that the young, freed of the yoke of humanity's past failings, will create a world that is qualitatively very different from the world into which they were born. Indeed, this is a metaphor we rehearse each year in the image of "old father time," representing the past 12 months, passing the hour glass to the "baby new year." The symbolism may also underlie the nativity theme of Christmas.

CHILDHOOD-ORIENTED INTERVENTIONS OF THE PAST

As has been pointed out by various scholars, the genealogy of programs in the western world aimed at enhancing child development is a long and venerable one. Powell (1982) traces the lineage of interventions directed at children via their parents back to Comenius, a seventeenth century educator who wrote a handbook on the rearing of children dedicated to "Godly Christian Parents, Teachers, Guardians, and all who are charged with the care of children." Schlossman (1976), who bewails the "ahistoricism" of social policy

makers and social scientists, directs our eyes backward to the Massachusetts "tithingmen," government-appointed agents who began to
oversee parents through direct intervention in the home during the
late seventeenth century. Ross (1979) cites several sources for
the U.S. colonial period including Cotton Mather who, speaking
about indigent children, expressed the view that the community
ought to ". . . be more concerned for their *schooling* than for their
clothing" (p. 23).

In the early decades of the nineteenth century, ". . . there was
a proliferation of pamphlets, tracts, magazines, and sermons on
child rearing" (Powell, 1982, p. 137). By the 1820s, mothers' study
groups, called Maternal Associations, sprang up throughout the
country (Ibid.). The end of the century saw the work of G. Stanley
Hall and the child study movement of the 1880s (Schlossman,
1976). In 1897, the National Congress of Mothers, the antecedent
of Parent-Teacher Association (PTA) groups, came on the scene
as the first nationwide parent organization whose goals included
working with poor families and disseminating up-to-date knowledge
on child care and family life (Powell, 1982).

In New York, reading courses for farmers' wives were provided
by the state-sponsored and agriculture-related home economics
program beginning around 1900 (Lipsett, 1979). The reading program for farmers' wives ultimately involved in its dissemination
efforts home visits and study clubs; and as the effort blossomed
under what was later to become New York State Cooperative Extension, neighborhood groups in cities were formed as well (Ibid.).

At the national level, the Smith-Lever Act of 1914 appropriated
federal funds to give ". . . instruction and practical demonstrations in
agriculture and home economics," to persons outside the framework
of the formal land-grant college system (Ibid., p. 6). Very soon after
the passage of this historic legislation two important foci of such
home-economics extension programs became child rearing and
family life.

Some who lack the information implicit in this historical
perspective may view as foreign, as intrusive, and as unwarranted
the concept of outside intervention in family life for the benefit
of the child, especially the child who lives in poverty. But the basic
idea and its implementation in varying forms have been with us as
an integral part of Western culture, and specifically U.S. culture,

for literally centuries. Indeed, our problem in this chapter is not to find sufficient evidence for such concerns and efforts in our history, culture, and legislation, but rather the difficulty lies in finding a way to put the case briefly.

The historian Richard Pells had attributed much of the abandonment of the old American ideal of rugged individualism to the Great Depression and its aftermath which ". . . encouraged the conviction that human problems would never be solved by the individual alone" (1973, p. 114). We have seen, however, that the notion that families need and merit external support as they foster their young *far antedates the Depression*, and is so much a part of the fabric of our society that it would be surprising if by now nearly all living in this land have not benefited in some way, at some time, in some degree, directly or indirectly from the support of resources outside the family. Today, as Schlossman (1976) points out, the challenge for educational or social reformers is to learn from past efforts at influencing parents, to try to capture in contemporary intervention the successes of the past, to avoid repeating the failures, and most of all, to recognize that parent education is not a panacea for all social ills.

THE EDUCABILITY OF INTELLIGENCE

Like the concept of buttressing the nurture of our society's offspring, the idea that "intelligence is educable" is far from a novel one. Blatt and Garfunkel (1969) trace the view back to Itard's work with the wild boy of Aveyron in the first decade of the nineteenth century, the egalitarian *zeitgeist* that burgeoned following the French Revolution, and the scientific discoveries of that age that led to the belief "nothing was impossible to science." Beller (1979) sees a delayed effect of the work of Darwin, Locke, and Rousseau which ultimately found expression in the twentieth century in the concept that cognitive ability can be enhanced through experience in the right sort of environment. Bronfenbrenner (1979a) and Zigler (1979) add the much later research of Bloom (1964), Hebb (1949), and Hunt (1961) to the list of those pointing in the direction of intervention to stimulate intellectual capability.

HEAD START: ITS ORIGINS AND GOALS

Thus, retrospective accounts of the origins of Head Start and similar efforts in the late 1960s that form the lineage of Family Matters speak of it almost with a sense of inevitability, as "an idea whose time had come" (Bronfenbrenner, 1979a). And, indeed, "between 1965 and 1968 findings were interpreted as meaning that Head Start had definite immediate and possibly durable benefits for children" (Datta, 1979, p. 405).

According to Zigler (1979), the earliest creators and movers of Head Start had set as their major goal the promotion of "greater *social competence* [italics in original] in disadvantaged children." Social competence is defined by Zigler (Ibid.) as "an individual's everyday effectiveness in dealing with his environment." This would include the "ability to master appropriate formal concepts, to perform well in school, to stay out of trouble with the law, and to relate well to adults and other children" (Ibid.).

All of this was to be accomplished by working "with the child directly" and "providing services to improve his health, intellectual ability, and socioemotional development" (Ibid.). In addition to attempting to foster the *child's* health, intellectual ability, and socioemotional growth, Zigler states that Head Start sought to enlist "family involvement" and to stimulate "community change." These last two aspects of the project were seen as means to "produce maximum benefits" for the child, since, it was thought, without family involvement and "community change," the other facets of Head Start's remediation attempts would be less likely to achieve optimal results.

HEAD START'S EFFICACY ASSESSED

Health

Of the four items on the working agenda of Head Start and conceptually similar programs, health, intellectual ability, socioemotional development, and family involvement/community change, the results of the project's efforts seem to have been most clear-cut in the first area. Zigler (1979, p. 496) points out that "more than one-third of Head Start children have been found to suffer from illnesses or physical handicaps." He also notes that "of these children, 75 per cent have been treated" (Ibid.). Speaking about this kind of intervention more generally, Shadish (1982) concludes that, despite the considerable controversy over the value of preventive child health care, a comprehensive review of the literature of empirical studies is encouraging of such care.

Emotional Development

Zigler (1979) has much less in the way of evidence of gains to submit with regard to social and emotional development of Head Start youngsters. He emphasizes the need for "healthy self image, expectancy of success, adequate aspiration level, mastery motivation," etc., a premise that social scientists or lay persons can hardly dispute. He points out that we have *over*emphasized changes in cognitive ability as desirable outcomes of childhood intervention programs and *under*emphasized socioemotional development. But while there are some indications that Head Start and comparable programs may enhance such development for some youngsters, the evidence is far from overwhelming.

For example, Lazar and Darlington (1982) show that in 1976, children who had attended early education programs were significantly more likely than controls to offer "achievement related reasons" for being proud of themselves. The generality of such findings, however, their durability, and their relationship to *actual* achievement have all yet to be demonstrated unequivocally. There is a dearth of well recognized and standardized measures of social competence for children, and sufficient research has simply not been done to justify characterization of Head Start's efficacy in this area either positively or negatively.

In addition to the paucity of evidence for Head Start-enhanced socioemotional development, there is also the question of the best means for influencing such development. Thus Baumrind (1972) has found that black mothers categorized as "rejecting" by bourgeois white norms were producing daughters who appeared to be successfully developing confidence. Gray and Wandersman (1980) have emphasized the difference in value systems between middle-class white and lower-class black families, pointing out that attempts to be supportive can lead to dependence or to expectations that will only end in bitter disappointment later on. In the absence of strong evidence for better socioemotional development, the apparent nobility of purpose or of means has not served as hard evidence for achievement.

Family Involvement and Community Change

As for Head Start's third goal, family involvement and community change, the 1970 Kirchner Report and the work of Lazar and Darlington (1982) suggest that as its mandate directed, Head Start is likely to have stimulated communities to improve their educational, health, and social services for the poor. Its effects seem also to have been felt in encouraging mothers to upgrade their vocational aspirations for their youngsters and to take a more active role in relation to their children's education.

These accomplishments, while having their valuable aspects, will not be viewed by all as completely in the public interest or even that of the families involved. Clearly, to the degree that child and family education and health were indeed upgraded by Head Start's stimulation of a proactive and constructive parental role in the areas of health and education, few would argue with the worthiness of such achievement. But Head Start's role in encouraging the demand for more social services and programs will not be seen universally with joy unalloyed.

We do not have specific information on Head Start itself on this particular point, but as we will have occasion to note later in this volume, some programs (e.g., the Child and Family Resource Program) inspired by or allied with Head Start have sometimes urged mothers to quit their jobs and subsist on public assistance so that they can devote themselves more fully to child rearing. This kind of lifestyle cannot be regarded by the most sympathetic of observers as anything but a *mixed blessing*.

We now live in an era when even ethnic minority scholars (e.g., Cross in Cross et al., 1977; Sowell, 1984) and opinion leaders (e.g., Raspberry, 1984 and Clarence Pendleton, the current chairman of the U.S. Civil Rights Commission) seriously question the ratio of benefit to detriment inherent in many of the services and programs for the poor. And if those who genuinely share the concerns of the underclass have their doubts about at least some of these interventions, those who are more neutral and those who are frankly indifferent or antagonistic, particularly to the degree that they perceive themselves as having to pay for such services and programs, are likely to oppose encouraging the "clamor" for services. Yet there can be little question that mothers who do devote themselves to child rearing, and who receive social or formal governmental support in their endeavor confer very real benefits not only on their immediate families but also upon the larger society as well. Head Start's achievements in this area thus constitute a classic "good news-bad news" situation.

In addition to the ambivalence inherent in stimulation of demand for external social services, there has been no way to assess the extent or efficacy of Head Start's own service efforts. Thus, Lazar (1979), a strong proponent of Head Start and its service component, admits, "While virtually every other aspect of Head Start has been formally evaluated, I was unable to find any evaluation of its social service component, and could not find much incidental data" (p. 286). Overall then, there is in the mind of thoughtful persons a good deal of ambiguity about the nature of Head Start's contributions in the area of social services.

Cognitive Development

Moving from Head Start's role in providing or stimulating the demand for social services to its fourth and last goal, one that had been its original emphasis, we must conclude that once again, the project's efficacy has been far from unequivocal. Early positive assessments of Head Start's influence on child cognitive development, especially on I.Q. scores, gave way to verdicts of "little or no impact," when what were then called *long-term effects* after the program were evaluated. It seemed that with Head Start and other similar or allied programs, short-term achievement might or might not be demonstrated, for example, the Family Development Research Program (Lally and Honig, 1977) or the Child and Family Resource Program (Abt, 1981a), but such effects tended to be reduced to nonsignificance within a few years after program termination (cf. Abt, 1981; Lally et al., 1982) or to "wash out" completely (Nicol, 1976).

In 1979, a creator, a director, and a vigorous proponent of Head Start, Edward Zigler conceded ". . . we have almost nowhere produced the degree of cognitive improvement in poor children we had hoped for . . ." and this ". . . has been a most sobering experience" (p. 502). Elsewhere (p. 496) Zigler says that ". . . if Head Start is appraised by its success in universally raising the I.Q.'s of poor children and maintaining those I.Q.'s over time, one is tempted to write it off as an abject failure" (cf. also, Ramey, 1982). Zigler speaks of "overoptimism" and "overselling" of the project's potential accomplishments in the cognitive area by its early proponents. Halpern (1984) provides similar evaluations of the efficacy of infant and toddler programs, whether directed toward cognitive goals or toward other aims. Unfortunately these realities and Zigler's appraisal of the gap between aspirations and achievement provide an excellent example, in the terms of this volume, of the passion for progress and the striving for high purpose overreaching themselves.

Such overreaching was evident at the very birth of Head Start. Although academic luminaries such as Zigler and Bronfenbrenner were among Head Start's intellectual godfathers, its midwife (or its "midhusband") was Office of Economic Opportunity (OEO) director Sargent Shriver. Bronfenbrenner (1979a) reports that when he and others sensibly recommended trying out the idea on a small scale before implementing it with large numbers of children, Shriver impatiently demanded something that would effect a major social change *immediately*. Bronfenbrenner (1979a, p. 82) quotes Shriver as saying, "We're going to write Head Start across the face of this nation so that no Congress or president can ever destroy it." The statement attributed to Shriver constitutes an excellent example of a passion for progress that brooked no delay, despite expert warnings that the program might prove ineffective or worse.

Especially during the early and middle 1970s, pessimism prevailed in the most highly touted area of Head Start's purview, intellectual development, and it seemed that the experts' warnings to Shriver were all too prophetic. Dour assessments of early childhood and preschool interventions nearly led to the project's extinction (Carnegie Corporation Quarterly, Summer 1978, p. 5). It was only grass roots efforts by Head Start parents and other advocates and the Report of the Consortium for Longitudinal Studies (Lazar and Darlington, 1982) that showed some durable cognitive gains produced by compensatory education, that are credited with lengthening Head Start's life.

The report demonstrated that in the eleven *high-quality* projects it analyzed, program children, as compared with controls

were significantly more likely to meet their schools' basic requirements, and *less* likely to be assigned to special education classes
or to be retained in grade. Stanford Binet measured I.Q. scores
were higher for program children for several years after the project
experience, though this effect did not appear to be permanent nor
general across all subgroups. There was also evidence of improved
achievement test scores in some areas for children who had received
early education, but here again the generality of such findings was
limited.

In the cognitive area once again, however, early education-
produced outcomes are by no means unambiguous, with even some
proponents today still expressing concern about the magnitude of
effects, even where such effects are statistically significant. Certainly,
by comparison with the expectations of the ". . . heady days of the
1960's . . . none of the projects succeeded in developing children
who, as a group, were significantly above average intellectually or,
presumably, academically" (Ramey, 1982, p. 149). Further, the
mean I.Q. score at follow-up for the four projects with the best
sampling designs was about one standard deviation *below* the national average for both program and control children (Ibid.).

THE WINTER OF DESPAIR AND DISILLUSIONMENT

Despite these qualifications on the Consortium report on the
long-range effects of Head Start, its overall findings of childhood-
oriented interventions were some of the best news proponents had
had for several years. Before the report, especially between 1969
and 1974, overall analyses of the midrange efficacy of compensatory
education had very little positive to say about Head Start. The
"wash out" (Nicol, 1976) of early effects of Head Start became
proverbial. This led to what Datta (1979) has termed "a winter of
disillusionment and some despair." It was within this mid-1970s
context of opinion surrounding Head Start's accomplishments,
i.e., that it ought to have produced dramatic effects, but that it
had not done so in the cognitive area or any other except perhaps
health, that Family Matters and its immediate predecessors were
conceived.

THE PROGRAM PROGENY OF HEAD START —
FAMILY MATTERS ANCESTRY

As a rule, Head Start intervention actually took place in the classroom, and was directed primarily at preschoolers. Although parents often were contacted and encouraged toward involvement in various activities, the chief emphasis was on the child. Thus, Head Start Programs may be categorized as largely (though not exclusively) school-based and child-oriented. In the latter 1960s and early 1970s, researchers interested in studying the acceleration of positive aspects of human development began to experiment increasingly with a dual emphasis on *both* parent and child, trying to benefit the youngster directly and indirectly through influencing the parent, usually the mother (Schlossman, 1976). White (1975), for example, argued that it was better to teach young mothers how to rear children more effectively in the home rather than creating new institutional settings for child rearing. Both White (Ibid.) and Schlossman (1976, p. 438) predict, ". . . that parent education will become the clarion call of reformers in the next two decades."

With this shift in emphasis on parent education that took place in the 1970s, intervention sites also shifted from the school to the home and to the center as the primary locations for betterment efforts. Among the earliest of the home-based parent-oriented efforts that were most like the later Family Matters Program were: Home Start, The Florida Parent Education Program, The Verbal Interaction Program, the DARCEE Infant Programs, The Ypsilanti Infant Education Project, and the Infant Intervention Program. Beller (1979) provides excellent brief descriptions of these programs (as well as those that were child or parent-child oriented and those that were center-based), and evaluative summaries of their achievements (cf also, Halpern, 1984).

The conceptualizations that shaped the home-based programs required that the major modality for embodying the intervention would be home visits. As mentioned previously in conjunction with the nineteenth century origins of Cooperative Extension in New York State, home visits to mothers of very young children were, of course, not a novelty in this country or abroad. Internationally speaking, home visits with a primary emphasis on health and nutrition are not an innovation. But instead of nurses or their surrogates, the more recent educationally oriented programs in this country utilized social workers, professionals with credentials in education or human development, or specially trained parapro-fessionals.

The visits might last from 30 to 90 minutes, with the modal frequency averaging about once a week (Beller, 1979). The visit program might last for a specified number of sessions (24 or 32), or for a period of months, for a year, or even for three years. Taking a strongly experimentalistic approach, many of the interventions provided different treatments within the same program that varied in their content, intensity, or duration, or utilized control groups in various forms. At first, most were targeted at low-income, often racial minority groups. Later, parent educational efforts began to turn equally toward the developmental needs of *all* youngsters. It became ". . . demoncratized," as the notion of 'cultural depriva-tion' gave way "to a more generalized theory of 'developmental deprivation' " (Schlossman, 1976, p. 439).

Program goals were generally quite similar: furthering the intellectual and personality development of the child, raising mater-nal self-esteem, promoting verbal interaction between parent and child, helping the mother to guide the long-range cognitive and intellectual growth of the child, preventing abuse and neglect, enhancing the child's physical and psychological development and making the mother an educational change agent, advocacy on behalf of the family, and linkage with needed services, etc. (cf. Beller, 1979; Halpern, 1984). The developmental span generally ranged from prenatal care through the early preschool years.

Of all these programs (other than the school-based Head Start), Bronfenbrenner and Cochran (1976) appear to have been initially most familiar with Levenstein's Verbal Interaction Program. Some of their early writings also acknowledge a debt of gratitude to Karnes' (1969) intervention, a mother-oriented, center-based pro-gram. Bronfenbrenner, as an important collaborator in the founding of Head Start, a leading expert on human development, and a re-viewer of the effects of early childhood intervention for the federal government (Bronfenbrenner, 1974), was familiar with the outcomes of these and other projects. Both he and Cochran knew something about their intervention techniques. Both of them therefore resolved that their Family Matters Program would embody the best of the home visit approach, but would not neglect the best of what was to be found in interventions outside the home (i.e., the neighborhood, the community, and later once again, the school). Thus we now examine the early conceptualizations and theoretical underpinnings of Family Matters, as a case study of an educational effort designed to promote social change, an experiment in human betterment.

3

FAMILY MATTERS

THE ATOMIZED FAMILY

Embodying the concerns of the founders of Head Start, of its successors, and of Family Matters, the years 1979 and 1980 were designated as the International Year of the Child and the International Year of the Family, respectively. Over the preceding decade (as we have seen), and subsequently as well, the U.S. family has been the focus of considerable attention. Social scientists, service professionals, political leaders, concerned lay people, and even "talk-show" hosts have been carefully scrutinizing this basic component of our society. Sometimes that scrutiny has been carried out with dispassion. Probably more often it has not. Perhaps the best analyses have been those that combine a reasoned empiricism with concerned advocacy of the need to strengthen family life.

There seems to be a fair degree of consensus about the need for such support (cf. Kahn and Kamerman, 1982), despite the optimistic, politically advantageous statements one often hears about the U.S. family being "very much alive and well." But among serious thinkers, the issue is neither simple nor susceptible to rosy generalization. In the United States, the Advisory Committee on Child Development and Public Policy of the National Academy of Sciences (1976, p. 92) has noted a trend toward "progressive fragmentation and isolation of the American family in its child rearing role." Abroad, the contemporary French revisionist historian

Donzelot (1979) points to the atomization and withering away of the family in the contemporary western world.

A disciple of Foucault, Donzelot takes the anomalous view that the family is under attack by an unlikely trio of foes — Marxists, feminists, and Freudians. Although the thinking of the Foucault school in this respect diverges quite markedly from that of the Committee on Child Development and from mainstream scholarly views in *this* country, generally there is a similar and growing tendency for those who study problems of family life to turn away from endogenous variables and to look increasingly toward exogenous ones. The problems of today's family are not seen as coming so much from within as from without.

THE FAMILY AND ITS CONTEXT

For example, Keniston (Keniston and the Carnegie Council for Children, 1977) has characterized as "mythology" the assumption that families are "free-standing independent, and autonomous units, relatively free from social pressures" (p. 9). This, says Keniston, is the myth of family "self-sufficiency," which "blinds us to the workings of other forces in family life." According to Keniston et al.:

> families are not now, nor were they ever, the self-sufficient building blocks of society, exclusively responsible, praiseworthy, and blamable for their own destiny. They are deeply influenced by broad social and economic forces over which they have little control. (p. 12)

THE SOCIAL CONTEXT AND
DEVELOPMENTAL DEPRIVATION

One of the corollaries of the thesis that families are "deeply influenced by broad social and economic forces" is that the children of families most adversely affected by socioeconomic factors are more likely to grow up in deprived environments that may adversely affect human development. Any number of studies in the 1960s and 1970s documented a relationship between social class differences in children's families of origin and various measures of their cognitive ability (cf. Coleman et al., 1966 and Deutsch, 1973 for reviews). Deprivation and associated maturational deficit may ultimately be translated into low and declining I.Q. scores, ". . . disturbed personality development, and, in extreme cases, death" (Lazar and Darlington, 1982, p. 2). Enriched environments, on the other hand, have been found to exert rehabilitative and ameliorative effects on youngsters from deprived circumstances (Ibid.). Thus it became an important prevailing view in the professional, scientific, and policy-making communities that without such enrichment, the developmental gap between advantaged and disadvantaged children would simply grow wider as they grew older (cf. Ausubel, 1964).

Rarely has the passion for progress had a more noble reason for intervention — the aim was to enrich the inner worlds of poor youngsters to prevent their falling even further behind children from economically more privileged circumstances in the course of their lives. In the preceding chapter, we examined a series of major social and educational experiments undertaken by U.S. society over the course of two decades. Their goal was not merely to bring the cognitive skills of economically disadvantaged children up to those of their more affluent counterparts. Early education in the 1960s was similarly seen as a veritable instrument of "social reform" and "to solve social problems" (Lazar and Darlington, 1982; Zigler, 1979).

Once again, Schlossman (1976) reminds us that such social change motivations for childhood interventions are not new. He reports: "Before World War I, parent education referred not simply to techniques of early child care but to a broad range of social issues which all parents were considered responsible for understanding" (p. 466). Schlossman adds that even PTA members ". . . certainly no radical group — easily integrated political lobbying into their thinking on parent education and would have considered themselves morally impoverished not to do so" (Ibid.).

Returning to the antecedents of Family Matters in the late 1960s and early 1970s, the very title (to say nothing of the content) of Zigler and Valentine's (1979) edited volume on the chief educational program of this era is highly indicative — *Project Headstart: A Legacy of the War on Poverty*.

Both the book title and its content are appropriate because, as we must remember, Head Start was originally launched by the Office of Economic Opportunity and only after an odyssey entered the domain of the Department of Health and Human Services component, the Administration for Children, Youth, and Families (ACYF).

Some of the other experiments of the day were defined clearly as educational, while others dealt with other aspects of the interface between the family and society. They ". . . began with the prototypes of Head Start in the early Sixties and continued with Head Start itself and Follow-Through during the middle and late Sixties. Next came the family income experiments of the Seventies, and, most recently, contemporary studies of flexitime and family life" (Bronfenbrenner, 1980).

SOCIAL PROGRESS?

Unfortunately, however, as with many of the interventions discussed in Chapters 1 and 2, the results of these programs fell far short of the expectations of those whose purpose and intent were so lofty. The progenitors of Family Matters were fully aware of this shortfall. Bronfenbrenner (1980) describes Halcy Bohen's carefully conducted study of flexitime carried out for the Family Impact Seminar that apparently yielded a rather surprising outcome: the only married employees who reported benefiting from flexible work schedules *are those without children.* Yet the chief family policy advocates who have lobbied for flexitime have always stated their hope that decreased rigidity in adhering to the workplace's timeclock would lead to greater opportunity *for families* to be together, hence an advantage for employees with children. Here we have still another example of an intervention whose effects have been very different from those intended.

Of even greater concern to those who have considerably more than a passing interest in family stability and human development were the "counterintuitive" results produced by the income maintenance experiments. Here, the sudden availability of greater financial wherewithal may have *increased* the likelihood of divorce (Ibid.: and cf. Knudsen, Scott, and Short, 1977, and Groeneveld, Tuma, and Hannan, 1980). From the perspective of those wishing to strengthen the nuclear, two-parent family, the remedy really did prove to be fatal.

As for the compensatory educational programs, especially project Head Start, we have seen that their effects did not prove to be negative, but neither did they produce the dramatically positive intellectual outcomes that had been hoped for and in many cases promised with a good deal of assurance (cf. Zigler, 1979). Preliminarily affirmative assessments of this major national effort soon turned to the Westinghouse (Cicirelli et al., 1969) evaluation of little or no lasting effect produced by Head Start. And although the subsequent reassessment of Head Start's long-range effects through a series of interviews with selected program recipients has shown at least some worthwhile positive effects (Lazar and Darlington, 1982), when the Comparative Ecology of Human Development Project and its Family Matters Program component were conceived in 1976, even these limited beneficial outcomes of Head Start had not been demonstrated. It was still Datta's (1979) "winter of disillusionment and discontent."

WHY FAMILY MATTERS?

The original creators of Family Matters and the Comparative Ecology of Human Development Project more broadly, Bronfenbrenner and Cochran (1976), have, like Keniston (1977) and others, placed considerable emphasis on *external influences* in human development and family life (Cochran and Brassard, 1979). Cochran has stated "Families have always been embedded in networks of relatives, neighbors, and friends. . . . Yet such social influences have gone virtually unrecognized by those studying child development" (Cochran and Brassard, 1979, p. 601). Similarly, Bronfenbrenner has seen the developmental ecology as ". . . a set of nested structures, each inside the next, like a set of Russian dolls" (1979b, p. 3). Influences in the ecological environment affecting a child's growth may stem from the home or the school, from the neighborhood or the community, from parents' workplaces or even "a location in a foreign land." Analysis of the environment into micro-, meso-, exo-, and macro-level components reflects a conceptualization of factors affecting family life that is not only exogenous in its approach, but also complex, highly differentiated, and systems-oriented. Thus for both Cochran and Bronfenbrenner, not only are families *not* free-standing or self-sufficient, they are tied to the rest of the world by a multitude of stronger or weaker strands of differing lengths that are woven together in intricate network.

Faced with the evidence of little impact on human development by Head Start and other educational interventions as well as of null, low-level, unanticipated, or counterproductive effects of other social programs, Bronfenbrenner and Cochran reasoned that more had to be learned about "social structural" variables and their influence on family life generally and on child rearing in particular. Bronfenbrenner argued that what was needed to obtain the desired developmental and societal outcomes was an "ecological intervention," an "alteration of those aspects of the wider external environment that offered the greatest possibility for influencing the functional effectiveness of developmental settings such as the family, the day care center, or the school classroom" (1980, p. 3).

He asked the question, "What particular aspects of the external environment should be the focus of such allegedly *super-potent* [italics mine] intervention efforts" (Ibid.). But unfortunately, ". . . the research data necessary to answer the question simply did not exist" (Ibid.). Bronfenbrenner also speaks of the "mounting frustration" he experienced over the years ". . . as a social scientist periodically called upon by decision makers, both in the government and in the private sector, to advise on policies and programs affecting children and those directly responsible for their care and education" (Ibid.). That frustration was the result of a "critical gap" in scientific knowledge in the area of environmental influences on human development and family life.

He saw the information base of developmental psychology as more complete when the topic was the children themselves than when it was the environments in which they live. But even the data on the children themselves were of doubtful ecological validity. Thus, Bronfenbrenner (1979b, p. 19) refers to laboratory studies of youngsters as dealing with ". . . *the strange behavior of children in the presence of strangers under strange circumstances for the briefest possible periods of time"* (italics in original).

What was needed then, was a broad-ranging research effort of the social structural conditions that affect young families in their child-rearing mission — a study that would be naturalistic enough to be considered ecologically valid, would provide clues about how to carry out the elusive "super-potent intervention" that would benefit human development generally and that of disadvantaged children specifically, and would thus serve as a guide for social scientists in their roles as consultants to policy makers.

THE COMPARATIVE ECOLOGY OF HUMAN DEVELOPMENT PROJECT

To provide the knowledge base through naturalistic research that would focus on the developmental environment, Bronfenbrenner and Cochran (1976) conceived the Comparative Ecology of Human Development Project, a cross-cultural examination of family and neighborhood life in seven cities in five different countries.

Much of what appeared to be wrong with social structure was concentrated in urban areas. Virtually all of the social unrest in the 1960s and the 1970s had centered there. It was toward the cities that many previous attempts at social engineering had been directed. Cities thus constituted a logical focal point for the Comparative Ecology of Human Development Project as well. The seven metropolitan areas chosen were: Goteborg and Stockholm, Sweden; Mannheim and Konstanz, West Germany; Tel Aviv, Israel; Cardiff, Wales; and Syracuse, New York (in the United States). Samples abroad were to consist of 80 to 100 families representing a minimum of eight neighborhoods in each of the four countries.

In all five countries, research was to be carried out that would target six social structural variables (in project writings they are sometimes also referred to as "social addresses" or "ecological niches"): (1) *race,* (2) *socioeconomic status,* (3) *family structure* (single- versus two parent families), (4) *entry of the mother into the labor force,* (5) *use of child care outside the home,* and (6) *neighborhood.* A relatively homogeneous set of research instruments was adopted by investigators in the five countries. The three fundamental areas of inquiry subsumed by the research instruments were: (1) child-caregiver activities (the number and kinds of activities engaged in jointly by parents and their youngsters); (2) social networks (the relatives, close friends, neighbors, and acquaintances who might or might not assist families in their child-rearing function); and (3) stresses and supports (those aspects of the physical and social environment that helped families, especially in relation to bringing up their youngsters, or might instead be sources of strain).

Ultimately a "transcultural" coding system was created to permit analysis and comparisons of the "nature and function of *the developmental ecologies* associated with the six major structural contrasts found in modern industrialized societies" (Bronfenbrenner, 1980, p. 5). The international team of investigators believed that evidence had accumulated showing these six "contrasts" have "special significance" for the psychological and educational development of children.

The whole research project was based on a complex and evolving set of hypotheses. Presenting them in detail here would consume a good deal of space that must be devoted to other topics. Indeed, Bronfenbrenner (1979b) has presented a set of 50 hypotheses that describe the potential relationship between the environment and human development. In brief, however, the projects' general orientation, in line with the topics of the research instruments described above was that: (1) joint activities carried out by parents and children (particularly those that involve variety and cognitive complexity as well as encouraging the child's initiative, independence, and perseverance in the pursuit of long-term goals) are likely to enhance the cognitive and social development of children; and (2) such nurturance of children is facilitated by the presence of social networks of persons who are supportive of the family's child-rearing and educational efforts both directly and indirectly in the face of the stresses inherent in contemporary family life. As stated and as conceptualized, these two hypotheses are not independent of one another. Rather, the state of affairs posited in hypothesis two, support from social networks, is a necessary mediating condition for the operation of the first hypothesized parent-child activities.

FAMILY MATTERS

This orientation or set of working hypotheses had been based on a previously published evaluation of research on preschool and school intervention programs by Bronfenbrenner (1974) that yielded two major findings. First, the most powerful and lasting effects were produced by programs not directed to the child alone, but rather to the *mother-child dyad*. The second conclusion was that potent and long-lasting interventions of the future would have to be "ecological," i.e., they would need to be addressed toward the broader developmental contexts in which the growing child moved.

These two conclusions suggested to Bronfenbrenner and Cochran that a powerful way to explore developmental settings and to provide fellow scientists and policy makers with the information needed to better understand human behavior and to produce the required "super-potent" intervention would be to actually carry out such an intervention, one that would influence the parent-child dyad directly and would also create positive changes in the child's and the family's wider developmental context. Thus, unlike the Ecology of Human Development locations abroad, the U.S. site was to provide the setting for an experimental program that was later to be called "Family Matters."

Significantly, a more recent meta-analysis of the research on academic achievement by White (1982) strengthens Bronfenbrenner and Cochran's emphasis on the importance of the home environment in relationship to cognitive attainments. Based on a review of nearly 200 studies, White (1982) contends that it is *family characteristics* such as "home atmosphere," not socioeconomic status that are more closely related to academic achievement when individuals rather than aggregates are used as the unit of analysis.

Thus, it appears that Bronfenbrenner and Cochran were moving very much in the right direction when in the original proposal seeking support for the Comparative Ecology of Human Development Project (e.g., Bronfenbrenner and Cochran, 1976), it was stated that the program they planned was to be strongly home and family oriented. Their undertaking was intended to be both a "true" experiment, a test of the effectiveness of intervention strategies that gave promise of being able ultimately to promote gains in the cognitive and social development of participating youngsters, and also as a "heuristic tool," an instrument of "scientific discovery." This instrument was to serve as a kind of probe to ". . . explore which aspects of the ecological environment are susceptible to change in ways that foster developmental processes and outcomes" (Bronfenbrenner, 1980, p. 19). But whether a "heuristic tool" or a bona fide social experiment, the two fundamental operating strategies of the Family Matters Program were based on the previously developed theories of Bronfenbrenner and Cochran that specified the necessity of a bifocal approach to the intervention, one that targeted both the parent-child dyad at home as well as the social support systems in which that dyad and that home were embedded.

Strategy I involved ". . . providing recognition and resources for participation by parents and other family members in joint activities with the child" (Bronfenbrenner, 1980, p. 19). This providing of recognition and resources was to be carried out by home visitors, U.S. project staff members who were to come to the homes of participating families periodically and to encourage parent-child activities by stressing the developmental value of existing activities and to convey information about new ones, especially those that psychological theory suggested would be most beneficial to the child.

The second strategy employed by the Family Matters Program, which, as mentioned above, was viewed as a mediating condition for joint activities and later developmental gains, called "for strengthening and extending social networks that support the family's efforts to maintain or restructure the environment in the family's own behalf" (Bronfenbrenner, 1980, p. 19). "Strengthening and extending social networks" was to be implemented programmatically by staff members who visited the homes of participating families and encouraged them to form neighborhood groups composed of other participant families. As the groups began to gel, program workers were to provide logistical support or to take an even more active role in the organizational processes of Family Matters. The aim in promoting these groups was to gain recognition for the parenting experience generally and for parent-child activities specifically. Also, as implied by the phrase "maintaining or restructuring the environment," groups were also to involve themselves in support efforts that went well beyond the home environment.

Thus, we may encapsulate the fundamental *modi operandi* of Family Matters in the two phrases, "providing home visitors" and "organizing neighborhood groups." Later in the program's history, the former strategy was to be known simply as "Program I" and the latter as "Program II."

THE BASIC RESEARCH DESIGN

Because of the interventive and experimental nature of Family Matters, the U.S. component of the Comparative Ecology of Human

Development Project, both a treatment and a control group were distinguished. In each of 20 neighborhoods in Syracuse, approximately 16 families were selected in a manner that aimed at stratified random sampling for participation in the research. Half of the 20 neighborhoods and the 157 families chosen within their boundaries constituted the main focus of the Family Matters Program. Two neighborhoods, represented by approximately 30 families, served as sites for pilot programming. In one of these neighborhoods, elements of the home visitor program were tested. In the other, group activities were tried. The plan called for the pilot interventions to run nine months (an appropriate gestational period for a study of human families) ahead of main study programming. This was an excellent and innovative strategy to gain feedback on the intervention's efficacy before the most critical aspects of the intervention were implemented.

The remaining eight neighborhoods and their approximately 130 families were designated as controls. Here no program activity was to be carried out, even though in some cases control families later requested it, having heard about the intervention from actual program participants. Only data collection was to take place in these eight neighborhoods at time intervals corresponding to the pre- and posttesting that was conducted in the treatment neighborhoods. In addition to serving in the traditional role of a contrast group with the experimentals, control subjects in this project also constituted an appropriate comparison group with the other above mentioned samples collected by the Comparative Ecology of Human Development Project abroad. We must remember that project families outside the United States had not been asked to participate in any program other than data collection.

In all 20 U.S. neighborhoods and in the international component as well, among the most important of the selection criteria was that the family had to include a child who was three years old at the start of the study. Project argot referred to this youngster as "the target child," and the home visits and later outcome measurements were directed importantly at this target child. The U.S. neighborhoods themselves were chosen and their borders defined according to a composite of criteria involving school district lines, physical boundaries (parks and streets, etc.), and social addresses such as race, ethnicity, and economic levels, as perceived by people living there as well as by outside observers. Each neighborhood defined had to be large enough to contain a sufficient number of families with three-year-old children. In the total sample there were middle, moderate, and low-income neighborhoods. Some neighborhoods contained families belonging predominantly to one racial or ethnic group; others were mixed. Special efforts were made to include a significant proportion of black families (around 40 percent) (Cross et al., 1977) and one-parent families (30 percent) (Bronfenbrenner and Cochran, 1976).

Family Matters Not Just for the Economically Disadvantaged

At this point in our description of Family Matters, we must pause to say a little more about the socioeconomic and racial composition of the sample. First, it is important to note that out of a social experimental tradition that had centered its concerns on socioeconomically disadvantaged youngsters and families (Head Start, Homestart, etc.), Family Matters had emerged as a betterment effort that was not "means-tested," i.e., you didn't have to be poor to receive its benefits. Indeed, during recruitment efforts, some middle-income families initially thought that they had been selected for participation by mistake. They protested that they were ineligible for inclusion in the program. But recruitment of families with annual incomes as high as 50,000 dollars was neither a sampling error nor a general inadvertence in research design.

There were two reasons for inclusion of relatively affluent families. The first was inherent in the study's interest in understanding the effects of *different* social structural characteristics on child rearing and family life and the whole spectrum of developmental ecologies associated with those characteristics. The second rationale for *not* focusing exclusively on poor families was embodied in the belief of the principal investigators that many of the problems of child rearing in the contemporary urban environment are not confined to low-income families. (cf. above, Schlossman's 1976 assessment of the "democratization" of parent education efforts.) They believed, and prior and subsequent investigation has confirmed, that high stress relative to available support systems is by no means the lot of families in poverty only; nor are the poor the only parents who don't or can't spend enough time in optimal forms of joint activity with their children. It was thus for both of these reasons, breadth in social-structural comparisons and the universality of the problems of contemporary child rearing, that all but the very highest income stratum families were included in the sample.

Emphasis on Families Most in Need of Support

The second point to be noted here with regard to sampling, however, does make it clear where the center of gravity of the intervention lay. The decision to oversample black and single-parent families was grounded in the belief of the investigators that although nearly all contemporary families experience stress in attempting to rear their children optimally, racial minority, low-income families, and families generally with the least amount of social support experience problems in greater measure than do others.

In the original plan for the U.S. research component, black families were to be included, but only as the result of random selection. Cross (Cross et al., 1977), a Cornell colleague of Bronfenbrenner and Cochran, with special interests in the Afro-American family, pointed out to them that blacks constitute only about 12 percent of the population of Syracuse, New York. This number was insufficient to permit systematic analysis of the experience of black families. He presented evidence suggesting that the study of the nature and impact of support systems on black culture in the United States has "special importance both for science and for social policy." He argued that racism has "increased the vulnerability of the black family by restricting access to external support systems." Also, in some instances, "the Black family has been demeaned, and its capacity to function impaired, by policies and practices that, in the name of rendering service, have in fact promoted stagnation rather than social mobility" (Cross et al., 1977, p. 2). Thus, it was critical to the study of urban developmental settings generally that a significant sample of black families be included.

Recognizing the validity of these arguments, Bronfenbrenner and Cochran asked Cross to become a partner in the investigative team, and the beefed-up sample of black families became a part of the sampling design of the research. Cross's most valuable theoretical contribution to the Comparative Ecology of Human Development Project was his stress on ". . . the development of the child's *sense of self in relation to others*, with particular reference to ethnic identity" (Bronfenbrenner and Cochran in Cross et al., 1977, p. 3, emphasis in original). Stated specifically:

> The basic hypothesis underlying this phase of the investigation posits that the child's emerging awareness of self in relation to others functions as a powerful determinant of the extent to which existing abilities and skills can be actually utilized.

Clearly this hypothesis is conceptually related to Bronfenbrenner and Cochran's first hypothesis which speaks of comparable aspects of child development, i.e., "competence, cooperation, sustained effort in pursuit of a goal;" and just as Bronfenbrenner and Cochran's second hypothesis set a mediating condition for Hypothesis I, Cross's thinking "stipulated an important mediating condition," i.e., reference group orientation, for the kind of development that was to be studied.

De-Emphasis of a "Deficit" Orientation

In the two preceding sections we have seen that while Family Matters was not designed to serve low-income families exclusively, it did place an emphasis on studying and helping families most in need of social support. This approach, which manifested itself structurally in the above mentioned oversampling of low-income, black, and single-parent families, might have led to an attitudinal manifestation toward participating families that has been called "the deficit model." In a presentation to the program staff on November 22, 1978 entitled, "Experimental Programs for Family Matters: The Biography of Some Dissident Ideas," Bronfenbrenner objected to the dominant practice of human service professionals of determining on their own what is best for growing children and families rather than being responsive to their clients' existing strengths and taking their cue from those being served. He found that the service professionals were oriented to "putting down" their clients on "honorable grounds." Bronfenbrenner, Cochran, and Cross all concurred that whatever forms the Family Matters Program took, and whatever the economic, racial, or social circumstances of its participants, program policy and staff-to-participant communication would have to avoid this deficit orientation and rather reflect respect for the values and capabilities of all families.

Later in program history, this shunning of a deficit orientation in approaching participating families, was cast in even more vigorous terminology. Phrases like "families have strengths" that need to be recognized and emphasized were utilized in both oral and written discussions of program philosophy. Still later we see that the word "empowerment" appeared in program-related documents and oral presentations. The term "empowerment" is a pivotal concept in the thinking of Freire (1971), and has been used *mutatis mutandis* by other family and childhood interventions (e.g., Lally's phrase describing one of the FDRP's aims, ". . . to increase their [parent's] potency in fostering the development of their children" (Lally et al., 1982, Appendix A). Sometimes the "empowerment" in Family Matters seemed to be related to child rearing in the home. At other times, empowerment appeared to be directed at parents vis-à-vis the community. But whether oriented toward the home or the social system, the decision by program designers was a highly significant one when they resolved to distance themselves as far as possible from a deficit approach in providing services. As we shall see later, it was a decision that had many, many ramifications in later program policy and implementation, some positive, some negative.

FAMILY MATTERS AND OTHER FAMILY AND CHILDHOOD INTERVENTIONS

Before we turn to a description of the implementation program policy itself, it is important that we reflect for a moment on the relationship between Family Matters and other family and childhood-oriented programs and to other kinds of interventions more broadly. Among other family and childhood interventions, Family Matters, like Head Start, chose a period that was relatively late, compared with those that began with prenatal care or early infancy. The scope of services was also more limited than some. In contrast, for example, with BEEP and FDRP, no health-care, diagnostic, or extensive nutritional services were planned; and while assisting families to benefit more fully from social services was contemplated, actually taking people to appointments (as was done at many CFRP sites) was not envisioned. There were no classes or play group for the preschooler, although child care was often provided.

In the original proposal Bronfenbrenner and Cochran (1976) *did* contemplate extending its purview to the wider community (for example, trying to influence parent-school and parent-employer relations) to help facilitate parents in their child-rearing roles, but the scope of Family Matters activities was, if anything, "middle-sized" compared with programs with four to seven major component interventions and those that offered only one.

The planned duration was much longer than most but shorter than some. Many interventions were to last for only a matter of months, while Family Matters was to run for at least four years. However, the program was not planned for a lifespan as long as the longest-lived interventions, some that went on for six or more years (e.g., BEEP and FDRP). Its planned intensity was also mid-range (for example, home visits were to be on an approximately biweekly rather than weekly basis, but this was more frequent than some other comparable intervention efforts).

Family Matters was thus in many respects of middling scope and intensity compared with many other programs of its kind, differing primarily in the strength of its research orientation, its concern for neighborhood-determined parent groups, and its emphasis (though this was not completely unique to Family Matters) on the family (rather than teachers or their surrogates) as the primary medium for influencing the cognitive development of the child.

The emphasis on neighborhood groups, however, and dealing with parent-neighborhood, parent-community, parent-employer, and parent-social service relationships did strengthen Family Matters, role as a program dealing with root causes of social problems. It was like other interventions designed to change the future by changing the child. But its attempts to change the future by making individual parents and neighborhood groups as change agents, puts it very clearly in the category of a program designed to effect progress in our social system.

But for now, we leave this broad description of the basic goals and design of the Family Matters Program, and its relationship to the Ecology of Human Development Project, to its older cousin, to Head Start, to other programmatic kin, and to the environmentalist or social change zeitgeist found among scholars or by people concerned with human development and family life. In consonance with the ecological orientation of Family Matters and other contemporary interventions, we now turn to a description of the urban context of the program and an assessment of the conditions that were favorable and inimical to implementation of the project's aspirations for human betterment.

4

SALT CITY: AT THE CROSSROADS

A GLANCE AT URBAN ECONOMIC THEORIES

Worldwide, the problems of the city today constitute a major preoccupation in both the scientific and the policy-making communities. Urban versus suburban residence, city versus extraurban taxation, overconcentration of populations within cities and overconcentration of cities within regions resulting in the creation of megalopolises, even the allocation of scarce food resources to metropolitan areas in preference to the needy of the countryside — these and many more issues are of no small concern to both social scientists and political leaders.

There is, thus, little wonder in the many attempts to make sense of the urban environment. Despite the relative newness of urbanology among the sciences, there is no dearth of macro-level theories that seek to explicate metropolitan growth, function, and decay. These theories have given rise to a variety of models, some spatial or geographic, others economic, political, sociological or psychological. But ardent disciplinary or even ideological commitments, highly idealized formal models, and the ever-present "simplifying assumptions" frequently give a view of the city which seems to bear only faint resemblance to reality (Mills and McKinnon, 1973). For the heuristic purposes of our discussion of Syracuse as the context for the Family Matters Program (and others like it), urbanological theories may be arranged along two bipolar continua that reflect: (1) individual versus aggregate levels of analysis; and (2) equilibrium versus conflict models of interpretation.

In pursuing their own disciplinary commitments, economists have evolved at least three major contemporary theoretical orientations toward the urban residential environment. These three orientations which bulk large in the pages of scholarly literature dealing with city life may be characterized as: (1) the neoclassical view; (2) manipulated city theory; (3) the Marxist or neo-Marxist variant of the manipulated city theory.

The Neoclassical View

The neoclassical view, as described by Richardson (1977), has its distant antecedents in the nineteenth century theory of agricultural land of von Thunen (1966). According to the neoclassical perspective, each present-day urban family, like von Thunen's nineteenth century farmer, seeks a residence that will maximize the utility of that portion of its disposable income allocated for housing. Because incomes and transport costs differ from household to household, families distribute themselves broadly across the urban landscape, thus achieving social equilibrium or "a fundamental harmony of interests in society" (cf. Cox, 1978) in the usage of available land. Politically speaking, these *pluralistic* interests receive expression in decision making affecting urban life, and in the main a variety of legitimate societal subgroups have power in the city. According to this viewpoint, democratic political institutions in most metropolitan areas function as they were meant to (cf. Dahl, 1953; Truman, 1958).

The "Manipulated City"

More recently, this micro-economic equilibrium-oriented perspective has come in for considerable criticism because of its alleged simplistic character. Opponents contend that individual preferences in housing are insignificant relative to the influence exerted on urban life by various institutions. Thus, the central thesis of Gale and Moore's (1975) "The Manipulated City" is that important institutions and interests (e.g., banks, government agencies, insurance companies, developers, real estate firms, the construction industry, etc.) control residential land in the city far more profoundly than do the preferences of individual families. In "manipulated city theory" there is little said about equilibrium in the allocation of land resources. Rather, the implication is raised that there is maldistribution of resources that results from the unequal struggle between individuals and institutions.

The Marxist "Manipulated City"

In the Marxist variant of manipulated city theory (Cox, 1978; Harvey, 1978), this concept of struggle is amplified to the point where competition is not viewed as a kind of social Darwinism, but rather as part of the age-old conflict between capital and labor. Residential land is variously seen as useful in: "entrapping labor close to the workplace in the central business district," winning labor's adherence to the concept of private property by giving it a trivial "piece of the action," extracting further surplus value from labor in the form of land rent, encouraging the reproduction of the labor supply, "keeping workers, mortgaged to the hilt" so that they will be solid citizens, and generally exerting the kind of control over labor at home that capital enjoys over workers at the workplace (Cox, 1978; Harvey, 1978). Thus Marxist proponents of this perspective see attempts at neighborhood mobilization and other similar efforts to raise their political voice by the urban poor as seldom successful endeavors by "the people" to counter the machinations ". . . of a greedy, powerful and unprincipled clique of individuals . . . to rape and dehumanize . . . the city, all in a merely pecuniary interest" (Roweis and Scott, 1978, pp. 48, 49). Clearly, then, both Marxist and non-Marxist manipulated theory is heavily aggregate-oriented in its class struggle perspective, and conflict, as opposed to equilibrium-oriented, in its nexus.

In looking at Syracuse as a "developmental context" and as the site of the Family Matters Program, we have tried to keep these three theoretical orientations in mind. As pointed out above, one of the general thrusts of the program was empowerment. Its origins were in the movements of the 1960s toward social change and combating poverty. Organizing neighborhood groups, one of its two main prongs of effort, was in effect an attempt at urban neighborhood mobilization. And most important, economic conditions within the city were hypothesized to be and indeed turned out to be among the most important stressors encountered by families in their attempts to rear their children with the support of the Family Matters Program. Before analyzing these economic conditions in light of the above three politico-economic theories, we provide some brief historical notes on the city of Syracuse, how those origins gave rise to its contemporary fortunes, and a snapshot of the broad developmental ecology in which program participants were attempting to raise their preschoolers. We will then turn to a discussion of the ways in which living in Syracuse and other contemporary cities makes child rearing easier or more difficult.

INDIANS, DEMONS, A PRIEST, AND SALT

Located in central New York State, Syracuse is situated on the south end of Lake Onondaga at a point where the Great Lakes plains and the Allegheny Plateau meet to form rolling hills and valley lakes and streams. An unwary observer in days of yore might have thought that a tribe of Indians, the Onondagas, were indigenous inhabitants of the area. But the name, Onondaga, means "people of the great hill," and these members of the Six Nations of the Iroquois Confederacy only maintained trails in the region (Hall, 1980). The land was swampy, overgrown by pines, sedge, and cedars, and prone to flooding and insect infestation. Area waters were briny, bad-tasting, and foul-smelling, leading Father Simone LeMoyne, a mid-seventeenth century Jesuit missionary from Canada to conclude that the source of the problem was salt sedimentation, not the demons hypothesized by Indian legend.

In the first quarter of the nineteenth century, the area and what is now downtown Syracuse remained so marshy that it was said that it would "make an owl weep to fly over it." (Ibid.) These environs had a reputation as the most unhealthy place in the state and were known as "the abode of pestilence and death" (Ibid.). After an initial settlement as a trading post in 1786, much of what is now Syracuse had attracted permanent settlers beginning in 1788 to take up salt production, thus converting what was previously a liability into a natural resource.

In light of the importance of this resource, the village established by the salt-producers had originally been named "Salina" by the New York State legislature, which had taken an active role in promoting settlement of the region. Indeed, Syracuse owed its very existence in its early years to government intervention. In 1788, the New York State legislature offered land grants as inducements to prospective settlers, and established the Salt Springs Reservation for the Onondaga Indians. Ten years later the village of Salina was "ordered" into existence by the same legislature. A tract of land near Salina became the site of a mill and an east-west, state-spanning highway. This area later became known as "Corinth" and after several name changes, Corinth became "Syracuse" when a student of ancient history noted that Syracuse had been a Roman city in Sicily situated near a lake with salt springs and a place called Salina nearby.

Salina and Syracuse coexisted as rival towns, with the former a center for salt production and the latter as a center for trade. In 1848, however, the two decided to join their fortunes and were incorporated as the city of Syracuse with a population of approximately 20,000. The Erie Canal, which had reached Salina and Syracuse in the 1820s, improved communication and transportation, also beginning the process of uniting the disparate and sometimes feuding German, Irish, and Italian ethnic communities. Polish, Jewish, and black settlers were attracted over the years by the growing economic success enjoyed by Syracuse as business and industry grew. During the same period, the water level of the lake was lowered, the swamps drained, and a "salt rush" began to bring prosperity to the area. During the latter part of the nineteenth century, the great canal brought grain from the midwestern United States producing a profound change in the regional economy from the raising of grain to general farming. This general farming along with urban manufacturing was carried out by workers from diverse ethnic communities, and constitutes the pattern that prevails to this day.

SYRACUSE TODAY – A TYPICAL U.S. CITY

In many ways, Syracuse is typical of other U.S. cities of moderate size, so "typical," in fact, that according to information received from the Onondaga County executive it is a "standard market test area," and thus the frequent target of marketing-research surveys by companies whose brand name products are distributed nationally. Unfortunately, it is also typical of other U.S. urban areas in suffering many of the same forms of societal malaise that characterize other cities in this the last quarter of the twentieth century. Inflation, high taxes and interest rates, slow economic growth, a short supply of low- and moderate-income housing, transportation and energy problems, unequitable distribution of employment and other economic opportunities among various social and ethnic groups, intergroup tensions, political corruption, crime, and delinquency — these all-too-familiar woes of the U.S. city are all to characteristic of Syracuse.

Unlike other towns in this country, Syracuse gets more than its share of precipitation in the form of both rain and snow. The city is first among municipalities of its size in the amount of annual snowfall. Its skies are drearily cloud-covered more than half of the days of the year, and in this respect, Syracuse is second only to Wheeling, West Virginia in climatic gloom among cities of comparable size. Consequently, the Syracuse sun cannot be counted on very often to brighten and gladden the human spirit. As we shall see later on, this pall and precipitation, as well as the city's icy winters, have contributed their share in driving residents to leave town in search of drier and warmer climes.

As various public officials interviewed (including two county legislators) have pointed out, it is fortunate that industry in the city is fairly well diversified, and Syracuse is not a "company town" whose fortunes rise and fall with those of one manufacturer. The largest *industrial* employer in the county is the Carrier Air Conditioning Corporation, providing jobs for about 7,000 persons. Within the city limits, Syracuse University employs the greatest number of persons and in many ways is central to the city's economy and future prospects. Though economically depressed in many ways, Syracuse was recently ranked by Boyer and Savageau (1981) as the seventh most "livable" city in the United States, primarily because of its educational and cultural facilities — a far cry from the erstwhile "abode of pestilence and death."

EXODUS AND ECONOMIC DECLINE

The Exodus

Like many other cities in the northeastern and midwestern United States, urban Syracuse has recently been experiencing a loss of population living within the city limits during the past 30 years (Connor, 1979; Peters, 1979). Census figures show that Syracuse inhabitants numbered approximately 220,000 in 1950 and 197,200 in 1970 (Sacks and Andrews, 1974). Figures for 1980 show a population of 170,105, a decline of nearly one-fourth in only three decades, and a drop of nearly 15 percent in the last 10 years alone (U.S. Bureau of Census, 1981). On the other hand, between 1960 and 1970, the black population of the city nearly doubled; and recent increases make the Syracuse black community one of the fastest growing within the nation (Sacks and Andrews, 1974). Some of the loss of white residents has been the result of their movement to completely different parts of the country, especially the "sunbelt" where they seek to forget cold, cloudy skies, and snow-drifts, and where they can search for jobs in a more favorable *economic* climate. Some of the city's population loss however, has been due to flight to the suburbs where the housing stock is newer than that in inner-city areas. Former urban-dwellers, now suburbanites, remain largely in the same county, Onondaga County, with a total population that has swelled to approximately 600,000.

Economic Decline

The exodus from the city to the suburbs and to the sunbelt has been accompanied by concurrent economic decline in the city (Connor, 1979; Peters, 1979). For example, between 1960 and 1970, the number of jobs available (mostly blue-collar and traditionally held by males) shrank 10.7 percent (Sacks and Andrews, 1974). It is difficult to determine whether the job loss caused the population to decline or vice versa. In all likelihood the causality was bidirectional, with the job market losses being more influential. But what is clear is that during most of the duration of the Family Matters Program, unemployment in Syracuse itself exceeded the national average (Mindick and Boyd, 1982). And this reality, of course, had the expected impact on many program families.

Some of the reasons offered for the defection of industry, commerce, and residents are: (1) high state taxes on businesses and individuals; (2) the search for cheaper labor markets; (3) a desire by both individuals and commercial interests to avoid the high energy costs mandated by the area's climate; and (4) a more general preference by employers and employees for the lifestyle of the newer sunbelt areas. The resulting outmigration by industry, commerce, and residents has had the dire ramifications for the city's economy mentioned earlier, making it the *sixth worst* metropolitan area in the country for economic opportunity, according to Boyer and Savageau (1981).

In Syracuse as elsewhere, the outflow of jobs, industry, and residents has also meant a marked shrinkage of the tax base, leaving political leaders with the task of providing municipal services from a drastically reduced pool of local revenues. Consequently these leaders in concert with the service and business professionals as well as labor union officials have adopted three major tactics to compensate for the lost income (Titch, 1980). These strategies have been: (1) to vie for state and federal assistance; (2) to attract new industry; and (3) to make the central city a commercial and cultural magnet.

Obtaining State and Federal Revenues

Since 1970, the city's four-term mayor, Lee Alexander, like many of his colleagues in other U.S. cities, has aggressively pursued the acquisition of external sources of support for the city (Connor, 1979). In 1979, for example, the combined city-school budget drew on federal and state moneys for more than half of its funding. But the latter 1970s saw cutbacks in federal revenue-sharing programs by the Carter administration, and similar budget slashing by New York State's previous governor, Hugh Carey (Bliven, 1980). These cuts and more recent budget tightening by the Reagan administration have seriously blunted this strategy to draw income into the city's coffers. And if current news reports are correct in relation to important decreases in Urban Development Action Grant (UDAG) funding as a result of deficit reduction efforts by the second Reagan administration, then municipal fiscal problems will grow even worse.

In this tale of relative abundance diminishing to more straitened circumstances, Syracuse is by no means unique. Indeed it is the tale of many if not most municipal governments pressed by dwindling federal and state support. But in Syracuse and in comparable cities of the northeast and midwest especially, the fiscal crunch is worsened by the kind of economic and demographic declines described earlier. Indeed, the weaning away from outside support is further complicated by the very exceptional success of Syracuse and other aggressive city governments of a decade ago in raising aid from outside their borders, aid that has now contracted drastically.

Attracting New Industry

As a result of this contraction of extra-urban and intra-urban revenues, a second strategy employed to bolster the city financially has involved a campaign to attract new industry to Syracuse. "Come-hither" signals have been sent to various commercial enterprises located both in the United States and abroad (e.g., Japan) with a view to luring them to the city. Syracuse boosters have been stressing the city's "livability," since, as mentioned earlier, the same Boyer and Savageau (1981) study cited above that damned the city's economy, rated Syracuse as the seventh most agreeable city to live in among 277 metropolitan areas (Lyman, 1982).

Efforts to bring back business and industry to Syracuse would arrest the population decline, broaden the tax base, and provide jobs for current city-dwellers. But unfortunately for such attempts to recruit industry, for existing Syracuse commercial interests, and for resident families, personal and business income taxes within New York State are quite high. According to figures taken from the recent past, years that roughly represent the early and mid-life of Family Matters (Boyer and Savageau, 1981), the tax bite (combined personal income and sales taxes) taken out of household income in New York State is one of the four highest among the 50 states of the union. State taxes on business and industry are similarly heavy and have provided the impetus for the outflow of business to nearby New Jersey and other neighboring states. Similarly onerous are local levies on residential and commercial property.

In the city, the high taxes are, at least in part, due to the prior defection of financial enterprises and residents, and (as the mayor stressed in a neighborhood meeting attended by our staff) because of the expansion of tax-exempt property. Those anxious to attract new business warn against "poisoning downtown" through excessive taxation, and call for higher assessments on residential property. At the very same time, residential advocates insist quite rightly that homeowners must be preserved from collapse under the taxation yoke (Connor, 1979; Driscoll, 1979), arguing that business must bear a greater burden than it does now.

The city has had some success attracting new industry, for example, a caustic soda plant, and a new enlarged brewery that was planned to employ 3,000 workers. To draw firms, efforts have been put forth and still continue to expand municipal airport facilities, to improve and extend highway networks, and to provide housing for middle- and upper-income-level employees, along with shopping areas and entertainment and cultural attractions. The attempt is quite comparable to "gentrification" programs found in many other urban areas, from major ones like Boston, New York, Washington, and Baltimore, to those as small as Worcester, Massachusetts or Ithaca, New York. All of these efforts are designed to revive the central city.

Making the Central City a Commercial and Cultural Magnet

Gentrification, of course, is not just designed as a lure to industry. In Syracuse, as elsewhere, the effort is intended to enhance the city's economy by bringing to the urban core a variety of magnet enterprises aimed at drawing people, hence shoppers and dollars, back into the downtown area. Several shopping malls and commercial centers have been built.

Another project which is bringing about an even more significant change in the city's ecology is the new 50,000 seat enclosed stadium, the Carrier Dome, built by the Syracuse University with the aid of the Carrier Air Conditioning Corporation and of the State of New York. The dome with its athletic and entertainment events, its parking lots, concessions and support facilities, has already become a major attraction within the city. Moreover, it also draws patrons for other business nearby (i.e., hotels, motels, restaurants, theaters, etc.).

All of this, however, has created a situation of considerable ambivalence for Syracuse political leaders. They are pleased about the jobs created by the university's entrepreneurial activity and the spin-off revenues the city derives from private businesses that are associated with the Carrier Dome complex. But, they claim that when the university brings rock concerts and other forms of mass entertainment to the dome, stadium usage should not be considered "educational," and income derived by the university should not be considered tax exempt.

The university, on the other hand, proclaims its status as a state agency and the breadth of the scope of its tax-free classification as an institution of higher learning. The city has countered by demanding that the university open its financial accounts related to the dome, hoping to show that the university is realizing large profits from noneducational activities, profits from which taxes of various kinds should be paid. They argue quite pointedly about the additional services, especially those related to policing, transportation, and traffic control, that are demanded by dome events. The university continues to refuse to open its books, and for the past several years the arena of conflict between the city of Syracuse and Syracuse University has been both the courts and the local news media.

In addition to the dome and other projects that are even more clearly commercial ventures, the university has been expanding its academic and administrative buildings in recent years as well as its dormitory space and other residence facilities. All of these moves both by the university and by private business interests who wish to become part of the entertainment and commercial complex associated with the city's core and adjacent inner ring have resulted in a steady incursion. Slowly, as in other urban areas, residences for city dwellers of modest income are either being demolished or remodeled in accordance with the interests of nonresidents.

FAMILIES VERSUS NON-RESIDENTIAL INTERESTS

There are other large-scale construction projects that have dislocated or threaten to displace Syracuse inner city dwellers. These projects may be as genteel as the new downtown cultural complex, or as unpleasantly intrusive as construction of a proposed garbage-burning steam generating plant. Sponsored by county government, one projected location for this plant was to be in the midst of the most populous area in Onondaga County, the site of one of the first (mid-1930s) low-income housing projects in the United States. This last encroachment seems to have been unpopular enough that the locations being presently considered are ones that will do no violence to any residential property (Andrews, 1981). The change of plans was brought about by effective mobilization, partly by private citizens, partly by dissenting political leaders (mostly from the city), and partly by Syracuse United Neighborhoods (an aggregate of small neighborhood groups). But here, as in many other metropolitan areas, the overall pattern is clear. Land within the central city area is attractive because of its location. Occupied by low- and moderate-income residents, it is comparatively inexpensive to buy, and the constituency that might protect such territory has limited political clout. Such land is thus a tempting target for purchase by commercial and other interests.

There is strong evidence of an alliance among political leadership, business, industry, education, and labor. It would be simplistic, however, to characterize Syracuse as a city consciously manipulated by a monolithic power structure against the interests of lower-income strata. The above mentioned attempts to attract federal and state aid and the uses to which that aid has been put, i.e., schools, CETA jobs, transfer payments, home improvement etc., show political sensitivity to the needs of individual households, especially those of lower income, in addition to the self-interested requirements of officials trying to run a city on a tight budget. Efforts to bring industry to the city involve cooperation of not just business, industry, and political figures, but of labor leadership as well.

Rather than capital against labor, competition or conflict is largely between those who are concerned about tax revenues or profits, and those concerned about residential lifestyle and families. The pluralistic perspective of Dahl and Truman is supported by evidence from the successful mobilization of individuals and small community groups around the siting of the projected steam plant and in other areas as well. Also contrary to Marxist or neo-Marxist views of urban conflict pitting business people and landlords against labor, we find that there is a strong support by both business and organized labor in Syracuse for the mayor in his attempts to attract industry. In addition, there is reason to believe that rather than an overriding interest in conspiring with owners against workers, city government's chief concern seems to be that of an institution in fiscal decline which is motivated to perpetuate its organizational life cycle (see Katz and Kahn, 1978; Kimberly, Miles, and Associates, 1980).

As for making the central city a commercial and cultural magnet, much the same analysis is applicable — a coalition of commercial, industrial, political, and educational interests; in other words, non-residents versus residents. Downtown residents are those most affected by such development, while other city residents, both middle and upper income, are ambivalent. These latter groups can enjoy the shopping and cultural activities, but they also need to endure increased traffic, and shoulder the tax burden resulting from "not poisoning downtown" by high taxes as well as from the rapid expansion of tax exempt property. Indeed, as we have seen earlier, the growth of cultural and educational enterprises within the city creates ambivalence even among city political leaders. They regard such enterprises as inherently good, as stimulating commerce, and as attracting industrial growth through enhancing the quality of city life. But fiscally minded officials bewail the loss of property tax revenues.

Sometimes, as business, labor, political leaders, and educational institutions vie with one another in pursuit of their own interests, there is considerable conflict among these competing factions. Indeed, at this writing the mayor is suing the city council because its members have refused to pass his recommended 11-dollar per thousand increase in property tax assessment for 1985. The council instead wants an increase less than half the size of the mayor's request. And here we are confronted with another principle that emerges from our scrutiny of this city — that there are few permanent coalitions among the large and institutional elements in urban life. Rather, "coalition shifting" is more the norm and cooperation, competition, and conflict are transitory phenomena depending on the issue at stake. But whatever the issue or the coalition, what is most important in the present analysis is that the very strategies taken by city leadership to offset urban decline are the same factors that most effectively weaken local community structure and affiliation. Attracting industry and making the central city a commercial and cultural magnet result in encroachment on residential neighborhoods or their outright destruction.

THE SYRACUSE RESIDENTIAL ENVIRONMENT

As in other urban areas around the United States, many central city neighborhoods are ripe for such encroachment and destruction. For several years now, the deterioration of the city's old and dwindling housing stock has posed a substantial problem. The tight consumer credit of recent years has made it extremely difficult to obtain money for home construction and mortgages (Newer, 1979). Hence, there has been very little new residential building within the city or in the suburbs. Even nonresidential construction has lagged except in a few specialized categories. High taxes relative to rental incomes have led to owner abandonment of property and to tax default. Houses may then be unmaintained, vandalized, and later condemned; or, in many cases, they burn down under circumstances in which arson is strongly suspected. Thus the state of the urban residential environment becomes a causal factor in the urban flight outlined earlier (cf. Orbell and Uno, 1972). Then, closing the unhappy circle, the outmigration and economic decline give rise to the coping strategies described above, which in turn have their effect on the residential environment for those who choose to remain in the city.

CENSUS TRACT 32 – A CASE IN POINT

The impact of gentrification and other coping strategies on local community structure can be seen in the demographic changes of the city's census tract 32 which includes parts of the central business district. The percent of black residents in this area went from 73.2 to 12 in the years between 1960 and 1970 (Sacks and Andrews, 1974). This census tract was the commercial and social core of the black community. The demolition of the area had a profound effect on over 3,000 families and individuals who were relocated through urban renewal. Thus, the former center of the black community is now a location for new offices, commercial buildings, psychiatric and medical centers, a theater, a museum, and an interstate highway.

Mobilization Efforts

Local cohesiveness and sometimes successful organizational efforts can still be seen in campaigns by individuals, neighborhood groups, and various political leaders to: (1) lower utility rates, property assessments, and related taxes; (2) prevent conversion of residential property to nonresidential use; (3) deter vandalism, arson, and crime in general; and (4) improve and increase the available housing stock for the elderly and other low-income and moderate-income persons. Syracuse United Neighborhoods (SUN), the Urban League, the Public Power Coalition, and the Syracuse Ad Hoc Coalition for a Just Society have been particularly active in all of these areas. Understandably, however, their efforts are frequently in direct competition with those exerted by nonresidential interests. Furthermore, city officials seek to keep a lid on services and to expand, or at least maintain revenues, by converting low-value residential property to commercial, industrial, cultural, or *high-income* residential use. As in the case of the black community cited above, such development generally results in the exile of the neediest residents who rarely return despite assurances to the contrary that are often given at the outset of gentrification efforts. Smaller proportions of central city area are devoted to residences, and these are occupied by young, single, and less rooted professionals and business people who are increasingly attracted to central cities because of transportation and energy problems.

The elimination of low- and moderate-income housing exacerbates the city's already short supply of reasonably priced good quality housing. It is thus no surprise that in an interview, the director of the Syracuse Housing Authority indicated that some families were presently required to remain on a waiting list for two years to obtain some form of subsidized housing. As for repair and refurbishing of existing homes, some monies have been available through private and public sponsorship, especially Community Development Funds, but for several reasons that cannot be elaborated here, progress in this area is very slow. SUN, composed of a coalition of 15 low- and moderate-income, racially mixed neighborhood associations, has tried to further such fix-up programs, and is even demanding federal investigation of the problems ("Group Wants City Plan Audited," 1980). Whatever the outcome, the outlines of the conflict in the city are quite clear — commercial development versus housing (Connor, 1979), residents versus nonresidents, macro-social versus micro-social (and local community interests).

MOBILITY AND FAMILY MATTERS

Moving from macro-level observations (that is, the city at large) to those at the micro-level (those made of program families), project data reflect similar patterns of shift, both with regard to population loss generally as well as the twin streams of movement. Table 1 shows movement by program families in each of the ten neighborhoods where the intervention was carried out. In some neighborhoods, attrition from the program was as high as 27 percent, with a mean rate of 10.8 percent. This attrition took place over the course of only a little more than two years, as compared with the above cited 15 percent population loss in the city generally, which has occurred over the last decade. Furthermore, approximately 25 percent of all program families have changed residences in those two years, causing considerable difficulty for a program whose aim is to develop wide-ranging, strong, and stable social networks for families by involving them in the activity of *neighborhood* groups. The effectiveness of the neighborhood group intervention technique was obviously much diminished every time a family moved out of a given neighborhood, even if the family remained within the city or county but lost touch with its former program family neighbors. But when movement was out of the county or state, or when families simply disappeared without a trace, obviously, they could no longer be served by the program. As Table 1 shows, 17 of the 40 families (42.5 percent) who moved were lost completely.

The picture that emerges from these data on program family transiency is simply that in only a little more than 24 months, fully one-fourth of the experimental group to a greater or lesser extent lost some of the benefits of the social-network-promoting "treatment"; and for nearly one-half of these persons, the treatment was no longer available at all. Examination of the demographic characteristics of those among whom transiency was highest showed that as might be expected, dislocation was highest in the city, as opposed to the suburban county areas. Change of location averaged 16.2 percent in the two county (i.e., suburban) neighborhoods, only about half of the 27.7 percent rate in city neighborhoods. Similarly, family loss to the program was only about half as great in county neighborhoods as in those of the city (6.7 versus 11.9 percent). In the two program neighborhoods where strong ties existed for many families through a European ethnic background, loss to the program was extremely low — only one family out of a combined total of over 30 families. Finally, we note that transiency was higher in low- and moderate-income black or racially mixed neighborhoods, as opposed to middle-income white neighborhoods.

TABLE 1
Program Families (N = 157): Mobility and Attrition 1979-81

Neighborhood code name, selected characteristics, and no. of families	Total no. of families that moved	Total percent of families that moved	Moved within city or county	Moved out of county	Moved out of state	Moved; address unknown	Total no. of families unknown/ lost	Total percent of families unknown/ lost
L-F(N = 14) City, low, black	4	28.6	3	0	1	0	1	07.1
SS(N = 17) City, middle, mixed	4	23.5	2	0	1	1	2	11.8
W-T(N = 16) City, middle, mixed	6	35.3	3	1	2	0	3	17.6
E (N = 17) City, moderate, white	7	41.2	5	1	0	1	2	11.8
TH(N = 15) City, middle, white	1	06.7	0	0	1	0	1	06.7

Neighborhood code name, selected characteristics, and no. of families	Total no. of families that moved	Total percent of families that moved	Moved within city or county	Moved out of county	Moved out of state	Moved; address unknown	Total no. of families unknown/lost	Total percent of families unknown/lost
T-S (N=15) City, low, black	6	40.0	2	1	2	1	4	26.7
S-W (N=16) City, middle, white	1	06.3	1	0	0	0	0	0.0
LBJ (N=15) City, low, mixed	6	40.0	4	1	0	1	2	13.3
Ne (N=15) County, moderate, white	3	20.0	1	1	1	1	2	13.2
L (N=16) County, middle, white	2	12.5	2	0	0	0	0	0.0
	40	254.1%	23	5	8	5	17	108.2%

aNeighborhoods are classified in terms of: (1) location within city or county; (2) low, moderate, or middle-income levels; and (3) racial composition of black, white, or mixed.

According to information from the project's liaison staff, which converges with our own observational data, much of this transiency in low-income neighborhoods involved poor families moving to stay one step ahead of landlords demanding rent payments. Thus, some families moved two and three times within a year, sometimes within the same neighborhood, sometimes outside it. Obviously, none of this facilitated the delivery of program services. This mobility accounted in part for the participation rates in Family Matters activities that will be discussed in later chapters, those related to home visits, but especially those associated with neighborhood groups. It would be hard to expect a family constantly on the move to have any great sense of neighborhood, territoriality, identification with neighbors, or even much time or energy for voluntary association.

MOBILITY AND URBAN PROGRAMS GENERALLY

We have presented an extensive description of Syracuse in the foregoing sections of this chapter, discussing the city's history, demographic shifts, economic and housing problems, the fiscal difficulties experienced by municipal government, and the steps taken by city leaders to counter these problems. We have seen the hard times experienced by the city at the macro-level and at the micro-level by families generally (including program families). We have noted that the very measures taken by city leaders to keep government afloat impact most severely on property taxes, on housing, or residential neighborhoods, and on families once again.

Our purpose in this extended excursus is threefold: (1) to account for the problems of service delivery and participation in the Family Matters Program; (2) to suggest that mobility is an important factor in the indifferent effectiveness of many kinds of urban social program regardless of hue or stripe; and (3) to document the assertion made in Chapter 1, that even positing the best of intentions, the social problems tackled by most social programs are simply not susceptible to easy solutions.

Program Participant Mobility and Attrition

With regard to the first point, mobility and attrition of individual Family Matters participants, we have seen how economic and housing difficulties affected fully 25 percent of the experimental group in a little more than two years, creating attrition from the sample. But more important, from the perspective of efficacy, mobility made the delivery of program services more difficult, and in promoting neighborhood social networking, it made the intervention meaningless.

This leads us to our second point, which suggests that similar causes frequently undermine implementation of other child- and family-oriented interventions and other urban programs more generally. Although program family mobility was high, it is lower than the national norm during the early 1970s when one in five U.S. citizens moved annually, and in recent years the same high rate of transiency has continued among certain population subgroups (cf. Heller, 1980; Trimble, 1980).

Syracuse is by no means atypical with regard to the mobility problems it faces or the steps taken to solve these problems. It may differ from the sunbelt or other cities experiencing population growth and/or economic upturn. But it does share much in common with many major and middle-sized northeastern and midwestern cities that are in decline. Furthermore, Syracuse's difficulties parallel those of many central cities, regardless of region or state of growth, in relation to the issue of suburbanization. Indeed, in many western and southern cities, there is even greater pressure being put on low-income families living in central cities by *growing* populations and economies. This pressure is translated into the displacement of families from housing and neighborhoods. Also universal is a desire by government to enhance revenues through taxation and to minimize services wherever possible. Syracuse is unique in none of these respects. As a matter of fact, Boyer and Savageau (1981, p. 382) have rated Syracuse as the third best metropolitan area (which includes the affluent suburbs of Onondaga County) for young families raising children because of the availability of affordable housing, the low crime-rate, the good schools, and the excellent recreational opportunities. This means that there are many, many metropolitan areas in this land where the problems of young families are more acute than they are in Syracuse.

Nor are the implications of mobility and counter-mobility strategies unique to Family Matters or other comparable interventions. It is clear that any social program will experience difficulties in delivering services to a population that is struggling for subsistence and that is likely to experience transiency. Program outcome evaluation reports often mention attrition (Knudsen, Scott, and Shore, 1977). But they rarely mention the segment of the sample who are available for outcome measurement but who have been only episodically available for the treatment. Also rarely discussed in simple pre-post analyses is the disproportionately large amount of staff time that must be allocated to service mobile populations.

No Easy Answers

Our detailed, ethnographic analysis of the urban environment, in addition to suggesting the difficulties experienced by Family Matters and likely to be the lot of other programs as well, also demonstrates very graphically the magnitude and interrelatedness of the problems Family Matters and other interventions seek to remedy.

Our analysis of the current urban scene illustrated by Syracuse has shown that there is a clash between the interests of business, industry, education, labor, and other nonresidents, and those of residents, especially nonaffluent families with children. Among these contenders stands municipal government. From a strictly fiscal or management perspective, government might be expected to maximize revenues and to minimize the expenditures to provide services. Education typically consumes a very large share of a municipal budget. On a relative basis, low-income families with small children are high consumers of services, and individually are small producers of municipal revenues. Commercial and industrial interests, and affluent households (especially those without children) require less in the way of expensive services and are more likely to pay taxes. Business and industry not only pay taxes of various sorts, but they also provide jobs.

From a political point of view, city officials cannot ignore voters, even poor voters. And municipalities must not only support education and basic services, they must provide amenities to attract or maintain existing "supplies" of residents and commercial enterprises. Thus, the dilemma. If city leaders are forced to provide too much in the way of services, this drives up taxes, and drives out those who pay taxes and/or provide jobs. Not only does this hurt city government. Ultimately such outflows of revenues and jobs hurt consumers of city services and those who need jobs. Syracuse and New York state are excellent examples of this problem. A recently published study carried out by the Center for Social and Demographic Analysis at the State University of New York at Albany, showed that the years 1975-80 (roughly contemporaneous with Family Matters) saw a veritable exodus of affluent and educated New Yorkers (Berger, 1984). This exodus was accompanied by a net loss of 300,000 persons in the state labor force. On the other hand, displacement of families from inner city lands, high property taxes on residences (to avoid "poisoning downtown") works the kinds of hardship on families that we have described above.

Interventions like Family Matters that urge maintenance of neighborhood strength, encourage parents to maximize the education of their youngsters by insisting on the high quality and the fiscal wherewithal that good education requires and that stimulate low-income families to utilize government services to the fullest, work in a direction that is likely to cost government more and produce less in the way of revenue. Yet the quality of life of both poor and middle-income families, the encouragement of child rearing and education, and the maintenance of strong neighborhoods are not only important humanitarian values, they are also necessary components of urban life that city administrations need to look to for their own survival. The analysis becomes even more complex when one recollects that one cannot really divide urban interests into neat categories of residents versus nonresidents. The business, industrial, labor, and educational "nonresidential interests" described above are personified in human beings with families who are themselves residents. And the "residential interests" we spoke of earlier turn out to be business people, industrialists, educators, white-collar workers, and laborers, who have a stake in a healthy city economy and a municipal treasury that can afford services. The distinction between residential and nonresidential interests has some heuristic value, but it is a concept limited by the reality that often both sets of interests reside in the same human being.

Thus, none of the three academic perspectives on the city whether individualistic or aggregate oriented is particularly successful by itself at capturing the reality of urban life today. To say, for example, as the pluralists seem to, that the interests of all urban groups are all pretty well represented, and that in the struggle between them, it all turns out pretty well, is to miss the anguish, the disadvantage, and the falling by the wayside of many urban residents (cf. above p. 58, what happened to Census Tract 32). On the other hand, the perspective of manipulated city theorists, especially that of the Marxist variety, perhaps misses the mark even more. This view, which sees a monied power elite self-consciously engaged in unbridled and nefarious machinations against labor and the poor generally with the connivance of political leaders, has overlooked the kinds of services cities provide, the electoral process, the compromises government officials must constantly make, the conflict and coalition-shifting that exist within the alleged power elite itself, and most of all the reality that in our political and economic system, without some incentive and/or grant of voice to those who pay the highest taxes and provide the jobs, revenues, services, and work would not be there for those who need them.

As for social programs which seek to intervene in this complex, interrelated system (i.e., save the neighborhoods, maintain and increase services, especially those related to education, keep residential taxes down), such efforts enter a maelstrom of competing interests and unknown long-range consequences. The good intent and the potential benefits of such interventions could be considerable from a humanistic perspective, but that will not prevent their encountering tremendous resistance to change, in the form of both inertia and (in some cases) active opposition. There is also the very real potential for reverse effects in urban programs (cf. especially Forrester, 1971). It is therefore not surprising that success does not come easily. As indicated earlier, the magnitude and interrelatedness of the problems confronted make it impossible for the size of positive effects to be otherwise.

All of the foregoing is *not* intended as an argument against urban or other programs. Indeed, as we will have occasion to observe in the final chapter, simply leaving the cities to their fate in laissez faire fashion could have serious consequences for the very underpinnings of our political and economic system as well as for the family life that is alleged to be of such concern to all. We will raise the question of whether current trends, if continued, might not lead to a veritable medievalization of our society. Rather than a simple hands-off perspective, the analysis in this chapter is intended as an argument for realistic appraisal of the strength of the forces urban interventions confront and the indissoluble nature of good and bad within those forces. This means that future interventions need to be carefully thought out, be premised on modest expectations, and implemented with a skill that is too rare on the contemporary scene. For now, however, we return to our heuristic case study of Family Matters, examining first the implementation of the Home Visitor Program and then the organization of Neighborhood Groups in the face of the vicissitudes of the urban context discussed above.

5

BENEVOLENT INTENTIONS AND DEEDS: HOME VISITS

A CAPSULE OF PROGRAM HISTORY

Main study activity began in nine of the ten program neighborhoods (five designated for home visits and four for neighborhood groups) in January of 1979. At that time, program activity had been underway for about a year in the two pilot neighborhoods (one assigned to each of the two intervention strategies), and as planned, attempts were made to incorporate what had been learned in the pilot activity into programming for the Main Study neighborhoods. The months between January 1979 and January 1980 were largely spent in this endeavor, and in implementing program plans for neighborhoods and families. Time was devoted to gearing up internal organizational structure, training, initiation of contacts with families, and actual delivery of program services.

Program Fusion

As a result of the experience gained during the first year of program functioning, a major change in direction was made. This course shift involved the integration of the two types of intervention strategy, so that families were able *both* to receive home visits and to take part in neighborhood groups, if they so chose. This fusion of the two types of programming was dictated by a desire to intensify services to families and also by the recognition that providing only one kind of activity to families who wanted or needed both types was artificial and not consonant with the ecological orientation of the research. Integration of the two programs was not complete, however, since many families decided against participation in the fused program, ultimately taking advantage of only one aspect of Family Matters offerings, usually home visits.

The Element of Choice

A key change in program orientation, however, was the element of choice. Instead of being assigned to a specific program activity through residence in a designated neighborhood, families were now able to receive the kinds of program services they regarded as meeting their own needs. There were indications that providing these options to families (home visits or neighborhood groups, or both), significantly increased participation. Shortly after the introduction of the integrated program in February of 1980, the number of inactive families dropped by 19 percent, from 44 percent of all program families to approximately 25 percent.

The Program's Midlife

The late winter and early spring of 1980, broadly speaking, represent the program's midlife period. Other changes in direction around this time were: reassignment of workers and families to accommodate the integrated program, establishment of a Family Matters Program Advisory Board, opening of Neighborhood Resource Centers to be utilized by program families, formation of a task-force of program workers to look into phase-out of programs in pilot neighborhoods, and a new initiative in Main Study neighborhoods to place greater emphasis on the interface between children, parents, and schools.

Family Matters, Last Months

Somewhat later in the history of the program, i.e., during the last months of 1980 and in early 1981, the last major substantive reorientation occurred. This reorientation involved preparation of, training in, and distribution of modular materials designed to assist families in their relationship with schools and in several other aspects of child rearing. The modules represented an effort to give families material that would be useful to them after the program ended.

About this time also, attempts were made to involve the tenth neighborhood in the intervention. Start-up in this neighborhood had been considerably delayed by an insufficiency of funds that did not allow for enough staff to provide services. Because the sampling design demanded inclusion of the low-income, racially-mixed inner city families that lived in the neighborhood, a belated attempt was made to initiate program activity there. The problems of program activity in that area of the city would have been great even with a more timely beginning. Efforts begun only a few months before program's end proved to be far too little and far too late. The program's demise occurred in June of 1981, and was a premature one. Family Matters had been designed to last four years, but it was terminated after about two and one-half years, at least partly because of insufficient funding.

Having scanned program history briefly and having examined the chief substantive events and course changes, we now turn to an overview of program implementation. The view presented here is one heavily influenced by our interviews with program workers and our observations of internal organizational processes that represented the everyday "in-house" functioning of Family Matters, but we will also include expressions of families' views about the program.

INTRODUCTION TO PROGRAM I – HOME VISITS

As mentioned earlier, the theory behind the Family Matters intervention had a dual focus. One aim was to help participants cope with the stresses of the larger environment so that child and family development could proceed more effectively. The neighborhood group program was geared to provide this kind of support for families. The other kind of program activity consisted of home visits. It was the task of the home visitors to encourage joint and increasingly complex activity on the part of parents and children to promote cognitive growth and social maturity within the family broadly, and especially for the target child. To facilitate the present analysis, we will examine these two program strategies separately and in greater detail. For ease of reference each of the two approaches was designated numerically by the project. The Home Visitor strategy is referred to as Program I, the Neighborhood Group approach as Program II. We begin by looking first at Program I processes.

THE GOALS OF PROGRAM I

Four of the goals of Program I were summarized by the Program Director, Frank Woolever, and one of the principal investigators, Moncrief Cochran in the following way:

(1) Give recognition to parents as experts.
(2) Reinforce and encourage parent-child activities.
(3) Provide information about child rearing from other parents and other programs/sources.
(4) Provide access to men as well as women interested in children — encourage father participation (Cochran and Woolever, 1980, p. 31).

REINFORCING AND ENCOURAGING PARENT-CHILD ACTIVITIES

Among the four enumerated here, the most salient one to the theory behind the program was goal number two, reinforcing and encouraging parent-child activities. Giving "recognition to parents as experts" was a *leitmotif* found throughout all program functioning. Like goals three and four, in practice, goal one was incorporated strategically within implementation of the substantive aspect of Program I, i.e., home activities involving the worker, the child, and/or the parent. We will discuss goal one more extensively later under the heading of "empowerment." Thus, we begin our examination of Program I processes by looking at the kinds of activities that formed the substance of the Home Visitor Program.

Imagination-Stimulating Activities

Interviews with program workers suggested that some of the most ingenious activities utilized in Program I were those that depended primarily on imagination and required few props. An example of this kind of activity is the "imaginary walk." The worker would take the child's hand and they would both close their eyes. One of them set the scene and then in their minds' eyes they walked together through some setting — a town, a forest, or pond. One child might comment about "how noisy the frogs are," while another, having noticed that they have "messed up a lily pad" in their wading in the pond would dutifully "return" to water's edge to make repairs.

Art and Crafts Activities

Program I activities included a considerable number of arts and crafts projects using various media of expression. Many workers carried with them a bag containing at least the most elementary supplies: felt-pens, pencils, crayons, paper, paste, pipe cleaners, etc. It was thought that arts and crafts activities would help develop imagination and creativity, and facilitate progress in manual dexterity as well. Some of the best success workers had in involving fathers was in conjunction with crafts activities. Also, arts and crafts had possibilities as media for school readiness activities.

School Readiness Activities

Having youngsters draw numbers or letters was an approach that combined an arts and crafts medium with another important emphasis in activities — promoting school readiness. Other school readiness activities favored by some workers were counting, reciting the alphabet or the names of colors, and paper-folding crafts. One particularly imaginative and effective ploy utilized by one of the male workers was the creation of a "book" at the behest of the target child. The worker began writing the story the child wanted to tell and illustrating the "magnum opus." But it was up to the child and the parents to finish it. One mother, in a variation on this theme, helped the youngster to create a "picture dictionary." The possible permutations of this approach were many.

Home Management Activities

Even when time, supplies, and parental patience are short, home maintenance activities may still be appropriate. Setting the table, helping with cooking, baking, or washing the dishes, were some of the tasks in which children were asked to share. Such help around the house may actually lighten a parent's workload, though this was not always so. Because the youngsters were preschoolers and dexterity was still developing, it might take a parent longer to do the household chore *with* the youngster's help than without it. It was anticipated, however, that enlisting the child's help around the house would further future gains in the target child's social maturity, especially in his or her sense of responsibility and willingness to work cooperatively. Also, learning to do tasks in stepwise-fashion, developing a feeling of family, as well as the advantages of just spending time with mom or dad, were expected to repay the investment in parental-time dedicated to this inefficient form of "home production."

The above examples of Program I activities are meant to be illustrative, not exhaustive. Several other categories might be singled out, e.g., games, sports, or family trips, and many more examples of each *genre* could be detailed. It is important, however, that we not only delineate what happened in Program I and what it was designed to achieve, but we must also look at the manner in which activities were to be carried out.

GIVING RECOGNITION TO PARENTS AS EXPERTS

In the course of encouraging parent-child activities (whether directed toward the child's imagination, school readiness, or home-making skills), attempts were to be made to give "recognition to parents as experts" (goal one for Program I). Program philosophy in its earliest stages stressed the view that parents knew more about their children, about themselves, and about the home milieu than any outside savant. Giving them credit for their knowledge and for the positive things they were already doing would encourage them and strengthen their self-esteem. Also, it would prepare them for the time when program services were no longer available and independent efforts were required. Later in program history, these attempts to heighten parental self-esteem and encourage independent action evolved into a concept referred to as "empowerment," an idea that had implications not only for intrafamilial activity, but for activities outside the home as well, including those of a political nature.

Building parental self-confidence meant that activities were not to be initiated by program workers unless there wasn't appropriate activity *already* in progress when the worker arrived, or when the family hadn't planned something specific for the worker's visit. In general, however, families were encouraged to do such planning so that an activity would be ready for the "doing." Not only were such activities utilized on the spot, the description of family-contributed activities was written down (with the family's permission) and archived in the Program I Activities Notebook at the Family Matters office. To reinforce the idea of family expertise, copies of the activity write-up were to be taken back to each contributing family. Where possible, other participating families who requested activities were to be given those taken from the Notebook and told that the ideas had been contributed by *other families*.

Thus, ideally it was the family members who were to become the experts on activities rather than the worker. Early interviews with program workers suggest that taking their cue from the family became a basic reality of everyday program functioning. There were some families who were knowledgeable, innovative, and creative, which left little to do for the worker except being an enthusiastic participant. Sometimes the impetus passed from worker to family from visit to visit. Most often, however, the entire responsibility for initiating the activity and supplying the excitement rested on the worker's shoulders.

PROVIDING INFORMATION ABOUT CHILD REARING

As for goal three of Program I, i.e., "providing information about child rearing," this aim was at first to be accomplished indirectly rather than directly. Rather than offering unsolicited instruction on bringing up children, workers supplied referrals to authoritative information (either books and pamphlets or resource persons and organizations) only when specifically asked for counsel by the family. Otherwise, workers tried to support and encourage self-confidence in good child-rearing practices already in use by participating families. Interviews showed that the issues raised ranged from the whens and hows of TV watching, to the prospects of surviving the adolescence of an older child while trying to raise the younger ones, to the question of whether to allow a young child to attend the funeral of a grandparent despite objections by other members of the extended family.

In response to such inquiries, program policy called for workers to be supportive where parents seemed to have made good decisions, and to refer the parent, when she or he asked, to sources of authoritative information. Whatever the parental decision, however, the worker was not to criticize those child-rearing approaches of which the worker did not approve. Certainly workers were asked to refrain from offering "unasked for expertise." Often considerable patience and forbearance was required of the program worker. For example, when excessively harsh or dangerous parental disciplinary tactics were suspected, the decision to hold back was extremely difficult.

It was similarly hard to keep one's own counsel when a worker saw a family steeped in drug-use trying to rear a four-year-old, especially when the little boy's only role model was a teenaged brother who was a homosexual prostitute. In the face of such circumstances, the worker had to watch quietly and seek to make a difference in people's lives where making a difference was at all possible, trying to accept what had to be borne as immutable. Affirmatively, however, where conditions were less desperate than the extremes just described, the worker, instead of preaching a child-rearing gospel, tried to model the kind of behavior she or he sought to inculcate — patience, tolerance, and respect for opinions of all family members both great and small, hoping that by identification and imitation, a lesson would be imparted that was likely to have been rejected if it had been taught didactically.

Cooperative Extension

Later in the program's history, however, a more active approach to sharing child-rearing information became possible without workers violating the principles that prescribed worker roles. Through collaboration with New York State Cooperative Extension (one of whose most competent local agents was assigned to the project), important materials on child rearing and other related family concerns were made increasingly available to Program families.

Cooperative Extension is an agency affiliated with the state university system. Its mission is to provide *information* rather than social services *per se*. Generally, Extension sets no income test for use of its resources. Its publications and consulting services are widely utilized by all Socioeconomic Status (SES) groups, from affluent home gardeners in Westchester County to inner city minority group members in Brooklyn seeking information on home repairs. The advantage of using Cooperative Extension materials was that they are not written so as to imply deficit in those to whom they are addressed. Thus, the materials were helpful without being condescending or taking over parent decision making. One important kind of child-rearing information made available to program participants dealt with family nutrition, and was sponsored by the Expanded Food and Nutrition Education Program (EFNEP).

A second valuable resource provided by Cooperative Extension was the monthly Extension Newsletter called "Impact" which contained considerable information on family concerns. Even more specific to child-rearing education, Extension also made available a second newsletter called, "Letters for Parents of Preschoolers." The fit between this Extension publication and the needs of program families could hardly have been better. Through the link between Family Matters and Cooperative Extension and through worker urging of participating parents, subscriptions to "Impact" and "Letters to Parents of Preschoolers" by program families were increased substantially. Cooperative Extension also appeared to have had a stimulating and salutary influence in other areas such as the Neighborhood Resource Center to be discussed later in describing Program II processes. But, most important, the effects of collaboration between Family Matters and Extension seem to have been felt in solving the problem of not making parents feel deficient, and still attaining the goal of providing them with good child-rearing information.

The Modules

In the spring of 1980, about a year before program termination, four committees called "task forces" were organized to enhance Family Matters, information dissemination capacity. The task forces were composed largely of program workers, though sometimes persons outside the program framework sat in on these meetings to provide their specialized information. Process analysts also participated in these committees.

It was felt that for too long, workers making visits did not themselves have authoritative information to share with families. Thus, the task forces were to work up both the content and the means for transmitting materials in four areas: (1) cultural/spiritual/ethical values; (2) survival skills; (3) child development and appropriate activities; (4) the interface between the home and the school to be attended by the target child.

What became known as "the values task force" had as its aim making families aware of their own value systems and encouraging them to respect their own cultural, racial, or ethnic identities as well as those of other diverse groups.

The "survival skills task force" attempted to assemble materials that would be especially helpful to low-income families living at a time of national recession and Syracuse's own special economic woes described in Chapter 4. Information was collected on budgeting/money management, do-it-yourself projects, unemployment/employment, inexpensive recreational activities, and low cost food and nutrition. The latter area was appropriately entitled "cheap grub."

The activities task force focused its attention on child development and the kinds of parent-child activities that would best foster the child's cognitive and socioemotional growth. As with all task forces, the approach was for the workers to familiarize themselves with the relevant information as a prelude to imparting their knowledge to their families.

The most successful of the task forces, at least in terms of producing material that was later incorporated into an identifiable end-product, was the schools' task force. As it was being formed, some of the program children were about to enter kindergarten. A year later, they would be beginning first grade. The goals of this task force were: enabling parents to participate in their children's education; cooperation with the school; getting the best out of the educational system for their child; and preserving their own and their children's self-esteem in the face of any negative experiences with the schools. Education-related modular materials produced for transmission to participating families included information on: being a school volunteer, parent-teacher conferences, knowing the child's first grade, report cards, home-school communications, parent as partners with their children in learning, and the values implicit in the educational system.

The values task force itself contributed information to the modules on family and neighborhood cultural values, and the above mentioned racial and ethnic identities of diverse groups. These particular materials are notable for their emphasis on activities involving the child, e.g., designing a family crest, building a model of the home that embodied its traditions, making a street history rubbing, "adopting a neighborhood landmark," etc.

The survival skills task force contributed material that resulted in a module on job hunting, and the activities task force worked up some suggestions for summertime pursuits for parents and their out of school youngsters.

It should be noted that while a good deal of the impetus and groundwork for these modules was done by the task forces, the materials produced were largely the responsibility of two highly competent professionals who were hired only a matter of months before program's end. It was they who put the task force thinking into polished form, contributed their own very considerable share of ideas, and trained the workers in the distribution and presentation of the modules to families.

Unfortunately, these excellent materials came at the tail-end of program activities, when both staff members and families were aware of and sorrowing about the impending premature demise of Family Matters. Also, the modules were not embraced enthusiastically either by all workers or by all families. Thus their impact was probably limited.

PROVIDING ACCESS TO NURTURANT MEN AND WOMEN

In addition to conducting the home visits with respect for parental expertise and supplying child-rearing information, workers tried to provide families with access to *men* as well as women who displayed an interest in children. As Bo (1979) has pointed out, it was a member of the Israeli component of the Comparative Ecology of Human Development Project who called special attention to the need for males as role models for nurturance. Otherwise, Family Matters would be sending "a message to the involved families that it is a woman's job to interact with the child" (Sharabany, 1978).

As a result, families, although generally allowed to choose either a male or a female as their primary worker, were encouraged to accept a worker of the opposite sex as their secondary worker. As the titles "primary" and "secondary" imply, visits by the one were more frequent than those by the other. But earnest attempts were made to break down sex-role stereotypy in child-rearing roles.

Where extraneous factors did not interfere, male workers enjoyed considerable success in Program I activities. One was known as a sort of Pied Piper, who attracted not only program children wherever he went, but also the young of nonparticipating families as well. Other male workers likewise had their moments of notable success as well as some that were less triumphant, but this is the kind of mixture of achievement, or the lack of it, that was common to workers of both sexes. Certainly it was quite clear that male workers could successfully carry out their assigned roles as nurturant men. It was equally clear that in several instances, previously distant fathers were drawn into closer interaction with their children as a result of the example of the male program worker.

As mentioned earlier, several fathers were initiated into program participation by soliciting their help in craft or home project activities. One male worker not only modeled this kind of role, he also devised a clever strategy to assure paternal involvement. Collecting materials to make a model truck, he brought them into an activity session involving himself, the mother, and the target child. It became apparent toward the end of the session that the child would be unable to finish the project at the time. When the youngster commented unhappily about this fact, the worker simply replied, "Well, I guess you and your *dad* will have to finish the truck yourselves." A subsequent report by the program worker revealed that not only had father and son done so, but also that it was evident from family statements and from the quality of the finished product, that the two had spent many hours working on the truck together.

But as mentioned earlier, despite successful attempts like these, at times extraneous factors, unrelated to the program itself or the worker's own efforts, interfered with the male worker's ability to do his job effectively. Sometimes, the problem was the cultural identification of the target family and a resultant refusal to bend its stereotypes. Certain families were of European background and had come to this country only recently. Among these families, the thought of a male engaging in "play" with children was itself quite foreign. Also problematic was the idea of a young male visiting a young wife in her husband's absence. Thus, among certain ethnic groups, male home visitors did not gain ready acceptance.

A second if less frequent problem for the male home visitor was one that might be expected to arise when the mother (often a single parent) was the usual caregiver at home with the target child at the time of the program visit. Occasionally, the male home visitor sensed the beginnings of an interest in him by the mother that went beyond his professional role. Our study of process did not uncover any evidence of a comparable problem among female home visitors, apparently because it was rare for the father to be at home alone with the target child. But whenever it appeared that "romantic complications" might arise, workers requested a transfer so that the primary worker was one who was of the same sex as was the primary caregiver, almost always female. These problems, although perhaps not fully anticipated within this program's conceptualization, are not uncommon in field research generally. For example, Zelnik and Kantner (1980) have indicated comparable though not identical problems with males who were to be employed as interviewers within private residences.

ETHNIC IDENTITY

There was a fifth goal that was part of the aspirations of Program I, but unlike broadening family horizons with regard to sex roles, its implementation began much later in the program's history. This goal involved providing encouragement for expressions of pride in minority ethnic identity and concurrently bringing multi-racial, multi-cultural, and multi-ethnic information to all program families. Goal attainment of the latter effort was to be mediated primarily by a method similar to that used with regard to sex-role, that is, by bringing families into contact with workers of diverse cultures and ethnic backgrounds. Although careful efforts were made to assign primary workers to families of similar racial or ethnic background (there was even an Italian-speaking worker for families newly arrived from Italy), attempts were made to involve as secondary workers program personnel whose backgrounds differed from those of their assigned families. Wherever possible, this kind of arrangement was tried, though acceptance of the concept by families was not very widespread. Other efforts to enhance the multi-cultural, biracial orientation of the program included the organization of a task-force of workers to deal with this area, an emphasis on it in the "Marketplace" event held by the program, and also the above described modular material dealing with ethnic/racial identity distributed to families at program's end.

SOME KEY ISSUES IN PROGRAM I ACTIVITY

In addition to the goals to be attained, Cochran and Woolever (1980) also distinguished several key issues surrounding implementation of program activities. One of these was "avoidance of the deficit perspective." Another was "finding a balance among parent-child, worker-parent, and worker-child activities" (p. 32). We have examined the "deficit perspective" issue in part while discussing the question of initiative in planning Program I activities. More will be said on this score later in dealing with the concept of empowerment, an important goal for both Program I and Program II.

The other issue, "the balance among parent-child, worker-parent and worker-child activities" also emerged in Process Study data-gathering efforts. Ideally, activity conducted during home visits was to involve the *full* triad, i.e., the caregiver, the target child, and the program worker. The object of the home visitor program was to lead parent and child into more frequent interaction with each other. It was hoped that while such activity would, at first, be "instigated" by the parent, later activity was to be more often child-initiated.

Ideally then, triadic activity with *worker* impetus should have evolved into dyadic activity with increasing *child* initiative. However, as with many three-person groups studied by social scientists or the "triangles" so familiar in everyday life, threesomes often resolve themselves into twosomes, and the third member may become a passive observer or even leave the scene. Of course, program workers tried to prevent this from happening. But in some cases, parents would leave the worker alone with the child and pursue other activities either inside or outside the home, leaving the worker feeling like a "glorified babysitter."

In some instances, parents preferred to view the program worker as a sort of tutor or special friend of the child. In other cases, the worker was seized·upon as the special friend or *confidant* of the parent. The same worker experienced different role demands from diverse families. As one worker put it, "My role is as different as the number of families I have." Too often socioeconomic or more personal stresses in the parent's life required the worker to serve as a sounding board for emotional outlet.

One interviewed worker stated it simply as, "If a mother isn't making it financially, and she's just had a fight with her boyfriend, and he's just split, there ain't no way I can just say to her, 'OK, let's you and I go play a game with the child'." This argument was seen as a valid one, and recognition was extended in program planning to the need for special time alone with either the child or the caregiver. Often, however, this kind of pairing off was forced upon the worker for too many sessions, and as the Cochran and Woolever (1980) document implies, the issue is one with which the program staff continued to wrestle on an ongoing basis.

THE REACTION OF FAMILIES TO PROGRAM I

In our two special waves of data collection with families (described in the methodological appendix) we found the reaction to the Ecology of Human Development Project generally quite favorable. About 80 percent of the families questioned described their experience with Family Matters in positive as opposed to neutral or negative terms. Reaction to the research component of the project (i.e., the interviews about home activities, social networks, and stresses and supports) was even more positive than that elicited about the program. However, the program was described in broad terms by the respondents as a benevolent presence in their lives.

Quantitative and qualitative analyses showed that the home visits were the most favored aspect of the program. About three-fourths of those who had received the visits described their experience in affirmative terms. Once again the comments were usually nonspecifically positive, but when pressed, some mothers singled out two areas. They felt good about the special dyadic relationship between the home visitor and either the target child or themselves, or among all three members of the visitor-parent-child triad. The second benefit mentioned by respondents was the opportunity to view the behavior of the child through the eyes of another adult.

When parents were asked if they felt that Program I had made a difference in their lives, about half answered affirmatively, though only about a third of the sample felt that program participation had increased the amount of time spent in activities with their children. Where changes had occurred, it appeared that it was in the *kind* of joint activities (i.e., less TV watching, or more selective viewing), the *quality* of joint activity (more enjoyment of them by parents and more of a sense of family), and in a *raising of consciousness* about the parental role. Thus, like most participants in ad hoc social programs (cf. Weiss, 1972; Costello, 1983), families were clearly positive in their expressions about the home visit program. Based on parents' own self-reports, however, evidence of program-induced change was far less strong. And as we will see, behavioral support for home visits through actual participation parallels the less than spectacular program effects common to comparable interventions.

UTILIZATION OF HOME VISITS

As Costello (1983) has pointed out, regardless of the level of involvement in interventions like Family Matters, program participants usually describe their experience in positive terms. There is thus an apparent divergence between what people say and what they do. Participation in home visits considered on an average basis was much less frequent than had been planned by the program's designers. Analysis of the total number of home visits for 126 respondents still within the sample during outcome data collection showed that each family received about 15.4 visits over the 30 months of program duration, about one visit every two months. The actual duration of the program, however, differed considerably among families.

Because Family Matters was part of a field research project, implementation could not begin in experimental program neighborhoods until premeasurement had occurred. In at least a few neighborhoods, this beginning was delayed for about a year, due to problems in the project's data gathering phase. For families in the four neighborhoods originally designated for groups only, home visits were similarly delayed until the integrated program allowed these participants to elect to enter into Program I activities. Also, in the tenth neighborhood, where financial considerations had delayed intervention initiation, families did not begin receiving services until only a few months before program's end.

Looking at the data on the duration of the program, we find that its median length was about 575 days, or about 19 months. This meant that for various reasons, some related to family preferences but more the result of implementation problems, about a year's worth of program activity was lost to many families. When we look at the rate of participation in home visits as a function of the average number of visits and the median duration of the program (admittedly a rough index), intensity improves only a little, with home visits occurring less frequently than once a month. The program's original design (Bronfenbrenner and Cochran, 1976) had set a standard of one home visit every two or three weeks. Even if we remove from consideration the six summer months (over the course of two years) when little program activity took place, and use 13 months and 26 home visits as our criterion, only about 10 percent of the sample meet the standard of biweekly home visits. Using the criterion of one visit every three weeks, intensity improves somewhat. Still, only about 30 percent of the families had as many as the required 19 visits over 13 months. Some of this low intensity was due to problems of implementation by the intervening organization. In addition to the difficulties mentioned above, conceptual, financial, and those related to data collection, some workers simply did not see families as frequently as the families wished, or at times that were of greatest convenience to would-be participants.

Part of the attribution for low levels of participation, however, must lie with families themselves. Some scheduled visits on an infrequent basis, cancelled, or simply missed appointments, or declared a preference for not meeting with their worker during the summer months. We have already alluded (in Chapter 4) to the struggle for subsistence that was being waged by a good number of parents, though family income and legal marital status (i.e., whether there were one or two parents in the home) were not the variables most closely associated with program participation. But whatever the source of the decisions affecting involvement in Program I, the fact that most home visits occurred less often than on a monthly basis put the Family Matters Home Visit Program in the category of an intervention that was at a lower moderate level of intensity compared with other similar programs. This was below its designers' expectations, and certainly well below the weekly participation recommended by Bronfenbrenner (1974).

PARTICIPATION AND OUTCOMES

Although our focus in this volume is on implementation and process rather than on outcomes, it must be stated that based on our formative evaluation, at program's end, positive effects of modest size were predicted for some subgroups among program recipients. Preliminary and unpublished findings of the project's outcome evaluation component available at this writing confirm this prediction. The home visit program appears to have had some effects on parent-child activities, the proximate outcome variable, and also some impact on the ultimate measure of outcome, the cognitive development of the target child as measured by school performance. The effects are apparently related to program participation, though only weakly so.

In general, like other comparable programs, the outcomes produced by Family Matters are not: unambiguous, universal among all participant subgroups, immune to reverse effects, or of a size generally considered to be very strong in the social scientific community. Furthermore, we do not know whether they will, as with other interventions, wash out in the long term, and then appear to assert themselves again in the still longer term. But for now, it does seem that the home visit program did produce something in the way of cognitive gain among those who tended to participate more actively.

FAMILY MATTERS AND OTHER COMPARABLE AND NONCOMPARABLE INTERVENTIONS

The above described levels of participation and the related attrition rates unquestionably had their effect on program implementation and hence on program impact. The question may then be asked by the discerning reader, "Was Family Matters unique in such problems?" The answer is, "By no means."

Attrition

Participant attrition is one of the most common outcome-defeating problems in parent education and other programs. Families simply move and leave no trace or fail to respond to inquiries by program personnel. Gray and Wandersman (1980), examining seven home-based interventions, noted that *where reported*, attrition ranged between 30 and 50 percent of the initial population. Powell (1984) cites examples of recent reports of education programs showing a 48 percent dropout rate for low-income parents in the course of two years, and a 41 percent rate in another program for middle-income parents in just nine weeks. Thus, Family Matters retention rates were rather good by comparison with the nine programs examined collectively by Gray and Wandersman (1980) and Powell (1984). Also, there can be no question that the stresses of low-income urban life impact on attrition as noted in Chapter 4 (cf. also Gray and Wandersman, 1980); but we note that working with middle-class parents does not guarantee a low-attrition sample at intervention's end of even a very short intervention. Indeed, Powell (Ibid.) cites the literature to show that the evidence is inconclusive in attempts to link early termination of program participation to socioeconomic status. Other factors, such as composition and extent of social network also seem to be important.

Attrition is a problem with many kinds of social programs. For example, Fetterman (1982) describes the difficulties in recruiting participants for a Youth Employment Demonstration Program, and retaining those participants when there were delays in program implementation. Even income maintenance experiments have their serious attrition problems not just with their control groups but with those receiving the maintenance payments as well (Poirier, 1977). Some try to track down dropouts and determine the reason for their attrition (e.g., Poirier, 1977), while others, even large and expensive programs like that of the New York City Human Resources Administration have "conspicuously" not bothered to follow-up on dropouts (Lyon, 1976). What is clear is that initiating a program that seems to be of even major benefit to participants does not ensure high retention rates. As mentioned earlier, attrition approaching the 50 percent level is not uncommon and is not necessarily related to socioeconomic status (Powell, 1984) or geographic mobility (Ibid. and Poirier, 1977).

Implementation and Participation

Attrition, of course, is not simply a gauge of circumstances external to the program (e.g., SES, mobility, and social networks). It can also be construed as a measure of both *participant motivation* and the *efficacy of program implementation*. As Gray and Wandersman (1980) have pointed out, whether families elect to participate in home-based interventions once recruited is not a simple matter, and sometimes depends on recruitment processes themselves. For example, whether or not people were assigned to experimental or control conditions by lottery or by residential location seemed to make for very large differences (on the order of 40 percent) in project involvement in Levenstein's (1972) work. Rosenthal and Rosnow (1974) have long ago shown that voluntarism generally is associated with various personal characteristics. Participation rates reviewed by Gray and Wandersman (1980) ranged from a low of 33 percent to a high of 95 percent. These authors concluded that voluntarism is not only person-dependent but also influenced by historical factors, "a complex and shifting phenomenon" (Ibid., p. 989).

Not surprisingly, in addition to personal motivation for program participation, program implementation and services offered are pivotal to participation as we have seen in our case history. The home visit program drew far greater participation than did the neighborhood groups for several reasons, not the least of which was its better implementation. Ramey et al. (1976) have reported excellent participation reaching 95 percent, but even their control group received health services and nutritional supplements. Home visitor characteristics can affect participation as Lambie et al. (1974) learned when they had to switch from college volunteers to paraprofessionals upon finding high dropout among families visited only episodically by the students. The decision on whether to use paraprofessionals or paraprofessionals as interveners has implications both positive or negative whatever the course chosen (Gray and Wandersman, 1980), though most home visit programs have employed paraprofessionals because of fiscal concerns (Ibid.). But regardless of professional status or services that are planned, intervention can succeed through ". . . the efforts of a unique talented staff" (Travers and Light, 1982).

Program Efficacy

Outcomes produced by home visit programs, both the Family Matters' variety and others, are like those produced by many other social interventions. They are typically *not* overwhelming. Halpern (1984, p. 33) reviewing more than 40 home-based early childhood interventions concludes that "statistical evidence in support of program effects is lacking," and few intervention designers bother to determine the nature of long-term effects of their efforts. Instead, reports to agencies sponsoring the research are often filled with a good deal of qualitative evidence of positive treatment effects, ". . . usually case studies of individual families, illustrative material, and self-report by participating families" (Ibid., p. 37). Because of the selective nature of such data and the self-interest of those generally reporting it, this kind of evidence must be open to some question. In sum, home-based early childhood intervention, for all of its individual bright spots, cannot be considered a dramatically effective intervention any more than most other social programs, especially when judged by the criteria of effect size, generality across most participants, and consistency across domains of outcome. As with many other social programs, the rosiest assessment that seems applicable to home visit interventions generally is that they only work for some of the people only some of the time.

6

EXPANDING SUPPORTIVE
SOCIAL NETWORKS:
NEIGHBORHOOD GROUPS

PROCESS WITHIN PROGRAM II

Having examined in detail implementation of and participation in Program I as well as its intensity and likely effects, we now turn our attention to a similar review of Program II. As with the Home Visitor Program, we begin with a statement of the goals of the Neighborhood Grouping approach. The Cochran and Woolever document cited earlier (1980, p. 32) summed up the five Program II goals in a fashion similar but not identical to those of the original proposal as follows:

(1) To reduce isolation.

(2) To share information about children, neighborhood services, work, etc. informally.

(3) To exchange resources available within the group (emergency child care, transportation, etc.).

(4) To take action in concert at the neighborhood and community levels on behalf of families with young children.

(5) To reach out to other families in the neighborhood.

REDUCING ISOLATION —
GOAL OF PROGRAM II

Feelings of loneliness appeared to be an important problem among at least some participants in the Family Matters Program, despite the physical proximity of many others in the congested urban environment. It is by now a truism that such isolation may be quite real at the emotional level whatever the surroundings. This was often especially characteristic of single parents participating in the program, and many had a particular preference for neighborhood grouping activities.

A sense of being alone can also result from being part of a two-parent nuclear family cut off from friends, relatives, and other support systems as a result of death, estrangement, or migration. Feelings of political or economic isolation, being alone in relation to those better off and those identified as the power establishment were prevalent as well. But perhaps one of the most notable forms of loneliness in the Family Matters Program was that associated with trying to raise children in today's complex society without benefit of extended family resources or counsel, and without being able to rely on the memory of norms from what seems like a bygone era. Process study evidence was quite strong with regard to feelings about being alone and insufficiently informed about child rearing. We have already presented some indications of these feelings in the previous chapter and there were many instances cited by program workers showing parental bewilderment about raising very young children, to say nothing of their teenage brothers and sisters.

But the neighborhood grouping program, where it took hold, did make some progress toward meeting the needs implicit in goals one and two. There were a variety of social activities which helped reduce isolation and set the occasion for information exchange. Activities with a social emphasis included: socials, pot-luck dinners, picnics, sledding parties, and at Christmas time, visits to Santa Claus. All of these activities, however, also contained a distinct element of *family* participation and the kind of activity favored by children. In this respect, they represented a kind of blending of Program I and Program II motifs, combining as they did, both interfamily and intrafamily themes. This was as it should have been since the goal of Program II was not simply organizing groups. It was to organize groups *supportive of the child-rearing mission* generally and of *family activities* in particular.

In contrast to the social activities, however, organizational meetings directed toward specific topics tended to be more adult oriented, and were held in such a way as to allow parents to meet separately from the children. Early evening was the favored time for such activities and child care was provided. The youngsters had their own activity in a different room of the building, near enough, however, so that the very young could peek in occasionally at their parents to assure themselves that they had not been "abandoned."

From comments heard by process analysts attending such meetings and from our feedback interviews with parents, it was evident that parents often welcomed the opportunity to be relieved of child-care responsibilities and to interact with adults. In some neighborhoods, the last half-hour of even these adult meetings was devoted to parent-child interactions. The activity that took place might have consisted of either informal conversation and play or more structured sessions — for example making puppets, or tracing the outline of the youngster on a large sheet of butcher paper. In line with this emphasis, a few neighborhood groups formed Parent-Child Interaction Planning Committees. The role of these subgroups was to design activities for both the group sessions and for use at home. Here we see an important beginning of a procedure that could facilitate the transition from worker-initiated to parent-initiated activities.

That the neighborhood get-togethers generally met certain social needs was quite clear. In one neighborhood where Program II main-study activity went on longest, the group was so tightly knit that at first they refused to allow nonprogram families to participate, even though some of the other project neighborhood groups did reach out to nearby residents or friends who were not formal participants in the program. In a second neighborhood, meetings were attended quite faithfully by two physicians and their families, something of a rarity in Syracuse and in many other places where similar functions are held. Both of these phenomena speak to the interpersonal bonds that were established in at least some of the neighborhood groups, bonds that appeared to be important to participants who were not from the lowest income strata of society.

INFORMATION SHARING –
GOAL II OF PROGRAM II

As for sharing informal information about children, neighbor-hoods, work, services, etc. (Program II, goal 2), in four areas, there is little room for doubt about the reality of such exchanges. These four areas are: neighborhoods, schools, child care, and child rearing.

Neighborhoods

Information-sharing about neighborhoods did take place in Program II group meetings under a variety of headings. A little later in this chapter we will see some examples of specific action taken by Program II participants at the neighborhood level to im-prove community safety. These actions were the result of prior information exchange at the informal level that identified neighbor-hood problems. In one case, the problem was crime in the area, crime that was not being monitored effectively by neighborhood residents. In a second instance, the issue was a creek-bed, fenced in on one side only and located so that it constituted a very real safety hazard to children at play.

There were other similar neighborhood problems, which were raised at Program II meetings, but the creek-bed and crime issues are two that we will see as not only having been subjects of infor-mation exchange, but also the objects of successful community action. In addition, besides identifying local problems, some neigh-borhood groups and their program workers took it as their mission to identify neighborhood resources.

Child Care

The matter of child care was also a topic of information sharing among neighborhood groups. Reports obtained by process analysts showed that there was also informal reciprocity of baby-sitting services among parents – arrangements of the form: "Tonight, I'll take care of your kids, and tomorrow you'll take care of mine." In one neighborhood, an attempt was made to structure a more formal baby-sitting exchange. This effort, while initially successful, later "petered out" (in the interview words of the program worker who reported on the effort). Apparently the informal arrangements and neighborly reciprocity had greater flexibility than the official structure in meeting the varying levels of child-care needs in the group. It is clear, however, that sharing of information and actual child-care services did result from Program II functioning.

Schools

Besides child care and neighborhood resources or problems, a major and (as time went on) increasingly important topic of interest to Program II families was the whole area of education. Here, as with neighborhood-need identification, discussion of school-related issues and child care, information exchange was in some cases only the prelude to actual constructive activity. Later on, we will discuss a school-visit program undertaken by one neighborhood group. A second program group (living in a community outside the city limits but within the county) felt they needed more authoritative information for the sharing, and invited the Director of Elementary Education for the Liverpool Public Schools to talk to them about education in the primary grades.

During 1980, Family Matters parents generally became aware that a study of the early grades in the Syracuse School system had recently been completed, and this was of considerable interest to program participants. Program target children in Main Study families soon were to enter kindergarten, or, in the case of pilot neighborhoods, first grade. Interest, therefore, in this area was by no means premature. As mentioned in the previous chapter, a "task force for schools" was organized among members of the program staff to respond to or stimulate family concern in the area of education.

But the school issue was a highly complex one in Syracuse because of the problems in contemporary U.S. education generally, because here, as elsewhere, there was the busing issue, and because fully a third of Syracuse children attend parochial rather than public schools. Therefore, there was much for the parents to discuss and to learn about schools. Even in neighborhoods where there were few issues around which parent groups might coalesce, it was expected that with the entrance of main study target children into kindergarten, and with increasing emphasis by program workers on school-parent-child relationships, schools would form a nexus of ongoing and increasing interest for neighborhood groups.

Child Rearing

During the critical period of transition between home and school, information about child rearing was especially salient to program families. What to expect and what not to expect were questions which vexed and perplexed parents. As mentioned earlier, young parents of today have little by way of extended family resources for information on what expectations they *should* have. The shifting sands of psychological and child-development theory, whether derived from media presentations or from the occasional college course, hardly offer a Gibraltar-like foundation on which to build an edifice of consistent and self-assured child-rearing practice. We have seen that the Home Visitor Program offered some help in this respect. But program workers reported two reliable reactions about child rearing that came up in discussions in Program II meetings. The *first* reaction was the feeling of "aloneness" itself, probably especially important among program parents because of the systematic inclusion of an oversample of *single* parents in project recruitment. The reaction *after* the report of isolation was very often a tremendous sense of relief at meeting other parents who faced many of the same developmental transitions and associated problems that they themselves had encountered.

Apparently, quite apart from any transfer of substantive information, just knowing that "I'm not the only one," seemed to make a big difference for many parents. It is interesting and curious how the responsibility of parent and children for each other's reputations has evolved through the history of family life. In certain times and places, it was the child who was responsible for behavior that would reflect credit on his or her parents. Today, probably due to the broad dissemination of serious social science theory, to say nothing of pop psychology, it is often the parent who feels mightily responsible for all aspects of the child's behavior. The attitude we found to be reflected often seemed to be, "If something's wrong, it must be my fault." Thus, seeing the consistency of certain phenomena and relationships across various persons, family backgrounds, and developmental stages was not only enlightening. It was also a source of considerable relief, or solace, or renewed confidence.

Exchanging Resources and Taking Concerted Action — Program Goals III and IV

It has already been suggested earlier that concern about child rearing, schools, child care, and neighborhood needs and resources led to both exchange of resources and the initiation of group action. In the section below, we will see examples of both of these processes. It should be stated at the outset, however, that generally as we contrast the information sharing processes with those involving overt action, there was more of the one than the other. That is, there was probably a good deal more social activity as well as discussion and exchange of intangibles than there was a sharing of material resources or concerted group activity. This was true for several reasons, not the least of which was the belated start of Program II activity in Main Study neighborhoods.

In the initial four neighborhoods designated for Program II, activities got off to a slower start than did those of Program I. As a matter of fact, initially many Program II workers made contact with their families through *home visits*, which closely resembled those in Program I, and which sometimes continued for several months. Later in program history, this early period was called, "the trust-building phase," a time when families could get to know the program, its goals and aspirations, and its personnel. It was also a time for dropping fears, suspicions, and resistances. In retrospect, it was decided that such trust building was a necessary precondition for later group formation, one that probably should have been built into the original design.

Perhaps as important to the slow start up of Program II as the need for a trust-building phase are the well-known realities of the dynamics of group process. Tuckman (1965) for example, has distinguished four stages of evolution in group functioning. These are: (1) forming, (2) norming, (3) storming, and (4) performing. That is, first people must meet (forming). Then they must set standards (norming) to be observed by group members regardless of individual differences. Such subordination of personal aspiration and style nearly always results in intragroup conflict (storming), and in some cases, the loss of certain group elements. Finally, concerted action (performing) to further the group's goals comes only in the last instance, after evolution through the previous three stages.

Neighborhood groups formed under the auspices of Family Matters had to go through these stages of development; and information received by the process study suggested that the evolution was not any easier for most *program* groups than for those constituted of other human beings. For example, in one instance even when concerted group action met with success, there was considerable "storming" on the part of a small faction that had not been in the leadership role in the successful effort.

The theory of group process also suggests that Program I activities, which involved dyads, triads, and larger groups (when the other parent and the siblings are counted) would also experience similar group dynamics problems as did Program II, but because of the narrower focus, the problems may have been more susceptible to quicker resolution. Indeed, Olson (1965) argues that the larger the group, the less likely it is that individuals pursuing their own "rational" personal interests will be able to take effective action collectively. In fact most of the neighborhood group meetings held during the history of Family Matters consisted of two or three mothers with or without their preschool children.

The group theories discussed here, whether those of Tuckman (1965) or Olson (1965) or others, are neither universal nor invariant in their applicability to program functioning, but the concepts do help illuminate some of the difficulties and complexities of neighborhood group organizing. Specifically, these fundamentals of group process help clarify two contrasts: (1) the difference between the more rapid development of Program I compared with the much slower pace of Program II; and (2) the above mentioned disparity between information sharing and discussions in Program II and the more concrete achievements that resulted from overt and concerted group behavior.

These contrasts and analysis of some of the underlying processes associated with group dynamics will be discussed later in more detail. Now, however, we will examine the very real and tangible results of Program II attempts to encourage families to relieve stresses and provide supports by sharing resources and taking coordinated action.

Resource Exchange

Resource sharing (other than information resources) in most of the neighborhood groups consisted primarily of small but helpful items. For example, one group sponsored a supermarket discount coupon exchange. In this arrangement, unused grocery coupons were donated by families to a common pool. Anyone who could make use of such a coupon might simply withdraw it from the pool, in the expectation that the beneficiary would become the donor on another occasion.

Sharing also took place on a more informal basis as well. For example, we know of one instance where a family had concert tickets that they were unable to use. Calling another participating family, they offered to donate the tickets and they also volunteered to babysit that night as well. These reciprocal child-care arrangements were probably the most frequent examples of resource sharing on an everyday basis in the neighborhood groups.

A more significant example of cooperative use of available resources in an era of high energy costs and inflation was found in one neighborhood that established a car pool for participating families. Because residents' jobs were located in different parts of the city, the car pool arrangement was not helpful in dealing with transportation to and from work. But it occurred to these neighbors that they frequented many of the same stores at a local shopping mall. Consequently, these families increasingly shopped by car pool.

Later in program history, another example of resource sharing produced by the conscientious efforts of Program II was the Neighborhood Resource Center. The germ of the idea came from the activities of the local Cooperative Extension agent who introduced the concept to program workers by taking them on a visit to such a center in a nearby county. The workers, impressed with the concept and its applicability to the Family Matters Neighborhood Program, suggested it to Program Director Woolever. He worked diligently to augment existing program funds by applying for grant support for two such neighborhood centers from the City-County Youth Board. Also, in line with his philosophy of "community empowerment" rather than relying on services or resources handed from the top-down, Woolever carefully and patiently elicited support and participation in the endeavor by other community people.

His efforts were successful and these funds plus some from the program budget proved enough for a beginning. One of the regular program staff members was assigned to the project on a part-time basis, and her efforts were augmented by those of teenage volunteers and of a student intern from LeMoyne College. Space for one site was provided by a local community center and for a second by the county school system. The resources to be shared were donated variously by participating families, by some of the program workers on an individual basis, and by local and outside business firms such as Fisher-Price toys, etc. One of the centers was open several days a week for a few hours each day so that mothers and children could visit and use the available materials. Also, both centers attempted to develop themselves as bases for outreach into the general community, so that their scope would not be limited by the physical space of their headquarters.

Taking Concerted Action

Establishing the resource centers was not just an example of resource sharing. It also represented achievement in the fourth goal area of the Neighborhood Group Program, i.e., taking concerted group action. This was true for the establishment of the two centers themselves, and also for an outgrowth of the center program — the Teen Caring Project. This effort involved training teenage members of some program families to provide informed and generally good quality baby-sitting services for the youngsters of other program families.

Another example of such action lay in the growing interest in the transition of the target child from home to school. One neighborhood group encouraged its members to begin visiting the schools where their children would be studying. This kind of activism by parents in school affairs had been one of the chief products of other programs comparable to Family Matters, for example the Boston Early Education Project (BEEP) and most Head Start components. There are suggestions in the literature that such initiative may be important both in what is accomplished directly, as well as in the example it sets for the developing child (Zigler, 1979). Increasingly, both Family Matters workers and program participants asked for information from school administrators and teachers. As discussed above, the task force on schools formed near the end of the program contributed to the production of modular materials distributed to families which urged them to seek a greater measure of involvement in monitoring the education of their children.

A third instance of concerted group action reflected the reality of the high crime rates in Syracuse discussed earlier. Both police and social scientists with interests in the urban environment have, in recent years, noted the importance of "defensible space" (cf. Suttles, 1972) in crime prevention. This means that where people simply exercise surveillance over areas which belong to them personally or which they treat as areas to be defended for the common good, criminal activity is lessened.

In Syracuse the police department established zones of crime prevention (cf. Abbott, 1979; Dunn, 1980), and within these zones, they attempted to secure the cooperation of local residents for "Neighborhood Watch" programs. One of the brighter achievements of Program II was the stimulus it provided to program parents in one middle-income, ethnic, white neighborhood who were concerned about their childrens' safety as they played in a neighborhood park. These Family Matters parents, assessing neighborhood needs, saw the necessity of such a program, and they, along with other parents in their neighborhood, as well as some parents in other city neighborhoods, were among the first to ask the police department to set the program into motion. Also, Neighborhood Watch became an important part of their own group activity. We have here, therefore, an excellent example of neighbors organizing to support one another to help relieve environmental stress.

A similar example, and one which is perhaps even more dramatic because it involved a real wrestling with the political system, was provided by another neighborhood's attempt to protect its children from serious injury or worse. We have already alluded to the presence of a creek-bed in this neighborhood, where group after group over the course of many years had tried to get the county to add to or move the existing fence on one side so that the area was properly enclosed. Despite the hazard to life or limb that the creek (whether full or empty) posed to youngsters at play, county government had steadfastly refused to complete the job of enclosure.

It took the Family Matters Neighborhood Group about six months of diligent leg-work to secure sufficient petition signatures, to learn the procedures to be followed, and to find the right political buttons that had to be pushed. However, *their* efforts succeeded in half a year where those of others had failed over the course of many years — an instance of truly successful neighborhood mobilization.

This success provided the group with considerable impetus, and this particular cluster of families became one of the strongest of the Program II groups. Even this organization, however, experienced a good deal of "storming" of the kind discussed earlier. Its example points out the difficulties and intricacies of collective action even under the best of circumstances and with the most successful of outcomes. As discussed earlier, it became quite evident that it was harder and took longer to make the Neighborhood Grouping Program work at the same level as did the Home Visitor Program. To gain a better view of some of these problems, the difficulties specifically associated with Program II processes, we will now look at some of the key issues in Neighborhood Grouping activities just as we did with Home Visits.

SOME KEY ISSUES IN PROGRAM II ACTIVITY

Among the key issues singled out by Cochran and Woolever (1980) are two that helped explain the slower progress in Program II evolution compared with that of Program I. In addition to the fundamental difficulties associated with group processes generally, there were problems associated with "scheduling" conflicts and "high turnover" rate (Cochran and Woolever, 1980). In our brief survey of the contemporary Syracuse scene, we have already noted the severity of the problems of economics, employment, intergroup tensions, crime, housing, and mobility. Unfortunately many of these came home to roost when attempts were made to organize for mutual support. Often the stresses were so great that they overwhelmed the very attempts to relieve stress.

Scheduling Conflicts

For example, because of economic pressures on many Family Matters families of moderate income (i.e., lower-middle-class), some parents held *two* to *four* jobs between father and mother in order to pay inflated rents, mortgage costs, energy bills, and the other well-known horrors of today's economy. As some project senior staff members put it, the *national* recession economics during program history *plus* the recession indigenous to Syracuse in recent years have probably had the hardest impact on those who had "just been making it" financially. Upper-middle-income families probably had some cushion, and did not feel the pressure immediately. The plight of those in the very lowest social strata had been serious and worsened still further. Indeed some Family Matters *workers* themselves were not far from this situation.

The only way to stay afloat was to take the extra job, or to work weekends, or an extra or graveyard shift. Balance is thus in many cases maintained, but family life suffers and family schedules become chaotic. Home Visitor programming could often accommodate itself to the bewildering variety of timetables and caregiver arrangements this kind of work-load engendered. But the problem of coordinating such schedules for Neighborhood Group members was nightmarish, to say nothing of the motivational difficulties of getting families who were increasingly stressed and growing desperate to emerge from their homes and to share with one another. It is thus not surprising that the earliest and most notable successes of Program II activity, the neighborhood resource centers, the school visiting program, the Neighborhood Watch program, and the creek-fencing initiative took place in middle-income neighborhoods rather than in those of moderate or lowest income.

Transiency of Families

But economic pressures impinged on areas other than scheduling and motivation for social activity. Also affected were the rents and mortgage payments we have spoken of earlier. These pressures plus the problems of housing and residential dislocation through commercial development discussed in Chapter 4 helped create extremely high levels of transiency in a program that was neighborhood based and hence location-specific. For example, as of November of 1979 when the program had been functioning in the two pilot neighborhoods for only a little more than 18 months, Woolever (1979) reported that 12 of the original 16 Program II pilot families had moved at least once, and three families more than once.

The Home Visitor Program had encountered comparable difficulties in the geographic stability of its pilot families, thus attesting to the power of the double impact of economic and housing problems in Syracuse. Of the original 16 pilot families in Program I,

7 had moved in the space of a year and one-half. But the Home Visitor Program had greater flexibility. Families who moved could continue to receive program services regardless of location as long as they remained within the county. This was clearly not the case with regard to the Neighborhood Grouping Program, where even when families remained in the general area, they often found themselves far from neighborhoods participating in the project.

It is thus abundantly clear why the processes of Program II implementation were more difficult in terms of contextual conditions having little or nothing to do with Program implementation. A somewhat later start-up of group activity, the problems inherent in group process; preexistent networks that already functioned as family supports, scheduling conflicts, high turnover of families within neighborhoods, other stressors associated with social, economic, housing, and political conditions within the city — all of these factors contributed to making the path for Program II a thornier one. Consequently our overview of Program II processes presented, at best, much more of a *chiaroscuro* scene when compared with the somewhat brighter picture of Program I.

FAMILY REACTION TO PROGRAM II

Our interviews with families about halfway through the program and at its end reflected a dimmer view of Program II than Program I, though not a negative one. About two-thirds of those who had participated in groups reported that they had had a positive experience. Content analysis of all interview comments about groups, however, showed that fully a third of the statements were negative, a much higher proportion than had characterized the family feedback about home visits. The dissatisfaction was centered in three areas: the lack of structure or of direction in group meetings, low levels of participation by other families, and the relevance of topics discussed. When families were asked what program elements they would like to keep the same, the modal response had been "home visits." Only about one-third as many respondents felt that the group meetings were an aspect of the program they most wanted to retain.

As for changes that might be attributable to Program II participation, less than half of the respondents reported feeling differently about their neighbors, and content analysis of the comments in this area showed that the feelings were as likely to be negative as positive. However, about half the families felt that closeness with people outside their family had changed, and such changes were seen very positively. Expansion of social contacts and of social networks were frequently mentioned and spoken of affirmatively; in some instances, helping to dispel loneliness for the parents, in other cases, helping to provide companionship for the target child.

As for increasing utilization of community institutions, agencies, or resources, about half of our interviewees reported attitude change in this area, and only about a third indicated differences in agency use patterns. When the subject of community was raised, however, the data suggest that in many instances, program participation had increased *awareness of issues* among families.

The above findings from families show the mixed pattern of light and shadow discussed above. There are the usual general endorsements that evaluators have come to expect from most program participants, and in our case study as in other comparable efforts, such favorability is certainly due at least in part to genuine satisfaction rather than to response sets and to considerations of social desirability alone. Participants in Family Matters Program II showed some relevant attitude change, some increase in issue awareness, and, more important, some increase in social contact and social networks as well as the reduction in isolation and loneliness for parent and child that was one of the major goals of the intervention. The magnitude and generality of effects achieved, however, remain at issue, based on the levels and breadth of participation by families, and based on results obtained by our study of implementation and those of the project's outcome research component. We turn first to the question of participation.

GROUP PARTICIPATION

The average number of group meetings attended by Family Matters participants was 3.98 (i.e., approximately three group meetings and one visit to a family resource center). As with home visits, the variability was very wide with some families taking part in about 30 meetings, and a large proportion (about two-fifths) of the families attending none. Even assuming about a 19-month duration for the program and subtracting 6 summer months (for 2 years) where little group activity took place, fewer than 20 percent of the families participated in any kind of Program II activity as many as 13 times, a level that would approximate a once-a-month rate.

Most of the meetings attended were not mass gatherings but rather "clusters," get-togethers involving two or three mothers, usually with their preschool children. In general, participation in Program II activities was more frequent by better educated, white, married, and single mothers working on a part-time basis and living in suburban neighborhoods or those of strong ethnic background. As a rule, the meetings would be in the home, but about one-fourth of the time, they would be at the Neighborhood Resource Center. Thus despite the notable success of a few groups in affecting the larger social context described earlier, most of the achievements of Program II were not mass efforts. They involved mutual support by parent dyads or triads who felt (in the words of several families) "very much in the same boat."

Even at this level, Program II intensity was very low on an average basis. Spread over 30 months of program duration, or the 19 months or the 13 nonsummer months of median participation described earlier, the levels of involvement would not normally be nearly enough to produce very large effects for most program families. We will have more to say later about outcomes and about the conceptual and organizational reasons for problems with Program II. What has been said previously about the competing needs, priorities, and problems of families that precluded participation must be factored in here, as must the implementation difficulties of the project that have already been described and will be discussed in the treatment of organizational resources. But whatever the difficulties of implementation, the option of neighborhood groups was not popular with Family Matters participants. Thus, when the integrated program was offered to families, there were many more Program II families who elected either to add home visits or substitute them for group meetings than there were Program I families who chose to add group meetings or substitute them for home visits. We can understand why people dissatisfied with Program II might, given the chance, abandon that option. But it is less clear why those who had never tried the meetings would have resisted trying out that alternative. We will examine this question further in a later chapter on the "need" for certain social programs. At this point, however, we will turn to a very brief look at the outcomes that appear to have resulted from involvement in Program II.

PARTICIPATION AND OUTCOMES

Despite the above mentioned low levels of participation in groups by most program families, there were some effects measured by the project's outcome research component that appear to be attributable to involvement in Family Matters. These analyses are as yet unpublished and not yet even final, but they do intimate that for certain subgroups of the sample, groups made a difference in social support. The most striking finding was that for unmarried white mothers, there was an increase in nonrelatives in their primary and functional networks, and a decrease in contacts with relatives during the years between pre- and postmeasurement.

Our own process study observations converge with these findings on the importance of group activities for single parents (Mindick, 1980c and Mindick and Maples, 1980). Thus although the need for and participation in neighborhood groups may have been low by some, it was clearly not so for all. Once again, however, the overall findings of the outcome research component do not display either dramatically strong effects, or ones that are wide spread across most of the families participating. Indeed a simple pre-post comparison between network size involving both program and control groups yielded no significant differences.

The major changes seemed to involve an increase in the importance of nonrelatives in the social support systems of white single mothers and a concomitant decline in the importance of relatives. Thus, the chief program effect seems to have been confined to one subgroup of participants, and involved a substitution of nonkin for kin in supportive functions. This rise in the importance of nonkin was not as general among black one-parent families, but where such gains did occur, they were associated with significant positive program effects in noncognitive school outcomes, and with increased joint parent-child activities (the finding was true for black two-parent families as well.) The outcomes may be of importance in future efforts to strengthen families, but they and the other quantitatively measured outcomes obtained also represent what we have come to expect from early childhood intervention programs: small effects, neither general across participant subgroups nor across outcome domains.

As for our ethnographically measured outcomes, some of these are dramatic and either permanent or at least not ephemeral. The creek-bed described earlier is fenced for good, and presumably will not be a hazard to children in that neighborhood ever again. The neighborhood watch program is likely to go on for several years. The school visits made by a few neighborhood groups will in all likelihood have their long-term impact. One suburban neighborhood group continued through the dedicated efforts of two program families and provided educational and other family activities for about two years after formal program activity had been terminated. All of these are very real accomplishments. The sum of these achievements and those documented by the outcome research component of the project for both groups and home visits suggests that further efforts and investigation are probably warranted. But on the scale between "gradualism and grandeur" (Nicol, 1976), we find that Family Matters, like so many other programs, is far closer to the former than the latter.

NEIGHBORHOOD MOBILIZATION MORE BROADLY

As mentioned in Chapter 4, Family Matters attempts to organize neighborhood groups were comparable to efforts aimed at neighborhood mobilization such as those described by Henig (1982). Such endeavors, unlike the parent groups typical of Head Start-like programs, which are most often school-based, start at the neighborhood level, usually in response to some perceived threat. This threat is often some form of development that would displace residents from their homes or otherwise markedly affect the quality of their lives. According to Henig, "Urban renewal in the 1950's and 1960's mauled many urban neighborhoods . . ." and, "Highway and housing policies encouraged suburbanization and sapped the urban neighborhood of its strength" (Ibid., p. 3). Henig also bewails the neglect of the urban neighborhood by social scientists as well as the fact that attempts to fight back, i.e., mobilization, are phenomena primarily of the past ten years.

Like Family Matters, such attempts at neighborhood group organization are usually characterized by low levels of participation.

Indeed, Henig (1982) has pointed out that in many instances no mobilization whatever takes place. Of the six neighborhoods studied by Henig in Chicago and Minneapolis, only one responded quickly, forcefully, and in numbers to impending threats of development. In two others, the response was slow, and in only one of these did residents turn out in significant numbers. In the last three neighborhoods, resident mobilization was sluggish and small, or didn't occur at all. When mobilization does occur, it is usually a relatively few better educated residents who are involved, and theirs is usually a losing, if sometimes prolonged, battle against the forces favoring development. In this respect three of the ten Family Matters neighborhoods compare quite favorably with the norm. Fencing in the creek-bed, getting Neighborhood Watch going, and establishing at least one of the neighborhood resource center which continued for a few years after program's end represent a better than average record as mobilization efforts go. The other seven neighborhoods are more typical.

We also have seen that Syracuse United Neighborhoods (SUN), an umbrella neighborhood organization, had its innings, winning some and losing some. It is unfortunate that the constraints of experimental design made it impossible to link the Family Matters neighborhood groups with SUN for mutual support and greater longevity for Family Matters. Also, there are national organizations linking neighborhood groups. Establishing such a connection might have enhanced Family Matters Program II efficacy. But as neighborhood mobilization, Program II's achievements were not trivial. On the national level, however, although neighborhood organization remains a concern of importance to many, gentrification programs are to be found in major cities around the country, and as shown in Chapter 4, it would be simplistic in the extreme to see renewal versus residents as a battle between evil and good.

PARENT SUPPORT GROUPS

We have commented on the low level of involvement in Family Matters neighborhood groups, but this kind of problem is by no means uncommon. Indeed Powell (1981) has found a complex set of relationships related to parent group participation, and alleged "need." Attendance at his twice weekly group meetings was significantly and positively related to number of children and to frequency of contact with relatives, but negatively to life stress. It looks like children create some need for parent group participation, but not having relatives seems to have the opposite effect. This latter finding appears to suggest that in the wealth of social networks, the rich get richer, and in the face of stress, the poor get poorer. Yet in Powell's (1984) analysis, when it came to special events such as picnics and field trips, involvement with friends appeared to make such participation unnecessary.

Overall, Powell (1984) distinguished two separate patterns of group participation, often influenced by the means used to *recruit* participants initially. When recruitment is relatively passive, i.e., through advertisements and posters, participants are more likely to be active persons who will often pursue a *peer-oriented* pattern of program utilization. When recruitment is very active — door-to-door search, phone calls, heavy public relations, or "sales" efforts — more passive participants are likely to be drawn in. These people will display a *staff-oriented* pattern of utilization. In the peer-oriented pattern of participation, parents maintain a strong friendship and close contact with relatives and friends, take initiative and leadership roles, and are highly self-disclosing. In the staff-oriented pattern of participation, participation is under higher stress and primarily is for medical and social service problems. Utilization is more passive. There is a lower number of friendships with other participants, and less self-disclosure takes place. In other words, the innovative program becomes just another agency.

As a parent support group, Family Matters probably achieved less, for example, than many comparable organizations linked to Head Start. As Valentine and Stark (1979) have noted, Head Start parental roles have bifurcated into two major areas: (1) decision making, and (2) learning in order to teach their children. There was a good deal of controversy and ultimately some policy change about the former, i.e., parents as political activists in their communities, and according to Valentine and Stark, there has been too little evaluation of the constructiveness of Head Start parents' political role. We have already discussed in Chapter 2 the Head Start parent groups in their attempts to improve social services for themselves and their children. Family Matters did not have similar effects, except perhaps in the school-related outcomes earlier. According to the project outcome research component, it appears that Family Matters parents were more willing to communicate with school authorities when their youngsters were having problems than were control groups members. But there does not seem to be a general or even a highly specific impact on the social service system.

As for parents as educators of their youngsters, both Family Matters and Head Start share the same fate in not being able to demonstrate strong and clear-cut effects (cf. Datta, 1979; Valentine and Stark, 1979). Parental involvement was "a cornerstone of Head Start policy" (Zigler and Valentine, 1979), and several dozen Parent Child and Parent Child Development Centers were established around the nation. In assessments of Head Start and Family Matters impacts there again appears to be an intimation that social programs promoting parental involvement in their children's education may provide some beneficial outcomes. There is abundant anecdotal evidence, testimonial from some highly involved and highly satisfied parents (Robinson and Choper, 1979), but the demonstrated quantitative effects are very modest and not likely to galvanize the general public or policy makers to demand expansion of such programs. Thus, there is consistency in the record of ambiguity for these parent *group* programs comparable to that described above in our discussion of interventions targeted at *individuals*.

7

INFORMATION RESOURCES

In our case study of Family Matters, we have encountered a general characteristic of family-based education programs and several other kinds of intervention — effects that are neither large (by contemporary social scientific standards) nor general across participant subgroups or domains of outcome criteria. According to the argument advanced in Chapter 1, this set of results is precisely what we would expect. We have seen the very benevolent intentions and deeds of both the designers of the program and the program staff members and the bright examples of their very real achievements. But in Chapter 4, we described in detail the magnitude of the problems Family Matters and its participants encountered in the urban context of the program — difficulties nested in major structural systems and subsystems of the city (and also of family life) that cannot be tugged at easily without the unraveling of fabric elsewhere (cf. also Twain, 1983).

In Chapter 8, we will look in greater detail at the deficiencies of implementation and especially of organizational resources that we believe were related to the nonspectacular outcomes of the program we have studied in detail and possibly also to similar outcomes that have characterized other comparable efforts. But we have stated that the difficulties experienced by social programs in producing the effects they seek and that policy makers and the public have been led to expect do not lie strictly within the domain of implementation. Our contention is that there is a dearth of information resources about how to intervene strongly (the elusive "superpotent intervention"), successfully, and with a minimum of negative fallout.

To document this dearth of information resources, we return to our case study and we examine closely the manner in which inadequacy of information influenced the planning of the Family Matters Program. To some, our consideration of the conceptual ebb and flow in detail may seem excessively microscopic. But it is rare that we have the opportunity to observe the evolution of ideas such as that presented here. The realism and candor reflected in our study of this conceptual development are too often obscured by retrospective rationalizations by many designers to justify what was actually done in program implementation. Thus what we have here is an unusual look behind the curtains of one workshop of program design. At the end of this chapter we will examine the question of information resources generally available to social scientists in their attempts to modify human behavior.

DEVELOPMENTS IN THE NUMBER OF PROGRAM OPTIONS

To demonstrate that Family Matters was not predicated on a firm base of social scientific knowledge because no such base exists, we will examine the developments in various aspects of program design, showing not only an evolution in that design, but something much more disconcerting. We will see that a good deal of vacillation and backtracking occurred. We pursue this line of inquiry not to set the designers of Family Matters apart from others in any pejorative sense whatever. They are all well motivated and caring men who have sought to make a difference in our society while others have merely ignored problems or offered rhetoric alone. They are particularly to be admired for opening themselves and the Ecology of Human Development Project to the glare of scrutiny, wisely recognizing in advance that outcomes are often not congruent with intentions, and that it is only by examining what occurs between intention and outcome that we learn how to make progress more successfully in human development and in human betterment generally.

Thus we now turn to that examination of conceptual processes in various facets of Family Matters design. We begin with developments in the number of intervention strategies that the program was to implement, and the allocation of those strategies to participating families.

Earliest Thinking

The original proposal was the blueprint for the Family Matters Program (Bronfenbrenner and Cochran, 1976), and envisioned *three* experimental "treatments": one oriented toward home activities, a second directed toward "neighborhood resources," and a third that combined the first two. The rationale for this kind of design lay in the perceived need to assess both the separate and the joint effects of two sets of independent variables, i.e., parent-child activities and social networks.

Some Reformulations

The first important indication of a change in thinking about the *number* of treatments was found in a memo from Principal Investigator Cochran (1977) to Principal Investigator Bronfenbrenner about a year after the original proposal. Cochran expressed considerable doubt about the home activities treatment, presenting as many as eight arguments for dropping the intervention that would bring a parent/child specialist to families on a regular basis. The fundamental concern behind these arguments was "exposing parents to a family advocate who is primarily interested in demonstrating 'good child rearing' activities to them in their own homes" (Cochran, 1977, p. 2). Cochran expresses hesitations on ethical, scientific, theoretical, and pragmatic grounds. Stated succinctly, his reasoning runs as follows.

Short-term success in communicating the "hidden curriculum" of child rearing (i.e., the values of cognitive style implicit in the way parents interact with their children; cf. Hess and Shipman, 1965) across class and culture has already been demonstrated, at least in part, in the work of investigators such as Karnes (1969) and Levenstein (1972). A further demonstration in the United States is largely superfluous. Furthermore, the kind of in-home demonstration proposed raises questions of "moral propriety," since it may appear to demean parents in the eyes of their own children. Worse still, it may have a paradoxically negative effect on the independence and initiative of children in the long run, whatever the short-term gains. Cochran (1977) is clearly *for* parent-child activities, but believes that these can be encouraged by a "Family Neighborhood Specialist" (a concept originally proposed in conjunction with Treatment III, the combined intervention) without pedantic show-and-tell in the home.

In addition, Cochran calls for dropping Treatment I (the parent-child specialist) on pragmatic grounds and those of policy relevance as well. Dropping the treatment would "streamline" the program. This would allow efforts to be focused more single-mindedly on the "neighborhood as a social unit." Reducing the number of treatments might save funds and allow the project to add more neighborhoods or families. The economies realized by dropping Treatment I might specifically be used to strengthen the black families component of the project, the particular interest of Principal Investigator Cross who had recently "joined the team." Finally, financial considerations are also relevant to those of policy. The home visits to be made by the parent-child specialists are relatively expensive, and in any cost-benefit ratio assessed by future policy makers, this intervention may be seen as not sufficiently cost effective.

In response to these arguments, Bronfenbrenner (1977) drafted a reply just two weeks later. He made it clear that recently he had also begun to have second thoughts about the parent-child specialist intervention. Bronfenbrenner was especially responsive to the ethical, scientific, and policy-related concerns raised by Cochran. He, too, was troubled about the practicalities of having enough neighborhoods to be allocated among three different treatments; generally he was concerned about their combined "ability to bring off" the "monumental enterprise" inherent in a *threefold* experimental intervention in one country, plus cross-cultural comparison studies in four other lands.

In his own mind, he had also resolved that the number of treatments must be limited to two. The question was, which two? There seemed to be little doubt about continuing with the Neighborhood Resources approach, although Bronfenbrenner expressed very real doubt as to whether expanding families' formal and informal social networks would *ipso facto* lead to the desired kind of joint activity among parents and children. It is possible, said Bronfenbrenner (1977, p. 3) ". . . that family support systems do not necessarily result in parent/child activity of any kind, letting alone the type that may be most conducive to child development." It is only "support systems that *provide opportunity, assistance, status, and approval for parents* and other adults *to participate in constructive activities with children*" (emphasis mine) that would result in greater parent-child activity.

Thus, Bronfenbrenner agreed that it would be wise to:

(1)   Reduce the number of treatments.
(2)   Limit the scope of the undertaking generally.
(3)   Remove Cochran's (and his own) scientific, ethical, and policy objections to the parent-child intervention.

Bronfenbrenner seems to have felt that he could not abandon the parent-child specialist intervention in favor of a combined approach, i.e., parent-child activities *plus* enhancing social support systems, because a program that studied two treatments, X and Y, by testing X and Y+X (but never Y alone), could not adequately illuminate the separate contribution of each treatment to later outcomes of the intervention. He concurred with the need for reducing the number of treatments. He saw the best solution to the dilemma as changing the *nature* as well as the *number* of interventions. Thus, in the winter of 1977, both Cochran and Bronfenbrenner agreed that the number of treatments would be reduced to two, and the nature of the program would be modified in a very profound way.

DEVELOPMENTS IN THE NATURE
OF THE PROGRAM – THE ISSUE OF CHOICE

Earliest Thinking

As noted earlier, the original proposal (Bronfenbrenner and Cochran, 1976) envisioned that Treatment I would be carried out by a *"parent-child specialist,"* who was to make a "direct effort . . . to encourage parent-child interaction and provide each family with a wide range of resource materials . . ." (Ibid., 1976, p. 4). In Treatment II, a *neighborhood resources specialist* was to "provide and strengthen informal support systems that can assist the parents in their child rearing activities." The *family neighborhood specialist* discussed earlier was to "conduct" Treatment III which, it will be recalled, was to be a combination of Treatments I and II. Furthermore, as the proposal states (Ibid., 1976, p. 4), "All three types of specialists will serve as advocates for the individual families that they serve." Despite this active ombudsman-like role that Bronfenbrenner and Cochran planned for the specialists, however, the two investigators envisioned giving participant families ". . . considerable choice in the activities they might wish to undertake at a particular time" (Ibid., 1976, p. 32).

Some Reformulations

Permitting participants to select the kind and timing of the home activities in which they took part was to be one of the elements of parental choice in the Family Matters Program and also one of its distinctive characteristics. This characteristic was designed to differentiate the intervention from previous home visitor programs devised by other researchers who had favored a more "fixed curriculum" of activity. In his memo of January 24, 1977 (Cochran, 1977), however, Cochran felt compelled to remark on the *narrow* latitude of options offered by the parent-child specialist's treatment.

> Let's face it, the parent really has only two choices under this condition; to let the specialist into the house or to drop out of the program. No room is left for the parent who has the feeling that s/he is being told how to bring up his/her own children even in a very nice way, by powerful outsiders, and is offended.

Cochran then goes on to point out his personal and ethical discomfort with this kind of program.

In his response to Cochran's memo, Bronfenbrenner (1977) acknowledged the validity of Cochran's concerns. Although recognizing that some colleagues and research sponsors might not share their views about the issue of parents' ability to exercise choice under the proposed Treatment I, Bronfenbrenner saw the questions about parental options as yet another reason for *not* leaving the intervention in its original form.

Within three weeks of Cochran's first memo, both principal investigators drafted a joint communiqué to the Cornell staff and the project's consultants (Bronfenbrenner and Cochran, 1977, p. 1). The memo reveals the reservations of *both* men concerning the "invasion of privacy" and the "calling into question the parents' competence" that is implied by Treatment I as originally designed. Even though the original formulation of Treatment I did allow parents "to choose activities from a 'cafeteria tray' with a variety of options," it is now their view that this small amount of choice ". . . is so trivial a grant of power as to confirm rather than counteract any parental feelings of inadequacy and lack of control over their lives" (Ibid.).

But rather than abandoning Treatment I, as originally advocated by Cochran (1977), Bronfenbrenner and Cochran (1977) instead agreed to *modify* the intervention. Two major "additions and alterations" were suggested: first, the parent is to be recognized as an "expert," and second (and most salient to the present discussion), a major effort was to be made to protect and strengthen ". . . *parental privacy and power in the choice of parent/child activities*" (Ibid., p. 3, emphasis in original). These objectives are to be accomplished by encouraging parents to present their own ideas and experiences in the area of parent-child activities, or by allowing parents to elect to utilize activities suggested by other program parents. But prior to any discussion of activities, program staff members are to state quite explicitly that it is ". . . very important that parents be the ones to decide what happens in their children's lives" (Ibid., p. 3).

Thus parents might either choose to continue activities they have used previously or they may learn from *other program parents*. In February of 1977, however, there was no mention of the possibility that either the Ithaca academics *or* the Syracuse paraprofessional staff might have suggestions of their own about parent-child activities, or whether there would be any active role for the Program I worker. From this memo, the worker appeared to be something of a switchboard operator — transmitting and facilitating the communication of others, but initiating none him or herself.

By November 2, 1977, a memo from the "Working Committee on Program I" (Working Committee on Program I, 1977a) to the project staff strengthens the switchboard idea by stating that the title "parent/child specialist" is to be dropped, and instead calling "the Program I person" an "Activities Coordinator." The document expresses the hope that when families see their own ideas in print, they will be stimulated to engage in more home activities, including the "trying out" of "new parent-child activities provided through the visits by the Activities Coordinator or through the activities newsletter" (Ibid., p. 2). The memo, however, still does not make clear whether there would be any initiating role for the Activities Coordinator.

As a matter of fact, the *title* "Activities Coordinator" seems to have had a very short half-life. Decay in its "atomic structure" was total just five days later. The same committee (Working Committee on Program I, 1977b), changed the position title to "Activities Home Visitor," in its memo of November 7, 1977. In this communication to the project staff, the Program I worker is referred to as "learner" (who assesses parent-child activities in the home) "as well as a teacher sharing activities that work for other families" (Ibid., p. 1). Again there is no mention of teaching that springs from the worker's own knowledge or experience, or from the expertise of the Cornell research team. The latter had already acknowledged that they were not certain about what activities would work best (Bronfenbrenner, 1977). As a matter of fact, the Working Committee (Working Committee on Program I, 1977b) document stipulates that home visitors are to make it explicit "that the information is coming from other parents rather than professionals" (Ibid., p. 2).

Selection of Program Workers in Both Programs I and II

Perhaps the most unusual suggestion in terms of choices for families lies in a paper authored by the Family Matters program director himself (Woolever, 1978, p. 1). Woolever suggests that, "The workers in Programs I and II can be selected by the families themselves." The director proposes that there could be preliminary screening of candidates, a list of finalists drawn up, exposure of the candidates to the families, and then families could vote by secret ballot on those persons who are to be hired. Woolever sees this procedure as having advantages for empowering families and for "quickening the trust relationship between workers and families." To the best of our knowledge, this innovative plan was not implemented, but it does reflect the range of ideas in program planning early in the winter of 1977-78, just before pilot programs began. The plan also illustrates the degree to which efforts were being made to depart from models set up by previous fixed-curriculum programs and to allow families elements of choice.

OPTIONS AVAILABLE TO FAMILIES
IN PROGRAM II

Other than thoughts about choosing *who* might be hired initially, planning for families in the neighborhood-centered program seems to have provided less in the way of *individual* choice than did planning for families who were in Program I, the family-centered program. This is probably because Program I came in for such large amounts of criticism as a result of its original design, which was seen as being inherently devoid of options for parents. Also, there could be no question that in the neighborhood-centered program, however much the worker might hold back his or her preferences, each individual family would ultimately have to negotiate its predilections with others. Parents could work in pairs, clusters of three to five persons, or in groups of up to twenty. But except in the unlikely event of total unanimity, the activities decided upon would have to emerge as a compromise in the positions of at least two parents. It is thus quite interesting that in the same document that the program director (Woolever, 1978) refers to the Program I worker as a "Home Visitor," the Program II worker is still being referred to as "The Neighborhood Resource *Specialist*" (emphasis mine). At that point in time, the idea that the worker would be an *expert* was less problematic in relation to Program II than to Program I.

Choice of Activities

As for choice in the kinds of activities to be undertaken in Program II, at least as far as *worker* influence in concerned, Cochran and Woolever (1978, p. 1) state that the program areas for neighborhood activities ". . . will be identified as important by parents themselves." The mechanism for such parental input, however, is indirect, and as such, it is of considerable interest. At least initially, i.e., during the pilot phase of program operations, no information on individuals was to be sought. Family needs were to be evaluated in summaries of findings from one of the baseline assessment instruments, the "stresses and supports interview." The field research director was to prepare summaries of family concerns on a neighborhood (not on an individual family) basis, and these were to serve as the foundation for early worker conversations with specific Program II families. After reporting the findings, the worker was then to solicit further information from families about their interests and needs, and such reassessment was to continue cyclically on an ongoing basis. But here again, thinking with regard to individual choices appears not to have been as preoccupied with letting the family take the initiative as was the case with Program I.

We will see later that in actual program implementation, however, workers were encouraged to allow family *clusters* and *groups* to take the initiating role. Workers were to minimize their own organizational and leadership efforts. This strategy plus the apparent absence of the proposed summaries of neighborhood interests derived from research data both seem to have led to a good deal of ambiguity at some of the early Program II group meetings. But this topic must be reserved for future discussion. We now examine perhaps the broadest jump in principal investigator thinking on the issue of choice, i.e., choice of participation in Program I, Program II, or both.

FAMILY OPTIONS AS A RESULT OF PROGRAM FUSION – REFORMULATION BASED ON FIELD EXPERIENCE

We have already discussed the distinctive characteristics of Programs I and II and their interrelatedness as well. Also, we have noted the intent of the principal investigators to keep the interventions separate in order to prevent confounding of the specific effects of each in analyzing experimental outcomes.

Several problems arose, however, as a result of this strategy of separation. The first was inherent in the natural evolution of the programs themselves. As Cochran and Woolever (1980, p. 3) put it, ". . . a substantial number of families in the Home Visitor Program have spontaneously expressed a desire to get together with other families in the program." Some of the considerations that apparently motivated Program I families to show an interest in the program's neighborhood groups were: curiosity about other program families living close by, an accumulation of trust in the program, the effects of the supportiveness it offered, and sometimes, simple feelings of being isolated in one's own neighborhood.

On the other side of the coin, the neighborhood-centered program had been notably less successful than its counterpart. In April 1980, about half-way through Family Matters history, Cochran and Woolever (1980) reported that, "Only about 50% of eligible families have been participating in groups." It was felt that if Program II families had the option of home visits that could be more flexibly accommodated to their individual schedules than could group meetings, and if dyadic interaction between parents and children could be worked out through Program I activity, the impact of the total of Family Matters on families might be intensified.

The issue of program intensity had been a thorny one for some time. Parent groups were to meet on a monthly basis, and home visits were to occur on an average of once every two or three weeks. But a site visiting team from the National Institute of Education (NIE) reviewing program implementation on November 13-14, 1979 had expressed concerns about the actual intensity of the intervention. While at least two N.I.E. site visitors had commented favorably on the attempt to emphasize "family strengths," they also saw this approach as creating ". . . a diffuseness of goals and organization" (Travers, 1979). Two important messages, among others, from the site team seemed to be that the program needed to be more intensive, and workers should take a somewhat more directive approach toward families.

It appears that the principal investigators themselves had felt for some time that there might be a need for closer supervision of program activities (cf. Pierce, 1980, April 16, and April 23), and perhaps some "fine-tuning" of the interventions in greater accord with their earlier thinking (i.e., Bronfenbrenner and Cochran, 1976), especially in light of lessons learned from the pilot phase of the research and also from the first year or so of program activity. Also, a confidential memo (Mindick, 1980b), had presented to the principal investigators process study findings and recommendations with regard to the active or passive nature of worker role, the issues of supervision and accountability (and implicitly program intensity), and the need for clarification of program goals, means, and information to be presented to program families.

For these reasons, and others as well, it was decided to integrate Programs I and II. That is, rather than being constrained to participate only in activities sponsored by the program component to which they have been originally assigned, parents would be *encouraged* to cross previously established boundaries and take part in both groups and home visits. It was felt that the dual intervention would supply an intensity and direction that the single approach could not. Thus, in February 1980, workers began a carefully prepared campaign augmented with visual aids to solicit commitment from families to participate in both kinds of Family Matters Program activity.

If the effort was to get all families to commit themselves to both programs, however, the results proved to be only partly successful. As of May of 1980, only 24 percent of Program I families and 11 percent of those in Program II had elected to participate in the fused program (Mindick, 1980a). These figures represented only about 18 percent of all program families. By July 1980, about a year from program's end, there was a bit more interest in the integrated program, with 26 percent of program families opting for both groups and home visits. But it also appeared that in some instances these families had recently begun "to drift away" from home visits. Consequently, on an overall basis, it seems safe to say that rarely did more than one-fourth of the sample actively participate in both home visits and group meetings. Also, program integration necessitated a realignment of workers and families. In many instances this meant reassigning a worker to new families and taking her or him away from those with whom strong rapport already existed. This promoted bad feelings among staff members and families and was a source of unfavorable comment by both these groups.

More encouraging, however, was the report by Cochran and Woolever (1980) that allowing families to choose home visits or groups or both had the highly desirable effect of reducing inactivity among program families. Most of the change was in the direction of families who were previously eligible for Program II electing to switch to Program I (i.e., home activities), but as a result of program fusion and the related options that became available, overall participation in the program rose by about 20 percent.

The upshot of all these changes was to transform a program that assigned "subjects" to an experimental condition by neighborhood into a program that allowed families to choose the kinds of supportive services *they* felt they wanted or needed. This was of course a *non*-"trivial grant of power" that was more in line with the empowerment theme adopted by the principal investigators in the winter of 1977. It is also more in line with recent findings in the area of program evaluation (cf. Weeks, 1979) and opinion in the public policy community (cf. Travers, 1979) that micro-level interventions and *planned variations* from macro-level programs are more likely to be successful than "shotgun" approaches that prescribe the same "treatment" for large national samples regardless of region, community, neighborhood, or individual difference.

DEVELOPMENTS IN THE NATURE OF WORKER ROLE IN PROGRAM I

In the preceding section we have reviewed the evolution of principal investigator thinking as well as developments in both program guidelines and implementation as they related to a fundamental change in the nature of the program with regard to the issue of parental choice. Next, we pursue further the topic of developments in the *nature* of the program, focusing on an area that is inversely related to the subject of parental choice, i.e., worker role. Here we will place our emphasis increasingly on a somewhat later phase of conceptual evolution and to aspects of program implementation itself.

Earliest Thinking

In the words of the original proposal, the parent-child specialist was to "present, demonstrate and explain the purpose of various activities" (Bronfenbrenner and Cochran, 1976, p. 32). It is interesting to note that in line with the experimental orientation of the project, at this early stage the home visitor program was referred to as "*Treatment* I." The "Rationale for Treatment I" states (Ibid., p. 33), "The key to facilitating the child's development lies primarily within the family," because of the impact of ". . . the activities to which the parents expose the child . . ." (i.e., the hidden curriculum in the home). "This hidden curriculum can be made explicit, communicated to parents through information and demonstration . . ." (Ibid., p. 33).

In analyzing the nature of worker role in Treatment I as it is outlined here, several key elements emerge with considerable clarity. The home visitor is described as a "specialist" rather than simply as a "*worker.*" The more egalitarian job title was adopted later. Noteworthy also was the accompanying characterization of the specialist's tasks, i.e., ". . . to present, demonstrate and explain the purpose of various activities . . . and to act as an advocate for individual families."

There is little doubt that the specialist was seen as an expert who was to provide his or her talent and knowledge to family members who required them. It is equally clear that this conceptualization implied deficit in those who chose to utilize the specialist's expertise, and it is precisely this view of research families as potentially deficient that had troubled Cochran and Bronfenbrenner in the winter of 1977. Ultimately, of course, the issue was resolved in the decision to use paraprofessionals (a subject we will deal with in the next chapter), and to change the title, the role, and the job description in such a way as to minimize any apparent expertise by the home visitor.

One interesting detour along this conceptual road from "specialist" to "home visitor" is found in a draft of Program I guidelines for families (Family Matters, 1977). Here the home visitor is referred to as a "peer/learner," a sharp contrast to the parent-child specialist who was to be much more of a teacher than a learner. Rather than "presenting, demonstrating, explaining" and "advocating," the peer/ learner was to "explore *with* (emphasis in original) the families those activities that foster growth and development in children." We have already discussed the November 7, 1977 Working Committee memo, in which the Program I worker was to be a learner/teacher, instructing families about activities contributed by other families.

Some Reformulations —
Worker Activities in Program I

Most important, changes in terminology were *not* merely cosmetic. They reflected a very real shift in program philosophy.

Bo (1979), describing early Family Matters documents points out that in program materials, the view reflected is that both parent and worker have something to contribute. "One is not more important than the other. They bring different resources and share these to a common advantage" (Bo, 1979, p. 13).

Bo, whose excellent account of early program processes proved to be an invaluable source of information, also notes that in documents dating from May 1977 to February 1978 (the latter date marks the beginning of program activities in the pilot neighborhoods), several additional changes can be discerned. In documents formulated during that eight-month period, there is no longer any mention of "parent-child activities kits" that were to have been brought by workers into participants' homes as potential sources of preplanned activities. Initiatives for suggestion and requests lay with the parents, not the workers. As a matter of fact, there is less stress placed on identifiable activities. "The visit is less restricted to activities and curriculum" (Ibid., p. 14). The home visitor's role is seen more in terms of being an "attentive listener, active recognizer of parents' strengths, encourager of parents' efforts" (Ibid., p. 14).

Where and when they did occur, the worker's task also included *collecting* accounts of the activities from families, and distributing the narratives to other families. All of this is a far cry from presentation, demonstration, and explanation. The worker was to listen attentively, to encourage parents in those joint activities in which they were already involved, and to point out to families those everyday parent-child activities that were already part of their routine, but might not yet recognize as being beneficial to child development. There were carefully drawn guidelines as to *what* activities workers "shall bring in" (i.e., initiate themselves), "*how* they shall be brought in," and *when* worker-initiated programming might take place. For example, program guidelines encouraged workers *not* to "bring in" an activity until after the seventh home visit, and then not until the parent suggested it (Ibid.).

These specifications about the Program I worker role led to a kind of laid-back attitude on the part of home visitors (and as we shall see later, by workers organizing neighborhood groups also) that proved to be nonthreatening to families. As one participating father put it, "The good thing about your program — not like other programs — is that you're not always telling us what to do!" But if the diffident approach by home visitors was initially advantageous in trust-building and in other respects as well, it also proved to be *disadvantageous* in still other ways as time went on.

There was concern by some workers and some families that the home visitor, far from taking over the parental role, was simply not doing enough. As Bo (Ibid., p. 42) put it, "The question, 'When are you going to bring us something?' came up in several families after only a few meetings." The workers *themselves* felt uncomfortable about the situation, one of them stating pointedly, "If we don't have anything to bring to the families they won't stay with us for four years" (Ibid., p. 40). As a result, Bo (Ibid., pp. 43-45) had recommended a more equal and active role for the home visitor, arguing for a partnership between parent and worker. As she put it (Ibid., p. 45), "The argument is that parents are more likely to find *this approach* indicative of respect, partnership, and support rather than a more distant and passive worker presence."

The Program I Worker as Advocate

Advocacy, the *most* initiative-filled area of the parent-child specialist's role, similarly underwent a profound metamorphosis. At first, there was even some hesitancy about offering unsolicited information to families, to say nothing of a more direct role for the worker in initiating contacts for the family outside the home. We quote Bo (Ibid., p. 14) once again as she describes documents dating from May 1977 to February 1978: "Information about professional resources and services is to be given only when it is asked for in relation to a stated concern." This description of preprogram documents, as well as Bo's characterization of the first six months of program activity in the pilot neighborhoods show that programmatic posture had turned 180 degrees on the question of advocacy. Further evidence of this policy shift is cited by Bo as she described guidelines used in early program implementation. The guidelines specify that (Ibid., p. 48), "Under no circumstances should the worker be in direct contact with services, organizations or institutions on behalf of the family."

Later in program history, there were fewer strictures on offering unsolicited information and advice. As a matter of fact, ultimately workers made vigorous attempts to encourage even Program I families to make contact with schools, to learn "survival skills," and to utilize agencies and services. But it remained a rarity for program workers to *initiate contacts for* the family outside the home. As a matter of fact, it was not only rare; such initiative was generally considered *verboten* according to the program's value system.

OVERVIEW

In the course of this analysis of the evolution of principal investigator perspectives on the attempt to encourage parent-child activities, and the translation of those perspectives into program implementation, we have seen rather sharp shifts in course. We have seen that treatments became programs. Parent-child specialists became peer/learners, and finally workers, and home visitors. The word "activities" was dropped from the job title of the "(Activities) Home Visitor," and workers given the message that listening attentively is as important as activities themselves. Still later, in a reconceptualization resulting from field experience (and one that also harks back to the original proposal), the principal investigators reemphasized the importance of activities.

In a similar evolution along the activity-reactivity dimension, we have seen the outside expert (the parent/child specialist) give way to the *"inpert"* (the parent), and initiative largely surrendered to the parent. Again as a result of field experience, attempts were subsequently made to work out a more equal distribution of responsibility (e.g., Bo's "partnership" arrangement); but as Bo noted in a visit to the project in the Spring of 1980, many home visitors appeared to fall unwarrantedly close to the passive side in the attempt to provide a balanced approach. The concerns Bo voiced echoed those expressed by several NIE reviewers who raised the issue of "program intensity."

DEVELOPMENTS IN WORKER ROLE IN PROGRAM II

Having described and analyzed worker role in Program I in its original theoretical formulation, in its conceptual development, and in its actual implementation, we now turn to a parallel discussion for Program II. Here we can be a bit briefer, because the pattern for Program II was very similar to that with Program I.

Earliest Thinking

Unlike the role of the erstwhile parent-child specialist, the role of the neighborhood resources specialist seems never to have been fundamentally questioned. The original proposal states (Bronfenbrenner and Cochran, 1976, p. 34) that there was less in the way of a "previous model" either to emulate or reject. As with Treatment I, the "Specialist" ultimately became "Worker" and "Treatment" was transmuted into "Program." If the basics of the role remained unchanged, however, many important characteristics of the treatment did evolve considerably.

In a way that differs remarkably from the outline of the role of the parent-child specialist, the original proposal presents a highly detailed job description for the neighborhood resources specialist (Ibid.). In January of 1976, Bronfenbrenner and Cochran envisioned five major functions for the neighborhood resource specialist. These were:

(1) Helping families to obtain needed services.
(2) Developing through activities a sense of community and patterns of support.
(3) Identifying and strengthening existing informal networks and facilitating new relationships.
(4) Encouraging and assisting parents to identify and utilize resources.
(5) Establishing communication between the family and major community institutions.

In more specific detail, the proposal speaks of the specialist "informing families about and helping them to obtain needed services (health, welfare, child care, etc.)." Also, the specialist's job is described (Ibid.) as seeking . . . "to develop a sense of community and support for each of the target families through activities . . . ." These "activities" should be designed so that "ultimately" they can "be carried out independently, without participation of the specialist." The responsibility of the specialist is ". . . to activate other individuals in the community in support of families and their children."

In helping to form, identify, or strengthen informal networks around the family, the worker was encouraged to "establish a *base* in the neighborhood," and if possible, to actually live in the neighborhood as well. Also within the scope of the specialist's task was helping parents identify and utilize neighborhood or community resources.

Here again, as with Treatment I, the characterization of the Treatment II worker is both that of one who brings expertise to the task and one who is an activist and initiator. Once again also, we find a sharp contrast between principal investigator perspectives in the original proposal and Family Matters training materials and guidelines that were developed later. Not surprisingly, the same kind of contrast is to be found in descriptions of program implementation during its early and intermediate stages.

The Program II Worker as Advocate — Some Reformulations

The most striking change in the role of the neighborhood resources specialist was in the question of *advocacy*. The original proposal shows the worker contacting schools, employers and supervisors, business and government leaders, and social services agency personnel. Workers are to enlist community volunteers, and persuade those who might be able to provide potential meeting space for neighborhood groups. The advocacy role is explicit and detailed. But later Cochran and Woolever (1978, p. 1) wrote, "The worker's function is not one of personal advocacy."

As Maddaus (1978, p. 1) has observed, "The role of the neighborhood worker in Program II has undergone repeated redefinition . . . ." The conception of the worker as ". . . a family advocate . . . was written out of subsequent working papers as the self-help concept became the primary commitment." Maddaus, cited here, was a veteran Family Matters staff member and supervisor of Program II activities. He is thus exceptionally well qualified to describe the policy discussions and implementation of the Neighborhood Grouping Program.

Chronicling staff discussions beginning in April 1978, Maddaus (Ibid.) describes how the self-help concept was first applied to "the *concerns* in which neighborhood groups would become involved, and later to the *ways* in which they would move toward actions on these concerns" (emphasis in original). Maddaus recounts:

The fundamental assumption became: "Families have strengths — they know what is best — they will find a way." And the corollary: "If the worker should err, it should fall on the side of doing too little, rather than on the side of doing too much."

A comparable statement found in the minutes of a July 26, 1978 project meeting says of workers, "It is better to not initiate when they should, rather than take initiative when they shouldn't" (Family Matters, 1978). Maddaus states that at a Cornell staff meeting in July of 1978, he "was discouraged from proposing a sample agenda to a parent group, or even bringing paper and magic marker and suggesting that the parents develop an agenda" (Maddaus, 1978, p. 1). As a result of this orientation, the basic unwritten law of program implementation seems to have become: no intervention, no matter how seemingly beneficial, should be undertaken by the worker if there is the slightest chance that it will threaten parent self-concept or parental image in the eyes of their children. Compared with the change in the advocacy aspect of the *home visitor's* role that came about later in program history, the foregoing analysis of the new conceptualization of the *neighborhood worker's* role shows that the contrast between the original proposal and later evolution is, if anything, even sharper.

Now, however, we must move from the above examination of the neighborhood worker as advocate to other elements of the fivefold role initially planned for staff members working in Program II. Only two of these elements ever emerged very concretely in actual practice. These were: (1) developing through activities a sense of community and patterns of support; and (2) identifying, strengthening, and helping to create informal networks. Attempts to implement both of these were embodied in organizing neighborhood groups; and where those groups emerged and functioned successfully at least for a time, the gains for some parents and some neighborhood projects were truly noteworthy.

Program Worker Role in Obtaining Needed Services

In the original proposal, however, the *first* function of the "Neighborhood Specialist" was to help families obtain needed services. But, in everyday practice, far from actively establishing the linkages between families and social service agencies, workers were asked to refrain from even raising the topic. Instead, they were to wait until a request for information emerged from the family. Even then, workers were trained not to initiate any contacts with agencies, but merely to provide three possible referrals *to the family*, whose responsibility it was to get in touch and request the service. In actuality, workers sometimes did take a "pushier" role than this, but they did so aware that they were going beyond established guidelines, and often had to proceed with considerable trepidation.

The Program II Worker Role in Identifying and Utilizing Resources

As for "encouraging and assisting parents to identify and utilize resources," the same kind of problem existed early on, but by no means to the same degree. Since the pilot phase of program implementation, workers encouraged and assisted parents in resource identification, in both the neighborhood and in the community. Furthermore, later collaborative efforts with New York State Cooperative Extension, the Family Matters Neighborhood Resource Centers (discussed earlier), and other similar endeavors *did* help connect families with resources. Still it was hoped during the pilot phase of program activity that individual parents and the groups as a whole would come up with their own ideas for utilization of available resources and of the more formal networks.

As Bo (1979, p. 63) puts it, "Program II workers went out with an assignment to become facilitators rather than leaders, and to be clearly non-directive in their approach to the group." One worker (cited in Bo, 1979, p. 66) said that workers' ". . . lips were buttioned. . . . What we were very conscious of was not making suggestions . . ." Bo herself comments that, "guidelines called for such behavior as an effort not to let workers' opinions lead the way, not to lay workers' values on the group . . ." In calling for a more balanced approach, Bo (Ibid., pp. 77-78) and Maddaus (1978, pp. 4-6) argued for a more active role for the neighborhood worker in the area of resource identification and utilization. Bo (1979, p. 78) makes this point with special clarity in her statements that ". . . the project and the workers also have values . . ." and that "We must be prepared to handle tension or outright conflict . . . (in values) . . . between the systems or parties involved." Bo thus goes on to suggest ways to resolve tensions and conflicts within the system constructively, rather than by simply surrendering to parental attitudes at every turn.

In some instances, it is quite evident that as a result of training in project values, of the workers' own values, and of Bo's influence, parents were exposed to resources that they might have otherwise overlooked. But the pattern here remained inconsistent, with some workers in some instances holding back, at least partly as a result of unclarity in program policy.

Program II Worker Role in Establishing Communication with Institutions

If assisting families in identifying resources was implemented inconsistently, there is little doubt that establishing communications between families and the principal institutions of the neighborhood and the community was carried out in only a very few instances, at least in the sense that this function was originally conceived. The proposal envisioned the neighborhood resources specialist arranging ". . . with the school for informal visits by the child and his parents . . .," engaging ". . . older school children in responsibility for the younger . . .," creating ". . . opportunities for employers and supervisors to become informed about and to take an interest in the lives of their employees as parents," encouraging local business executives, administrators of government agencies, and employers to develop personnel policies that can reduce conflict between the demands of job and family . . .," and encouraging ". . . friendships between adults in the world of work, on the one hand, and children and their families on the other" (Bronfenbrenner and Cochran, 1976, p. 36).

As discussed earlier, one major agenda item that *was* implemented lay in the area of extending families' lines of communication with schools. After many months of uncertainty and inactivity in this area, the spring of 1980 saw the program working with some effectiveness on the link between home and school, and this undoubtedly had its impact on the school-related outcomes of the program discussed earlier. In some instances, these efforts led to some promising beginnings in the task of building good parent-school relationships which may some day lead to further enhanced performance by program children in the school environment. If realized, this achievement would, of course, constitute evidence of confirmation of the original research hypotheses (Ibid.) that supportive social networks and parent-child activities would lead to sociocognitive gains by the project's "target children." These gains were expected to be apparent even in "extra-familial situations," the most important of these being the school (Ibid., p. 36).

Turning from schools to the workplace, however, to the governmental and political arenas, and to the business world, we must observe that these areas did not receive much attention by Family Matters. One exception to this rule was one instance in which workers encouraged families to lobby against reductions in the Syracuse city school budget. We have already chronicled two additional examples — one in which program families were encouraged to participate in a "Neighborhood Watch (Crime Prevention) Program" and another case in which a program-sponsored neighborhood group succeeded in getting county government to fence in more adequately a dangerous creek-bed. Otherwise, the areas outlined in the earliest planning of this research project remained largely "off limits" in actual program practice, especially in the activist sense of workers making contacts *for* groups or families.

It must be pointed out, however, that the absence of Family Matters efforts in these domains was not an "error of omission." Here, too, a conscious decision was made *against an ombudsman-like* role for the neighborhood worker to prevent excessive leading, or activism, or the freighting of unwanted values by workers on program families. Suffice it to say that in this area, which requires the most outgoing role by program workers, we see the greatest disparities between original intents and later conceptualizations and program implementation.

OVERVIEW

In this chapter we have looked at both Programs I and II with regard to several issues to show the conceptual uncertainty and the back-and-forth of Family Matters Program designers as they first preplanned, then changed, and then changed again in major ways the blueprints for the program. The number of "treatments" started out at three, was reduced to two, and later was effectively increased to the same three originally proposed. Home visits as a main program thrust were first advanced, then nearly dropped and then reinstituted; and this was fortunate, since process analysis shows that Program I clearly turned out to be the better implemented and the better received of the two intervention strategies.

Worker role in both programs was conceived in terms of expertise, was reconceptualized so as to make the worker a silent partner, and later returned workers to something approaching expert status with training in the presentation and distribution of a fairly fixed curriculum of modular materials — this from a program that originally had eschewed any "fixed curriculum" and proscribed a worker's bringing a magic marker to a group meeting to write down an agenda. Correspondingly, as worker role shifted from active to passive to active once again, parental role shifted from passive to active to passive once again. Documentation of other comparable zig-zags in course could be multiplied. For example, the location of Program II activities was originally to be in neighborhood centers. The idea was abandoned for various reasons; and then neighborhood resource centers ultimately became the sites of fully one-fourth of Program II activity. Considerations of space and balance, however, suggest that the illustrations provided here must suffice.

We have engaged in this lengthy exercise to demonstrate how brilliant men, leading experts in the area of human development and men who were aware of family and child interventions between the mid-1960s and the mid-1970s simply did not yet have a solid informational foundation on which to build their intervention. Indeed, in the above cited exchange of memos in February 1977, Bronfenbrenner confesses that he is not at all certain whether he knows what kinds of activities are best for families.

All of us can, of course, understand the need for evolution, flexibility, and responsiveness to contextual factors in any comparable program or in virtually any human endeavor. We can all appreciate the need for "fine tuning." But in this instance where major directions were precharted, then reversed, and reversed again, we must attribute such vicissitudes not to fine tuning, but rather to a lack of sufficient and reliable information resources from the outset.

A BIRD'S EYE VIEW OF SOCIAL SCIENTIFIC
RESOURCES FOR SOCIAL PROGRAMS

As mentioned at the outset of this chapter, our intention here is not to set apart the highly competent, well intentioned, and concerned men who designed Family Matters for any kind of opprobrium or blame with regard to the information needed for program implementation. On the contrary. The argument advanced here is an *a fortiori* one. If academic luminaries such as Bronfenbrenner, Cochran, and Cross do not have *definitive* information about how to intervene successfully and without equivocation in human development systems, then who among us does?

Indeed, in recent years Bronfenbrenner (1979b) himself has reflected on the state of social scientific knowledge as being insufficient, especially in relation to policy matters. We have cited him previously to the effect that prior knowledge bearing on family policy is very much wanting when he and other scholars are asked by policy makers to provide them with the information base needed for their decision making (Bronfenbrenner, 1980).

A major purpose of the Ecology of Human Development Project and its component Family Matters was to help provide this information base. And undoubtedly much will be contributed by both the evaluation of Family Matters effects and by the nonexperimental findings as well, both here and abroad. But in accounting for the indifferent success of Family Matters, of other early childhood interventions, and other social programs of the past as well as those of the foreseeable future, this insufficiency of informational resources must be assessed and acknowledged.

Public Policy-Related Knowledge in Psychology

Scientific psychology is generally dated from Wundt's work in his lab in Leipzig, making it only a bit more than 100 years old. The work of the psychophysicists and the faculty psychologists, while interesting and relevant to some areas of perception, is not immediately applicable to policy issues.

The next 50 years or so of psychology's efforts were heavily committed to comparative psychology and behaviorism, which Beach (1950) has called "rat learning." Beach, himself a comparative psychologist, urged his colleagues and the behaviorists to abandon their preoccupation with the Norway rat and with the noncognitive and the nonsocial types of behaviors typically studied, if they wish to generalize their findings to other species, especially to humans. Some cognitively-oriented learning theorists have wryly referred to the Skinner box as a "powerful tool for decorticating" an animal, because it allows the researcher to refrain from studying cognitive, social, or other forms of complex or sophisticated behavior. Indeed Beach (1950); in a rare and vivid form of statement in a scientific journal, accompanies his article in American Psychologist with a cartoon showing a huge rat, wearing a piper's hat and holding a flute to its lips, merrily piping a mass of little psychologists into the sea.

From about 1950 onward, there has been a rise in the use of human subjects in psychological research, usually college freshmen, who are presumably higher on the phylogenetic scale than *rattus Norvegicus*. Also, the behaviors studied have been more relevant to public policy, especially social behavior. But there are numerous critics of the artificiality of the experimental situations in which the research has been carried out (e.g., Barker and Schoggen, 1973), and the compliance and limited sampling of the subjects studied (Orne, 1965; Rosenthal and Rosnow, 1974). Still more recently, ecological and policy relevant research *has* been carried out, but most of it is less than 20 years old, and we can hardly say that we have anywhere near the amount of information we need for making solid recommendations for action programs.

Cole (1979) has recognized the limitations of psychology by reiterating the jest now familiar to psychologists that *Henry* James (the novelist) was a great psychologist, while his brother, William James (the psychologist) was the novelist. Indeed, Bronfenbrenner (1979b, p. 8) has argued that ". . . *basic science needs public policy even more than public policy needs basic science*" (italics in original).

The State of Public Policy Relevant Knowledge in the Other Social Sciences

Nor is psychology unique in its deficit of relevant knowledge. Sociologist Coleman (1972) has appraised the situation, broadly stating, "There is no body of methods, no comprehensive methodology for the study of the impact of public policy as an aid to future policy." Rist (1981, p. 485) argues that, "Nearly a decade later, Coleman's now famous quote rings true." Indeed, Rist speaks of a *worsening* situation in the area and "more disarray." Similar methodological critiques have recently been directed against sociological sampling bias (e.g., Berk, 1983) generally, and against research on school desegregation specifically (Crain and Mahard, 1983).

In Chapter 1, we saw not only disagreement between distinguished sociologists about substantive matters, but acrimony about methodology and even about the two sides' respective scientific workmanship. As Kuhn (1962) has pointed out, this kind of acrimony is particularly characteristic of young sciences where there is not a large body of widely accepted knowledge, but where even theoretical paradigms are still at issue. Confirming Kuhn's diagnosis of the ailment, Chen and Rossi (1980, p. 42) contend that ". . . the social sciences have yet to develop an adequate set of theories that are relevant to social problems." And the kinds of theories that are needed, according to Chen and Rossi, are those that model both the social problem and the social program.

In a similar fashion Leamer (1983) has criticized applied econometrics in a paper entitled, "Let's Take the Con out of Econometrics." Leamer (1983, p. 31) has challenged the imprecise nature of generalizations from available data, likening the applied econometrician to a ". . . farmer who notices that the yield is somewhat higher under trees where birds roost," and thus infers that "bird droppings increase yields." Leamer's criticisms, while pungent, are not unique. The vicissitudes of the U.S. economy over the past decade offer mute but eloquent testimony that despite input by the nation's best advisers, economic projections are too frequently inaccurate, and applied economics is hardly a precise predictive science.

Many more instances, citations, and quotes could be adduced from learned authorities, but perhaps the time has come to "rest" our case history and our broader comparisons with regard to the current inadequacies of applied social science as well. Our contention in this chapter has been and remains that despite an accumulation of real knowledge and increasing sophistication of theory and method in the social sciences, we are quite some distance from having strong and definitive information on how to intervene successfully and without untoward side effects or reverse outcomes. Indeed, speaking of the gap between the knowledge implicit in naive or common sense psychology, and scientific knowledge in the same area, Heider (1958) stated that because of the accumulation of wisdom acquired in the course of each human lifetime, there are areas of common sense psychology which transcend our more systematic scientific knowledge. In some fields, social science will need to compile and organize considerably more knowledge before it can match what we already know informally as individuals and (we might add) our accumulated lore as a species. All of this is not meant to damn contemporary social science. Rather, we seek a more realistic appraisal of its record relative to the social programs of the past and what it can achieve at present, in the hope of bettering its future efforts toward social progress.

8

PROGRAMS AND THEIR ORGANIZATIONAL RESOURCES

In documenting the assertion that despite our passion for progress, the resources that we bring to our complex and system-bound task are generally highly inadequate, the previous chapter has been devoted to showing that more than a century of formal social scientific research notwithstanding, the informational resources that are typically available in social betterment efforts are just plain insufficient. This chapter will deal with the similar insufficiency of organizational resources that is generally characteristic of the social programs designed to better the human condition. Once again, the Family Matters Program will serve as an illustrative case study and a basis of comparison.

SOCIAL PROGRAMS AND HUMAN SERVICES

As noted in Chapter 1, Family Matters was not typical of all social programs in all respects. But as we will see, the issues involved in the delivery of its services to clients and the fallibilities of organization and management that contributed to those problems are far from unique in either the innovative Great Society programs of the past or the more institutionalized efforts that continue today. Lynn and Salasin (1974) have written of the failure of "government and agencies" to deliver social services of adequate quality and quantity, referring to "the human services short-fall." (cf. also

Twain, 1983). No less an authority than Fredericksen (1984), editor-in-chief of the Journal of Organization Behavior Management, currently writes of ". . . our costly and notoriously inefficient human service service" system (p. 1). A similarly august social scientist with expertise in the area of program evaluation, Peter Rossi (1981), contrasts innovative social programs run by charismatic and dedicated individual leaders with the reliably less successful efforts of what Rossi calls, "YOAA, Your Ordinary American Agency."

Indeed, as we will see in this chapter, it appears that what is necessary for better social programs is a combination of innovation, charismatic leadership, strong organizational structure and management, especially the kind of management technology that has yet to be applied to human services generally either because of the earlier-noted insufficiencies in our social scientific knowledge, the lack of adequate utilization of such knowledge as now exists (cf. Fredericksen, 1984), or the politics and economics of much of human service effort under either government or private auspices (Horowitz and Erlich, 1974). To document in detailed and illustrative fashion the above mentioned difficulties of organizational structure and function programs often experience, we will target several areas of our study of Family Matters. These include: structure and staffing, training, supervision and feedback, and documentation.

FAMILY MATTERS ORGANIZATIONAL STRUCTURE AND STAFFING

Organizational structure within the Family Matters Program itself seemed straightforward enough. Throughout much of program history, there was one director, one supervisor for each of the two programmatic thrusts (parent-child activities and neighborhood groups), a staff of approximately ten additional workers, and one or two liaison staff members. The latter served as intermediaries between all participating families (including controls) and both the research and program components of the project.

The director was a man of intelligence, whose primary education had been as a theologian, but who had some training and experience in neighborhood organizing. He had excellent connections with the religious, educational, and community service networks in Syracuse. Fully committed to the fundamental goals of the intervention, he was a man of enormously benevolent intention. As one worker said about him in debriefing, "The worst thing I can say about Frank is that he's a nice guy." But throughout our observations, his very goodheartedness stood in the way of the toughmindedness and organizational management skills needed for the endeavor.

The two (later three) program supervisors were also bright individuals, highly dedicated to the program's basic goals of supporting family child-rearing efforts, but the sum of the combined professional training of the three was not great, and their experience with and knowledge of human service management was very small indeed.

What now seems like an important lack in the area of professionalism and organizational skills was not simply an oversight. In Chapter 3, we discussed principal investigator concern about the deficit orientation of most service professionals toward their clients and their disposition to take too much of the initiative in providing family support services. It was believed that not hiring an overly professionalized or service-trained staff would allow the impetus for action to flow from program participants themselves. Here again the legacy of Head Start was important. This national program, too, relied heavily on paraprofessionals who were given special training for their tasks (Zigler and Valentine, 1979). The slogan, "If you give them opportunity, they will become active," had developed in early intervention circles when approaching parents (Fabian and Pitkin, 1979) and the same watchword was adopted by Family Matters.

In addition to this conceptual factor, there were also other influences on the preference for hiring paraprofessional rather than professional types. There was the chronically tight budget of the project (more will be said on this score later) relative to the magnitude of the entire enterprise that lay ahead. This fiscal concern was at issue not just for the program to be implemented immediately, but for comparable efforts of the future as well (cf. Gray and Wandersman, 1980). It was thought that such endeavors would also be chronically underfunded. If effects could be demonstrated by employees who did not require the very extensive training of professionals and hence did not demand correspondingly high salaries, this would enable future programs to function inexpensively. Also, such an achievement would show the generality of the positive effects, and might even be accomplished with volunteers some day.

Furthermore, there was the feeling conveyed by the Syracuse minority community, especially prior to program inception, that staff members had to be both *in* and *of* the community in the fullest sense if initial distrusts and suspicions precluding participation were to be allayed (Fabian and Pitkin, 1979). For a time, especially during the project's baseline data collection, a prominent leader of the young black community served as the project's associate director for "Community Relations and Liaison Activities." But concerns remained about Cornell academics from Ithaca doing research on Syracuse families often of low-income and racial minority status. These concerns helped shape the decision that program personnel had to be very much like the people they were to serve — not upper-middle-class white professionals trying to impose their values in Lady Bountiful-fashion on people from other circumstances, cultures, and value orientations.

It should be stated, however, that while community influence made the issue more salient, this approach to staffing was by no means foreign to the principal investigators' own thinking. Rather, it seemed very much in harmony with their own perspectives at the time. Much later in program history, there was some shift toward hiring more highly trained individuals, but at the time, the principal investigators even expressed the view that the project should try to hire part-time, paraprofessional personnel to increase the amount of part-time employment available to area wage-earners, especially mothers who needed to work.

For these and other reasons, program staff recruitment, especially recruitment of program workers, emphasized paraprofessional rather than professional training and little in the way of service management skills. What was stressed instead was "connectedness" with the relevant community groups in Syracuse, life experience rather than academic qualifications (preferably some experience with education or child rearing), and commitment to the program's general ideology.

In retrospect it is also possible to say that staff members had a flair for self-presentation both individually and collectively that was later to endear them to many program families, the process analysis staff and its director, to community members they encountered broadly, to the project's principal investigators, and even to the site visit teams that research sponsors repeatedly sent to evaluate progress. Indeed, on one such occasion a site visitor who was highly critical of the program's achievements to that point, stated that program intensity would have to be increased considerably if any effects were to be demonstrated in the future; "but," he added, "if any group could do it, [i.e., produce positive effects] this staff can."

Thus, we may say that through most of program history the program workers were a collectivity of persons who, with few exceptions, had highly engaging personalities, were sincerely committed to the program's major goals, but who, like those in the upper echelon of the program (as opposed to the larger project) organization itself, did not have much in the way of advanced degrees, professional training, or even a great deal of formal knowledge about provision of human services. Indeed, most did not seem to have an overwhelming interest in formal knowledge, as evidenced by a lack of response when, toward program's end, efforts were made to try to arrange for academic credits and/or coursework for staff members who wanted to enhance their employability after their Family Matters work was finished.

ORGANIZATIONAL GOAL CLARITY

The use of paraprofessional workers in service occupations is of course a very legitimate approach when funding is tight, and when efforts by such personnel can be shown to produce the desired results. Successful use of paraprofessionals has even been demonstrated in the sensitive area of psychotherapy (Eysenck, 1952). But if personnel without specialized skills are to be utilized, and unless it can be shown that anyone can do the job without guidance or tutelage, it is clear that paraprofessionals need, at minimum, two types of information: (1) an explicit delineation of the major and minor goals of the effort; and (2) specific training in the means to bring about attainment of those goals.

The clarification of the goals of the Family Matters Program unfortunately only took place with thoroughness and sharpness with regard to the intervention's major long-term aims. Staff members knew quite clearly that they were there to be supportive of families, to facilitate parent-child activities, to promote the formation of neighborhood groups, to encourage parents to extend their social networks, and to urge families to seek solutions for their problems where necessary and/or possible from formal educational institutions or service agencies in the area. When it came to the short-term objectives, there was far greater uncertainty. The retrospective but extensive summary of short-term objectives of the Family Development Research Program outlined by Lally et al. (1982) provides an instructive contrast to the failings of Family Matters in this respect and those of other similar interventions, and to those of the national Head Start program.

Uncertainty at the Top

This uncertainty stemmed from quite a number of sources. The principal investigators' own objectives were by no means static or immutable as shown in our discussion in Chapter 7. The back and forth about proximate goals, means, and policies that came about through the lack of unambiguous knowledge for intervention probably had its most profound impact in keeping workers confused about what they were and were not to do. Also, there were differences of emphasis among these three program designers, as well as between them and the program director (for example, as to the importance of pure experimental method versus helping people in any way that worked).

There was the uncertainty at the top as to what would work and what was ethical, especially on the question of the degree to which they might be imposing white, middle-class values upon groups that might find such values either culturally distasteful or even downright maladaptive. For example, at least a few families appeared to be making a comfortable living from highly illegal activity. The program's wholesome emphasis on family and group connectedness and working within the system was far from the orientation of these families. And while such program participants were not representative, there was, as we might expect, a continuum of value orientations from this extreme to that represented by the intervention's "hidden curriculum," the value system implicit in the program goals. This meant that the *values in practice* of many participant families were very different from those espoused by the program.

For example, as we will describe later, some families grew impatient with the details of the research and program implementation.

They felt that they simply ought to be given the money being spent on the entire effort, and that would do them more good than all the scientific investigation and what they regarded as off-target programming. We cannot evaluate the generality of such feelings. Social desirability would militate against many respondents expressing such sentiments. But we do know that such clashes between program and family values did exist, and the principal investigators were not insensitive to such concerns.

Transmission and Reception Problems

Communication of short-term objectives from the top down was sometimes fragmentary for various reasons, and sometimes regarded by those implementing the program as being the impractical visions of academics out of touch with the realities of the street. There were the usual diffusion of information problems customary in all groups and especially in hierarchically structured organizations. These communication difficulties were complicated all the more by the existence of four "different authoritative sources," three principal investigators and one program director, and even certain equivocal decision rules as to *who* was to be considered authoritative on *what* occasion. Then, of course, there was also the usual *filter problem*, i.e., each individual listening to ambiguous, multiple, and evolving ideas that each worker could interpret according to his or her own programming, prejudices, needs, or interests.

The result was a great deal of confusion and contradiction that came through repeatedly in our interviews with program workers, confusion that translated itself into program practices that were often less than adequate and sometimes even counterproductive. One of the chief areas where this was true was in decision making about the nature of the desired parent-child activities. We have already mentioned the instance of the black worker who wanted to bring reading readiness activities to her assigned families, but was berated for doing so by her white supervisor.

This well-intentioned and hard-working supervisor had the idiosyncratic view that ". . . children read from the cradle to the tomb," and that what the families needed was "creative" and imaginative activity. The equally well-intentioned black worker who knew better what her families needed and what ultimately proved to be the outcome emphasis of the program broadly, had to pull back somewhat from her aspirations to enhance the future reading ability of the program's youngsters. All of this, of course, resulted in friction between both supervisor and supervisee and had its ramifications on the level of interracial tensions within the staff itself.

This lack of fit between subgoals and implementation culminated in the paradox that a program that was later to be evaluated at least in part in terms of the reading ability of its participating children, was foiled in some measure by the instructions of a well-meaning supervisor who directed supervisees *authoritatively* but *erroneously* to avoid working on reading skills. Other important if less dramatic instances of unclarity in objectives could be multiplied, especially with regard to the questions arising from the issue of the active or reactive role of the worker. But space considerations dictate limits to this discussion. Consequently we now turn from this discussion of communication of program objectives to the issue of training in achieving those objectives.

TRAINING FOR PROGRAM IMPLEMENTATION

In some organizations, the minor or even the major goals may not be communicated to relevant persons as explicitly as they should be, but there is a lore of practice or implementation in which objectives are implicit. Thus, aims can often be inferred from training and usage. Unfortunately the pragmatics of program implementation were the least clear elements of training and practice at Family Matters. This is not to say that a considerable amount of time and effort were not devoted to training. Indeed the amount of time set aside for meetings, for discussions, and for training sessions especially was quite exemplary.

Through most of our observations, there were weekly staff meetings and a training session preceded each one. A variety of topics were covered and external (and internal) resource persons were brought to the staff for the enhancement of their efforts. Early in program history, there was one worker who was in charge of "R and D," which officially stood for research and development, though this person claimed not to be a researcher-type and referred to her role as "resource development." Also, at the beginning of the fall of 1980, before the last ten months of program activity, an entire week was set aside for further training of the existing staff for a final programmatic push. Still later in program history two well-trained and highly qualified individuals were brought in to develop the above mentioned modules and to train staff in their use, but unfortunately, this excellent last effort was largely belated.

In general, the problems of training for implementation were: (1) the unclarity of goals that led to unclarity of means; (2) the uncertainty about the worker's role as being reactive or proactive; (3) the lack of authoritative written materials that could be used for training and everyday reference; (4) the lack of highly specific techniques to be employed in program implementation, or practice time in and/or supervision of such techniques; and (5) a large amount of time set aside for training was used inefficiently either in unproductive discussions and conflict or in expressions of concerns about organizational problems having nothing to do with the topic at hand. Much illustrative material could be cited here, but at least one example in this instance should cross-cut a number of the problem areas and be highly instructive.

As mentioned, the extensive amount of time devoted to training often brought to workers excellent ideas that might have produced better program services. Such an idea and some technique to go along with it was the (originally psychotherapeutic) strategy of "active listening" (cf. Rogers, 1954). Like many contemporary therapists, Family Matters workers were exposed to the idea of listening (rather than doing too much talking), listening closely (rather than inattentively), and offering either nonverbal or verbal cues to families that the hearing they were getting was an attentive and active one. After the training session, but without any role playing, practice, supervision, or feedback, one worker tried to employ this active listening technique with his or her families.

Later, process study research encountered a criticism of this home visitor by a program family to the effect that ". . . gives me the creeps. (S)He just sits there and stares at us. If (s)he has nothing to contribute, what's (s)he doing here?" The program worker, for his or her part, had just completed a training session on *active listening*, and had spoken to fellow workers with pride about his or her new found skills as well as their recent utilization with this same program family. It was only several weeks later that word reached the worker via his or her supervisor that this family wanted him or her removed as their assigned worker because of what they regarded as the strangeness of his or her noncommunicativeness. All of this came as a rude shock to the worker who thought that she or he was doing an excellent job. All of this was the result of an absence of practice, role playing, rehearsal, feedback, and direct supervision, and also the result of what proved to be a chronic need within the program, the need for definitive clarification given both to staff and to program families as to the nature of the worker's role.

This illustration shows how shortcomings in three of the five areas discussed above, goals and means, worker role, and supervised practice of technique, contributed not only to worker misunderstanding, but even worse, to a counterproductive effort. Rather than "active listening" bringing the worker and the family closer together, it created a barrier of suspicion. And although the *degree* of difficulty experienced by this worker in this instance was unique, the problem of workers who didn't know quite how to relate to their families or who didn't know when to initiate and when to wait for family initiative, were general difficulties that persisted for most of the program's history. This issue was a source of frustration experienced and voiced by many staff members. It was also noted and commented upon by several different observers of program functioning (Bo, 1979, 1980; Molnar, 1979).

Authoritative Written Material

Further complicating the problems of training for specific aspects of implementation were serious gaps in the written materials that were to guide worker practices. There were supposed to be two manuals written to help staff members carry out the two basic missions of the program — parent-child activities and organizing neighborhood groups. Preparation of the manual for Program I was completed tardily. That designed to provide authoritative direction for Program II was never completed. The neighborhood group program was much the weaker component of the entire effort. Yet no concerted effort was ever made to finish the training manual for this intervention even though it was sorely needed. In fact, attempts ultimately were made to put together a combined manual of procedures, but this material was still being discussed and added to during the very last months of program history. And while an evolutionary approach of "writing the book as one goes along" has a lot to commend it by way of avoiding rigidity and learning from experience, in this case critical areas required for both training and procedural guidance were completely omitted, especially, as mentioned, in the area of procedures workers needed to help them in group organization.

In addition to a lack of authoritative written material about organizing neighborhood groups, oral training sessions also neglected this area as well. More than half-way through program history, the process study component of the project took the initiative of putting together a training session on group dynamics for its own internal needs. When word of this reached the program component, the program director asked that his staff be included in the training. It was then that we learned to our surprise and consternation that this was the first major unit of training in this area for program staff members — this despite the fact that an intimate knowledge of group dynamics was really quite pivotal to carrying out successfully the program's aim of organizing neighborhood groups.

Lack of Systematic Training

Despite the large amount of time devoted to training, there were other important gaps in the information workers needed to function more effectively. These gaps were in such areas as: the kinds of parent-child activities that were most desirable, the best means of putting families in touch with the social service system, and general information for workers and/or parents about child development.

There were a variety of reasons for these gaps. In this last instance, information about child development, there was a conscious decision made by the principal investigators *not to share* their expertise with workers and through the workers, with families. This decision was primarily predicated on the concern that "a little information might prove to be dangerous." Since neither workers nor families were equipped to handle full-fledged training in child development, it was felt that fragmentary knowledge would do more harm than good. A site visit panel representing NIE offered a different view of this matter. After a recommendation that the Cornell team share its knowledge more directly with families, more authoritative information was provided through the modules discussed earlier, and through materials prepared by New York State Cooperative Extension. But once again, based on our interviews of participating families at program's end, we must observe that most of this came belatedly and did not appear to make a substantial impact.

A second cause of the lacunae in training lay in the lack of a systematic approach. There was no master plan of topic areas to be covered that might have minimized the omissions. Part of the problem was the innovative nature of the program, and as discussed above the very real lack of definitive social scientific information in many of the relevant areas. But part of the difficulty lay in the view of the principal investigators that their efforts were more innovative and more unique than was actually the case. For example, the Brookline Early Education Program (BEEP), which predated Family Matters by about five years, had both home visits and group meetings. The latter were center-based and had strong ties with the school system, but there were distinct parallels to Family Matters in BEEP, in the Family Development Research Program which preceded Family Matters right in Syracuse, and in many Head Start programs in their various permutations. This last element was also the subject of comment of the NIE site visitors mentioned earlier, who pointed out that the project had failed to benefit from the knowledge and experience gained in other comparable efforts by other investogators out of a mistaken sense that Family Matters was a pioneering effort with few, if any, parallels.

Training Time Wasted

The final problem with training to be discussed here was the inefficient use of training time. Here part of the difficulty lay in the fact that topics discussed too frequently remained unresolved in terms of policy for action. The pros and cons might be debated repeatedly, but too often workers left the training session feeling that they simply didn't know what to do.

A second source of inefficiency lay in what seemed like endless amounts of time spent in discussions of organizational problems. Topics reflecting organizational discord included: salary parity with the research component of the project; the requirement to fill out time cards that applied to some workers and not to others; the delay in receiving travel and similar reimbursements from Cornell; the obligation to provide documentation of services carried out; the adequacy of workspace provided; workload in terms of families assigned to various workers; whether each worker was doing his or her share and carrying out work that was claimed; interracial issues; and the adequacy and fairness of supervision provided to workers.

None of these problems is unique in the organizational life cycle, although some, such as whether or not one has to fill out a time card, usually are settled in fairly short order. Unfortunately, the concatenation of the above (and other) issues persevered too long, and was too acrimoniously debated in Family Matters. Issues seemed never to go away because of uncertain decision making and leadership. All of this resulted in a staff that became highly demoralized, lost much of its effectiveness, and while impressive in self-presentation to others, was internally dissident and disaffected with one another. Ultimately a group of very likable people ended up after three or more years not liking or trusting each other very much. Naturally all of this detracted from training, and more important, from group function generally.

SUPERVISION, FEEDBACK, AND DOCUMENTATION

The discord in the Family Matters staff was attributable to any number of causes — the lack of clear-cut objectives and service techniques that would allow for a satisfying sense of achievement, the low salaries paid to staff members who themselves lived on the edge of financial insecurity (complicated by bureaucratic delay in authorizing purchasing or expense reimbursement at the Cornell end), the difficulties inherent in the job of working with families who usually had other concerns that were of higher priority than those on the Family Matters agenda, and the simple problems of locating families who moved constantly, had no telephones and/or failed to keep appointments. There were also the limitations imposed by working as part of an intervention whose conduct aspired to be that of a rigorous experiment — meaning that workers often had to refrain from helping behavior because it meant crossing the lines of the prescribed treatment in degree, geography, or concept.

But for all of the external and internal sources of discontent, two of the key issues that we see at the root of low staff morale were supervision and documentation. There was constant and ongoing conflict over the question of whether workers should maintain the two major sources of documentation required of them — one of them involved making brief notations of contact (visits, meetings, phone calls, or letters) that was the responsibility of all project personnel and program workers, as well as research or liaison staff members. The second area of record-keeping specific to program workers was a log describing in detail home visits or group meetings that were the substance of the work done by intervention staff members. The two arguments advanced by workers were: (1) such record keeping was extraneous to their task and detracted from the time available for direct service; and (2) the logs might be of historic interest and of value to comparable interventions of the future, but that they did not want the information used to evaluate their own performance.

These arguments are understandable if only marginally valid, and have probably been heard, *mutatis mutandis* by every administrator since the days of the pyramids. In the case of Family Matters, the problem was exacerbated by the general lack of direct observation of service provision. Except in rare instances (when, for example, a supervisor or the program director and a supervisee worked together with a group) there were no regular instances of oversight of program services. There was a feeling that especially in the home visit situation, having a supervisor present would detract from the spontaneity of the effort, creating an artificiality that would vitiate program objectives.

Thus, workers were unsupervised during their work in the field, even at the outset of program activity when they were still learning. We have already seen an example of the counterproductive results of this lack of oversight. But worse still, the lack of field observation made documentation the only medium for any supervision to be carried out. Workers were supposed to bring their logs in on a monthly basis so as to use them in discussion of their work. There were "team meetings" that periodically involved workers operating in a given neighborhood, but most of the service delivered by workers was unobserved by anyone except participants and the process study.

The process study observed much in the way of excellent effort by some workers on many occasions, and it was this kind of effort that led, we believe, to the genuinely positive outcomes achieved in the home-visit program even though such positive outcomes were not consistent across all program families. Where the work that we observed, whether in home visits or in group meetings, was not adequate, under the terms of our agreement with workers, we were, of course, not at liberty to make this known to supervisors. In the much larger share of cases where no observation was carried out by anyone, reconstructing what went on and providing feedback to workers for their own benefit, to say nothing of program quality control, was extremely difficult. Often, in the case of those workers where it is likely that the least amount of work was being done, the supervisor had only the worker's word, which frequently was that the session had been adequate, had been cancelled, or the family was not at home. Logs were often in arrears for months at a time, and in at least two instances, it appeared that the workers had submitted no logs for periods approaching two years. This made it impossible to carry out even the remote supervision utilized in the program.

Later we were informed in an interview with a minority community leader that one of the staff members who had failed to document his or her work and a second program worker were also employed by this organization in apparent conflict with their responsibilities with Family Matters. Also, some of the modular materials that "disappeared" from the program storeroom found their way into the hands of this other community organization. This meant that not only was Family Matters work not being carried out adequately, but it is also possible, although we have no way of knowing for certain, that families in control neighborhoods may have received services and/or printed materials that were to be provided only to program families. Despite this possible vitiating of the efforts of the experiment, this failure to keep records for two years, the apparent conflicts of interest, and what seemed to be seriously inadequate performance of duties, none of the workers described here were terminated before the end of the program.

Overall, there was in this organization an attitude (as in many others) with which many of us have become all too familiar — an attitude that I would refer to as "the Robin Hood rationalization."

Low income or racial minority personnel were excused from responsibilities on the grounds that they had little in the way of resources. If they got more than their share relative to others, that was to be considered compensatory of their deprivation, or just something that you simply had to tolerate. Needless to say, this kind of Robin Hood rationalization, while implicit rather than explicit, did little to enhance the morale of workers who carried heavier loads in terms of numbers of families, who kept records conscientiously, and apparently did more work without moonlighting in ways that constituted conflict of interest.

This unhappy state of affairs was especially noticeable toward the program's end, when knowledge of the premature demise of the whole effort and the need for staff members to enter the inhospitable world of job search exerted their depressing influence on worker morale. Not unexpectedly, even the most diligent of workers began to slack off in the waning months of program activity. This was especially unfortunate, because, armed with hard-won knowledge from the previous years of program implementation and with some excellent informational materials, Family Matters might have achieved more in its final days than it did if it had not been for all of these morale problems.

This description of Family Matters' last days of intervention in Syracuse, however, is germane not just for our discussion of the problems of supervision, feedback, and accountability specific to Family Matters alone. It also raises the life-cycle problem characteristic of most innovative programs. Thus, we now turn from our primary focus on Family Matters, and instead direct our attention to early intervention and other social programs in which life cycle and other related organizational issues are highly salient.

THE ORGANIZATIONAL LIFE-CYCLE ISSUE

In recent years, the biological concept of life cycle has been applied to organizational research to illuminate implementation processes in settings as diverse as medical schools, child-care agencies, and the food industry (cf. Kimberly et al., 1980). In such research the issues of creation, transformation, and decline are added to the more traditional topics of organizational behavior, and in our analysis of the sufficiency of organizational resources typically available in social programs, we will deal with these traditional topics. At this point, however, we consider a relatively new perspective on the problems of efficacy in innovative social programs — the life-cycle issue.

The Short Life Cycle of Innovative Social Programs

A truly neglected subject in assessing the whys and wherefores of innovation effectiveness is the reality that social programs typically have a short lifespan. Some programs last a matter of months. The more fortunate few, like Head Start, may endure for a decade or two. But compared with successful business enterprises like Lloyds of London, governmental institutions like the U.S. Congress, religious organizations like the Catholic Church, or university Methuselahs like Heidelberg, the one-to-five-year lifespan of a social program is like that of the fruitfly. Or to use a more anthropomorphic simile, the life cycles of innovative programs are like those of undercapitalized small businesses with their typically high "infant mortality rate," most of them dying before they reach age ten (Boswell, 1973).

Organizational Learning

Old organizations, of course, have their own problems. But the chief problem of fledgling groups, especially in new areas of endeavor, is to acquire the kind of information they need and to adapt themselves to the contextual conditions they encounter. Kimberly (1979) has argued that the first two problems new organizations need to cope with are: (1) "getting off the ground," and (2) institutionalizing the structures and processes that prove to be effective. Miles and Randolph (1980) have referred to these processes as "organizational learning" which occurs in the infancy of "new and different" organizations. This stage is characterized by "high uncertainty in decision making" (Ibid.) of the kind we have noted in the management of Family Matters. Chapter 7 has been devoted to documenting the dearth of informational resources for the program and for other comparable interventions, and now we note that the problem is exacerbated by the Drosophilia-like lifespan of most social programs. Not only do such interventions generally not have the knowledge that they need to function more effectively, but their need to live for the funded moments they have usually precludes their acquiring that information in time to survive. Barely are they through Kimberly's "getting off the ground" stage when they are terminated.

Noting this short lifespan for innovative efforts at social progress would, for some, simply be an argument for long-range funding and hence greater longevity for such endeavors. And, indeed, in the final chapter of this volume, such an argument will be advanced, though on a selective basis. We say, "on a selective basis," because it would be useless to simply fund all social programs indefinitely in the hopes that they will ultimately find their way. As Miles and Randolph (1980) have pointed out, organizational *learning capacity* is critical for innovative efforts to succeed, especially if there is time pressure, and the conditions to facilitate such learning must exist if the information gathering is not to be an interminable and catastrophically expensive process.

Unfortunately, however, our examination of the Family Matters case as well as material examined on other social programs suggests that the very elements of motivation that animate our efforts toward social progress frequently militate against the conditions needed for organizational learning. Thus, Miles and Randolph (1980) have demonstrated that *proactive* organizations learn and perform better at new tasks than organizations that are comparable in talent, but that follow an *enactive* approach to implementation. That is, groups containing members who first seek out information relevant to the task, have a planning group, and consult with persons with expertise before involving themselves in performance, are more likely to achieve better results than those who "plunge right in," hoping to learn by doing. Furthermore, Miles and Randolph (1980) point out that one of the most consistent findings in the literature on organizational learning is that ". . . the stress produced by negative performance feedback is an important condition for organizational learning" (p. 49).

In plain terms, this means that short-lived social programs, if they are to learn their business quickly enough to succeed in producing recognizable results, must start with as much information as they can, consult with those who have the needed expertise, plan very carefully, and then proceed decisively, utilizing supervision and feedback (including the negative variety, where required) to maximum effectiveness. Unfortunately, these conditions did not prevail at Family Matters, nor are they likely to in similar innovations.

We have seen that such definitive information is often lacking at the design level. Thus, it can not easily be utilized at the service level. Furthermore, many of the social programs examined are designed by leaders with strong charisma, who, while bright stars themselves, are not prone to seek consultation or to find ready agreement with other leading lights about either conceptual or implementation issues in their innovations. Nicol (1976) describes some of these problems associated with the brilliance and with the personality of one of the leading designers of BEEP. We have chronicled the problem of insufficient consultation by Family Matters leaders with other comparable programs noted by NIE site visitors. Even more dramatic is Orton's (1979) admission that Head Start's attempts at accountability were hampered by a lack of good instruments to measure change, and that "the reason we didn't have the instrumentation was because we could not reach agreement nationally on the basic objectives of the program" (p. 133). Orton's statement reveals several problems with a major national social program — accountability and outcome measurement — but more than anything else, the disagreement at the top that makes organizational learning and just about every other aspect of implementation more difficult.

In addition to the leadership qualities at the top, two other factors inimical to organizational learning in many innovative interventions are the compassion and strong egalitarian spirit animating the entire endeavor. Frequently, the project's ends also become its means, its form as well as its substance. As we will see in the next few pages, the organizational model implicitly adopted by most social programs fosters such an internal climate. But it is mightily difficult for those who manage social programs to adopt a "just plain folks" posture toward staff members and then to provide the kinds of supervision and negative feedback necessary for rapid organizational learning to take place.

ORGANIZATIONAL MODELS OF SOCIAL PROGRAMS

Thus if Miles and Randolph (1980) are correct about the requisites of organizational learning, i.e., good information to begin with, plenty of consultation with those having expertise, planning implementation very carefully and proactively, proceeding decisively, and making good use of supervision and feedback, then many social programs have less than optimal conditions for organizational learning to take place in the short time they have.

In addition to the problems inherent in the short life cycle of innovative social programs and the difficulties for organizational learning this reality creates in an area where there is a shortage of informational resources, there is the question of the *organizational model* implicitly adopted by social programs both innovative and institutionalized. We have already observed that the organizational models characteristic of many programs may be inimical to rapid organizational learning. This makes consideration of organizational models all the more salient.

Elmore (1978, p. 188) has argued ". . . that there is no single coherent body of organizational theory that will serve as a basis for analysis" of the implementation of social programs. He therefore develops a typology that includes four models: systems management, bureaucratic process, organization development, and conflict and bargaining.

Implementation Styles and Implicit Organizational Models

According to Elmore (Ibid., p. 191), the systems management model decrees that program implementation should maximize the rational value of goal-directed behavior, be hierarchically organized, allocate responsibilities rationally, define a set of objectives, assign personnel, monitor performance, and make appropriate adjustments. The examples he offers of this kind of organizational model include various businesses, a defense planning agency, and the U.S. Forest Service. Elmore also points out that this organizational model is rarely associated with social program implementation because it does not work well when the cooperation of several federal agencies is needed, and because the model is a normative one — that is, it can be used to judge organizational functioning but it is not often that one finds it working as it was meant to, especially in social programs.

More common with *institutionalized programs* than the systems management model is what Elmore calls the "bureaucratic process model" which emphasizes discretion and routine. Power is dispensed among small subunits and decision making consists of controlling discretion and altering routine. According to Wilson (1973, p. 203), bureaucracy's central problem is "getting the front-line worker — the teacher, the nurse, diplomat, police officer, or welfare worker — to do the right thing." As we have seen, it was precisely this hierarchical, bureaucratic professionalized and routinized organizational model the Family Matters and other comparable interventions sought to avoid.

Elmore's (1978) third model, *organizational development*, more than any other approximates that which we found to be inherent in the implementation of Family Matters and many other social programs. Also, Elmore cites the Rand (1975) study of educational change interventions, the genre to which Head Start and Family Matters belong, to show that it is the organization development model that such innovations resemble most closely. Organizations of this kind attempt to satisfy the psychosocial needs of their employees for autonomy, control over their own work, participation in decision making, and for commitment to organizational goals. Hierarchical structure is minimized and instead effective work groups are to be created. Consensus building is important and especially accommodation between policy makers and implementors (Ibid., p. 209). This description aptly characterizes Family Matters, especially from its early days until about nine months before its end, though elements of systems management, bureaucratic process, and conflict and bargaining models were by no means totally absent in actual practice.

One of the major differences, however, between the organizational development approach to implementation and the other models is that in the latter paradigms "*policy is made at the top and implemented at the bottom*" (Ibid., p. 212, italics in original). Organizational development reverses this center of gravity and puts policy making in the hands of the implementors. As a result, it is especially effective with well-trained professionals, homogeneous work groups (because interpersonal relations are extremely important) and persons highly committed to the ideals of the organization. In the presence of conflict, it works rather poorly.

In the case of Family Matters, the only condition of these three that was satisfied, was the last, the high level of dedication with which nearly all workers operated, especially at first. But as

Elmore points out, criticism of the model comes from its strongest supporters, because unfortunately it is perhaps even more highly idealized than the systems management model. It seems to be appropriate under conditions of "trust, truth, love, and collaboration" (Bennis, 1969, p. 79). Furthermore, it is our observation that unless these ideal conditions prevail, the organizational development paradigm is a much less satisfactory model for organizations with short life cycles, low levels of information, and the need to learn rapidly, especially by comparison to the systems management model. In the long run, organizational development may indeed be the best approach to implementation, but implicit adoption of this paradigm by many innovative programs along with the attendant organizational life cycle and learning problems, go a long way to explain the pallid character of the outcomes of our attempts at social betterment compared with our intentions.

Much more could be said by way of analysis of the organizational problem of many social programs. We could cite sources about the need for goal clarity and lines of intragroup communication, for the nondiffusion of authority, for equity in the treatment of staff members, for an incremental approach to both decision making and associated implementation strategies as well as stepwise evaluation of both goals and means, but much of this is subsumed under the rubric of the organizational models chosen by programs. We could also discuss the common tendency of organizations to see self-maintenance as their real but unstated goal to the detriment of fulfillment of agencies' avowed goals (Perrow, 1978), a very real problem with service and other organizations. Space considerations, however, dictate a limit to our consideration of the issue of organizational resources, and that we sum up at this point.

Unfortunately, in relation to implementation, "the single most important feature of organizational theory is its conceptual anarchy" (Elmore, 1978, p. 187). The conflicting and contradictory theories have not provided and cannot now offer a firm body of concepts and data to help program designers and managers improve service delivery. We have seen why the bureaucratic process model, the bane of institutionalized and sometimes ossified programs, has been abandoned by the innovators. But a clearly superior model in practice, rather than just in theory, has yet to emerge. The systems management model (or some appropriate combination of organizational development and systems management) seems to offer good prospects for social program implementation and for producing better outcomes, but translating this approach from idealization to reality will not be achieved with ease. Organizational models and associated implementation should prove to be a fruitful area of inquiry for both theorists and would-be social engineers. For us, however, the time has come to reexamine the argument put forward about the efficacy problems of social programs, to summarize, and to see if the hypotheses advanced are supported by the evidence presented in this and the preceding chapters.

9

RECAPITULATION AND CODA

In traditional symphonic music, the end of a composition is often marked by a recapitulation or restatement of musical themes followed by a concluding section resolving the dynamic tensions built up by the previous contrasting tonalities and rhythms. In scholarly work, such recaps take the form of a summary and conclusions, though rarely is there a resolution of the issues raised. Although it would have been desirable to be like the composer and end this opus on some harmonious tonic chord, all the author can do is to recapitulate, interweave the relevant themes, and end, not on the tonic, but on what he hopes will be "the leading tone," a prelude to what will someday be a better resolution of some of the tensions between intention and implementation than has been available heretofore.

RECAPITULATION

This volume began with the premise that there is among human beings a strong drive for bettering one's own lot and a corresponding desire to improve the conditions for other societal members. We have put forward no empirical evidence for the former assumption, believing it to be largely self-evident. Not much more space has been devoted to documenting the premise that many of our species are highly motivated to work for better societal conditions. Such an exercise seemed largely unnecessary, given betterment efforts with which we are all familiar in history through our present day. As a matter of fact, among methodologically and conceptually rigorous psychologists (e.g., Campbell, 1975) there is now a respectability about the concept of altruism. Unlike past emphasis on hedonism in human motivation, today even "hard" social science types like psychobiologists are dealing with comparable concepts. Thus we have not consumed the reader's attention with attempts to demonstrate that there is an altruistic passion for progress. Rather, we have dealt with the questions of how social betterment interventions work and how they don't.

Restating our thesis in its barest outline, we may say that attempts at social progress confront large, complex, and deeply rooted problems, but have inadequate resources to meet those problems. Thus despite benevolent intention, and the other assets brought to bear, it is not surprising that results are less than expectations. The time has come to reexamine the elements of this thesis in detail in light of the evidence from our case study and from the broader universe of interventions to determine the goodness of fit between the data and the hypotheses.

Deeply Rooted Problems

We have argued that social programs typically confront problems deeply rooted within interlocking human and physical environmental systems. Chapter 4 provided a description of the urban context for Family Matters as an example of the forces that can impinge upon programs. We have seen the stresses — economic, social, and political — that affect employment, housing, family life, neighborhoods, transiency, program participation, etc. It became clear that arguing for more human values in city planning is needed, but that there are tradeoffs such that education, jobs, the city's economy and services, and ultimately the welfare of many low- and middle-income families could be adversely affected by human values-oriented planning if carried out too single-mindedly. This confirmed the part of our first thesis that stated that "even where effective betterment strategies can be found, there is invariably a risk-benefit tradeoff that must be accepted."

The Dearth of Informational Resources

We have said, "Even where effective betterment strategies can be found," there must be a weighing of pros and cons. But the reality is that from the viewpoint of efficacy, there is little that has been found to work in recent years. Many of the major advances in Western societies have been achieved earlier in this century (Rossi, 1966). In Chapter 7, we have tried to show that from the perspective of clearly relevant, systematic, and solid knowledge, social science has little as yet to offer beyond what individual human beings and our species generally have accumulated through experience. Even large programs like Head Start with leading human development and educational experts as founders and planners did not begin with the kind of informational base that would allow for clarity of goals and means, or for definitive measurement of outcomes.

We believe that there will not always be a paucity of policy-relevant knowledge, but that is the state of affairs now, and this situation will not change overnight given the current state of paradigms, theories, methods, and stocks of accepted findings in the social sciences. As a matter of fact, the time for truly concerned persons to worry is when we reach the era when social science really can produce "superpotent interventions," without fully understanding their consequences. If the examples of physics and chemistry, the more advanced sciences, are any criteria, we must be wary of such reverse outcomes as "nuclear family fallout," "societal resource depletion," and "stream of consciousness pollution" on the day when well-designed and implemented socio- and psycho-technologies are instituted before their long-range outcomes are manifest.

Organizational Resources

We have examined the relationship between the current status of informational and organizational resources, showing that we do not yet know as much as we need to know in order to make implementing organizations work optimally or even, for that matter, very well. Both case study and comparative material show that very few social programs can show either a smooth-running management style of any kind or highly intensive implementation efforts or the kind of long-range outcomes that prove organizational effectiveness. Here again, it was evident from the organizational literature that the information needed to organize effectively for implementation is not well understood. Thus, it is not surprising that the technology of implementation organizing is not widespread.

Financial Resources

In Chapter 4, we have tried to show the magnitude and system-bound character of the problems confronted by Family Matters, other family and childhood interventions, and other ameliorative efforts more broadly. We have also examined the informational and organizational resources brought to bear in our attempts to foster progress toward social betterment, finding them inadequate to the task. We have not, however, examined in detail our assertion that the financial resources marshalled for intervention are customarily inadequate also. Here we address ourselves to that issue.

Considering the size of our budgetary allocations for education and human services, some may quarrel with this contention. Rossi, Wright, and Wright (1978) have pointed out that one-fifth of our national budget is devoted to welfare (see Grace, 1984). As we will see, such arguments are not without merit. Our contention as a result of this inquiry is that perhaps we have tried to do too much, too quickly, too superficially, and too often, in a manner that is off-target. The question of the magnitude of social service expenditures and the kinds of programs our society wants to promote is a political one (Chen and Rossi, 1980), not so much one for scientific evaluation. It is germane for an evaluation of program implementation, however, to state that what we do, we ought to do well. This does not mean "throwing money" at social problems. It is clear that relatively well-funded but poorly targeted interventions of the past decades do little but waste taxes, inflate wages and other commodities, and sometimes achieve results opposite to those intended. But programs that are inadequately or falteringly funded cannot help but limp along inefficiently at best, and, in all likelihood, will fail.

The Ecology of Human Development Project as a whole received millions of dollars worth of funding over the course of approximately five years from a multitude of public (NIH and NIE) and private sources (the Carnegie Corporation, Kellogg, Kettering, Eli Lilly, Mott, Needmor, Spencer, and other foundations). But relative to the research and intervention objectives outlined for the project, the moneys allocated were highly inadequate. Generally speaking employees were compensated on the lower side of what might be paid for comparable work in the private sector. Tremendous amounts of time by the academic investigators and by graduate students were contributed to the project. There were no junkets or boondoggles that we were able to observe in the course of five years. On the contrary, there was a frugality implicit in project expenditures that sometimes caused problems in terms of worker salaries, office space for the Research Program and Process staff in Syracuse. This same chariness was associated with operations in Ithaca.

Uncertainty in funding began when one foundation, one of the chief sponsors of the project, withdrew precipitously early on, requiring a tremendous scramble for funds by the principal investigators, chiefly Bronfenbrenner, an effort that had its costs for the research and intervention and which lost much time and energy that had to be reallocated to fund raising. Another foundation had as one of the stipulations for its funding the proviso that employee salaries could not be regularly increased from year to year. This naturally created considerable financial strain within the project budget in paying employees during several years when double-digit inflation was abroad in the land.

Support by one of the sponsors was relatively secure at first, but was diminished sharply later. From the point of view of oversight, the same sponsor alternated between neglect during the early part of project history, and repeated and large site team visits (undoubtedly a drain on its own resources) toward project's end. The same sponsor demanded very frequent and detailed reports that we believe sapped staff energies for the intervention, for the other aspects of research, and for scholarly publication. But most crucial to program functioning was the uncertainty of funding, its inadequate magnitude, and its early termination forcing the program to end at least a full year ahead of schedule. Of course, it is hard to assess whether the designers should have cut back on the scope of the intervention or the sponsors provided more funding. But whatever the causes, there was considerable incongruence between scope and support.

Similar problems with support are reported by Nicol (1976) for the BEEP project. Here, simple attempts to communicate with a federal agency, the Bureau for the Educationally Handicapped (BEH), and to secure funding demanded tremendous allocations of time and effort. Here, too, support was terminated prematurely despite assurances to the contrary. Here, too, program planning faltered, at least in part, because of uncertainty and inadequate levels of funding, in the face of a tremendous amount of contributed services and voluntary effort.

The Youth Employment Training Program (Fetterman, 1982) discussed earlier and the Oakland Project (Pressman and Wildavsky, 1979) provide further illustration of uncertainty and delay in communication, decision making, and provision of funds by sponsors, all multiplying the problems of program implementation and hence, efficacy. Even where programs are adequately supported, attempts to evaluate the long-range effects of such interventions may go unfunded.

For example, unlike many other program designers, Lally (1982, p. 2) says of his six-year and apparently reasonably well-implemented Family Development Research Program (FDRP), "The program had clearly stated goals, sufficient time and funding for implementation to occur, and highly relevant, objective indices to determine which outcomes of the intervention matched its aims." Unfortunately, however, Lally was unable to secure funding to evaluate the question of whether significant short-term FDRP effects that were reduced at mid-range assessment, did prove lasting in the long run like those of Head Start programs that were well implemented.

The above material is not meant as an argument against oversight by sponsoring agencies or accountability to them. Nor it it to be construed as an appeal for prodigal expenditure. It simply appears that communications, requirements for proposals, and reporting should be clear, consistent (not episodic), timely, and should foster rather than overburden the research and/or intervention effort. If programs are begun, funds should be fully adequate to the task and be committed for the duration of the project and not subject to prior termination (pending satisfactory performance, of course). Otherwise, it is quite silly in the last instance to evaluate programs as not working when allocation size or intermittency wouldn't have permitted them to work in the first place. We repeat —

the political process must determine how much social engineering we will do, and the areas in which we will act. But what we do, we ought to do well.

Furthermore, in allocating funds in our national, state, and local budgets for social programs we must be willing to recognize the above described insufficiencies and fallibilities of human knowledge. We have much to learn in social science about everything, including how to bring about progress. We must also remember that fallibility and insufficiency in human knowledge is not confined to efforts at human betterment. When one considers the millions of dollars that are spent to develop one national brand product that appears on our supermarket shelves and stays there rather than disappearing after a year, then we must recognize that collectively we pay a high price for shampoo or dog food. Similarly, we must recollect the hundreds of millions of dollars involved in the innovation and development of one weapons system. Again, the relative importance of consumer products, defense of life, lifestyle and freedom, and of human betterment efforts is a matter of our values and politics. But it is important in light of the contemporary antiprogram *zeitgeist* to state that any objective analysis of the areas where innovation is carried out requires us to recognize that fraud, waste, abuse, mismanagement, and most of all a simple lack of knowledge are not the exclusive sins of only one sector. The latter are unfortunately necessary evils bound up with change, whether to the new and unprecedented, or perhaps even back to the old and the heretofore traditional.

BENEVOLENCE, CREATIVITY, CHARISMA, AND NEED

The third of the three assertions made in Chapter 1 argued that despite benevolent intention, creative, intelligent, and at least somewhat knowledgeable program design, charismatic leadership and what appears to be genuine need by those served, it is of little surprise that action programs are, at best, only moderately or inconsistently successful. We briefly consider the four parts of this assertion.

Benevolent Intention

Anyone who has spent five years close to a program like Family Matters cannot help but be impressed with the genuineness of the aims and sincerity of good will of its designers, staff, members, graduate students, and virtually everyone associated with the endeavor. Among program designers and implementors, and in the academic circles where such efforts are created, or evaluated, or studied, nobility of purpose appears in abundance.

On the other hand, about four or five years ago, a leading U.S. newspaper carried an editorial accusing the U.S. middle class, faltering in its support of social programs, of suffering from "compassion fatigue." Yet we would argue that it is possible that an excess of compassion and of the desire for progress may contribute to the ineffective implementation of social programs. We have previously discussed the Robin Hood rationalization that was applied to some Family Matters workers, and also was to be found among some families who thought that they simply ought to be given money rather than being required to participate in the program.

Raspberry (1984) points out the dangers inherent in excesses of pity. He urges those who design such compassionate programs to do so as if they were themselves going to be intervention recipients if they want to learn the perils of pity. Gray and Wandersman (1980) have similarly warned against compassionate excess and the dangers it sometimes entails. Perhaps more important, we have seen in our analysis of organizational models that when compassion becomes the very substance of a program, instead of a means to implement our aspirations for human betterment, the implementation, accountability, morale, and the very purpose of the program may suffer. Indeed it is no favor to the disadvantaged to implement a program poorly and to produce little or no effects, because this merely confirms the antagonists of such efforts in their perceptions that all programs are useless.

Also, we have observed that there is a self-righteousness that sometimes accompanies the passion for progress that leads to complacency and an immunity to constructive criticism that make the design and execution of excellent programs all but impossible. For example, the author was recently asked to comment on the design of an intervention hastily handwritten on a few pages from a source (one *outside* the Ecology of Human Development Project and *not* associated with Cornell University) that was seeking support in excess of a million dollars. In response to comments offered that the specifications of goals and means were inadequate in the extreme, and that there was simply insufficient detail to convince anyone that the potential implementors knew what they were doing, the reply received was to the effect that, the program was a very worthwhile one, "and besides the federal government wastes millions of dollars on other ineffective programs."

Indeed, the response to many scholarly and other criticisms of social program inadequacy has been that the critics are simply not kindly enough. But while it is true that *some* opposition to social engineering undoubtedly springs from self-interested, selfish, and mean-spirited motivation, it is also true that the criticisms have a very real basis in fact (Travers and Light, 1982), and that they are often put forward by social scientists who remain advocates of social programs. Furthermore, what is less often noted is that along with what is certainly genuine benevolent intention, there is also an element of self-interest among those who teach and train those who provide innovative or traditional social services, those whose job it has become to study, evaluate, design and champion social programs, and the large population of professionals and paraprofessionals within government and outside it who render educative and support services to those who are believed to need them. Thus, here as with the question of contending urban factions, it seems unduly simplistic to characterize the conflict as one between the "forces of light" and the "forces of darkness." In summary, we would argue as do Travers and Light (1982), that it is not an insufficiency of compassion but an insufficiency of information that is the more important cause of ineffective social programs, and that compassion and pity, as we have seen, are *sometimes* part of the problem rather than the solution.

Creative, Intelligent, and Knowledgeable Design

In addition to benevolent intention, we have argued that social programs are often the products of creative, intelligent, and somewhat knowledgeable designers, but this has not prevented their lack of consistent or convincing effects. Here, we can be brief because we have devoted considerable space to the contention that we do not yet have enough knowledge to further ameliorate conditions in this country without the risk of producing the problems and the fallout we have experienced when we have tried intervention in recent years. Yet the fact remains that some of the best minds in the country, both academic and political, created Head Start, other child and family interventions, and other social programs.

The reality is also that the effects produced by many of these efforts are not overwhelming. However, there have been enough effects often enough to intimate that some attempts to continue this kind of effort nationally need to be made. The question still remains as to whether greater intensity, wider scope, or greater longevity in programs might not achieve not only outcomes of greater magnitude for participants, but cost-effective solutions to social problems for the polity at large.

Charismatic Leadership

Any number of sources reviewed in the preparation of this volume have concurred in the view that strong leadership is important to: organizational success (Kimberly et al., 1980), neighborhood mobilization (Henig, 1982), and social program implementation (Rossi, 1981). Our experience with Family Matters has shown the importance of such leadership especially where innovative programs are being attempted, in order to involve sponsorship of the effort, to win adherence of staff and program participants, and to gain community cooperation.

In Family Matters, the leading movers Bronfenbrenner, Cochran, and Cross are men of the charismatic cast. Bronfenbrenner, a scholar of international repute has participated ". . . in the Head Start Planning Committee, two Presidential Task Forces, and other scientific advisory groups at the national, state, and local levels, as well as testifying for and collaborating with politicians and government officials on legislation . . ." (Bronfenbrenner, 1979b, p. xiii). Nicol (1976) speaks of the charismatic qualities associated with BEEP leadership, as does Rossi (1981) of the leader of a program designed to prevent recidivism.

Yet our experience with Family Matters, Nicol's with BEEP, and Miles and Randolph's (1980) characterization of the organizational learning process all suggest that charisma too has its risk-benefit-ratio, especially in terms of the ability to establish collaborative arrangements and to profit from the expertise of others outside the inner sanctum. On balance, there is no question that charisma is a plus in program leadership, but the message needs to be communicated that especially at this stage of our knowledge of "implementation," cooperation and consultation must not be neglected.

Genuine Need

In trying to understand the less than spectacular success of social programs, the final part of our third thesis has been that progress has not been achieved despite the existence of what appears to be "genuine need," for the interventions that have been carried out over the past several decades. Yet as we have examined the Family Matters Program, other child and family programs, and other interventions, it seems necessary to raise questions about the definition of "genuine need."

As Nicol (1976) has pointed out, "the impetus for BEEP came from educators and not from a grass roots campaign within the community" (p. 11-18). So too with Family Matters and many other family and childhood intervention programs. The initiative in many cases was that of university professors and their cadres of graduate students. It is they who have set goals and proposed strategies for programs they at first thought would benefit disadvantaged children and families specifically. Often the purview of such interventions has later been expanded to include all children. Yet the consistent threads that run through so many of these interventions are: (1) modest gains as shown by the most *proximate* measures of program impact; (2) little in the way of scientifically significant outcomes in the longer term; (3) a strong need to conduct public relations or sales campaigns to gain initial participation especially among those who appear to "need" the intervention most; and (4) relatively low levels of participation in such programs, despite the fact that the services are almost invariably provided without payment from recipients.

The concept of need generally implies that if an insufficiency is made good, then there is likely to be a change in some outcome state that was previously affected by the lack. Yet we have seen that with programs like Family Matters, results show modest short-term achievement, primarily in their intermediate goals. The Child and Family Resource Program (CFRP), carried out in 11 large or medium-sized U.S. cities during the 1970s, provides an additional illustration of an intervention that achieved only a modicum of short-term success. Results reported by Abt Associates (1981) from this intervention show that there were some gains in time spent by program parents with their children while under observation in contrast with a control/comparison group, and that the interactions of CFRP mothers with their children included more teaching and more language information. The CFRP children also made more attempts at language mastery.

But although these differences between CFRP and non-CFRP participants were statistically significant, the absolute magnitude of the differences was not all large, despite the fact that only highly active CFRP participants (also highly motivated?) were compared with a retrospective comparison group, and other methodological strategies favoring the CFRP group were employed in making the comparison. And when we move from these intermediate goals to the ultimate aims of the program — enhanced child development and achievement — "after a year to a year and a half of program participation, CFRP children were not found to differ significantly from control/comparison children in mental and physical development scores of the Bayley Scales of Infant Development" (Abt Associates, 1981, p. 2-16).

Similarly disappointing results are reported by Dawson and van Doorninck from their Parent-Infant Project in formal outcome measures such as: the Broussard neonatal perception inventory, accidents and hospitalizations of the infant, mother's income, employment, self-concept, confidence with the infant, and life change events in the family. Dawson and van Doorninck (1979) say that they "couldn't believe" that their home visit program had no results. Thus they reviewed the case histories of their participants and say they found "substantial evidence of benefit in at least half the cases." Yet what they call "substantial benefit" involved intermediate rather than ultimate goals. Also, some of the outcomes cited as beneficial are highly equivocal as to whether they were positive or negative (for example, "seven of the mothers saw a lawyer" — neither the purpose nor the outcome of the visit to the attorneys is described).

When these two researchers from the University of Colorado "looked to see which mothers showed most benefit," they decided retrospectively that it was the mothers who had the greatest "psychosocial need." These women kept their appointments for a greater number of home visits. Yet, because this analysis is retrospective, we do not know whether the conclusions drawn are essentially tautological (i.e., that need has been inferred from participation rather than the reverse), and whether the cause-effect relationship exists only in the minds of educators who "couldn't believe" that their designed home visits were of no benefit.

Certainly, in the Family Matters Program, apparent need was inversely related to participation. According to both the scientific or social change literature, those who on an *a priori* basis would have been regarded as most in need — single parent, low-income, and/or racial minority families — should have participated most. Table 2 shows that the factors affecting participation most consistently were mother's education, race, and neighborhood. Better educated, white mothers living in suburban or middle-class ethnic neighborhoods were those who took most advantage of program offerings.

All of this suggests the oversimplified nature of categorization of participants based on the inference that more need means more

TABLE 2
Significance of Statistical Tests Related to Seventeen Indices of Program Participation

	Number significant[a]	Number near-significant[b]	Number non-significant
Gender of target child	0	0	17
Family income	5	1	11
Mother's education	10	3	4
Race	13	1	3
Neighborhood	16	1	0
Work status	9	1	7
Legal married status	5	8	4

[a]p Less than .05, 2-tailed.

[b]p Less than .10, 2-tailed.

utilization. More need, or at least more stress, probably means less utilization of voluntary organizational or more optional activities as long as the meeting of (Maslow's) primary needs (for food, shelter, etc.) is in doubt. Head Start and other interventions that require a primary investment of time and energy from the child rather than the parent are probably an exception to these generalizations about participation.

Our study of Family Matters where parent participation was essential to success, leads us to believe that indeed the relationship between need and participation is, if anything, curvilinear, especially when it comes to activities not related to primary needs. Those least in need find them superfluous. Those in greatest need can't afford to spend time on them. And it is only those intermediate in need who will benefit.

In Family Matters, when it came to referral to social services, as might be expected, the relationship appeared to be linear, i.e., the more need, the greater the participation. But when we speak of home visits and parent-child activities, it appears that the utilization was intermediate between the *staff-oriented* and the *peer-oriented* patterns discussed by Powell (1982). The impetus of the home visit came from without, and the allocation of time and effort (and sometimes financial outlay also) was smaller than required for group meetings. There seemed no call for Powell's (1982) above mentioned peer-orientationed activities. Yet workers said that they were there to learn. This is probably what caused the greatest confusion in the minds of families who were staff oriented, and were waiting for the worker to tell them what to do. It also explains many of the difficulties we have described about worker role. Other individual difference factors probably also determined utilization, but differing needs and associated peer versus staff orientations were undoubtedly pivotal in participant receptiveness to the services provided.

This means that broad-gauged interventions, especially those that come from the theorizing of upper-middle-class social scientists, are likely to be very much off-target for a large number, perhaps even a majority, of their intended recipients. Unless individualized, they will be perceived to be of marginal value, even where they deal with important issues. For example, of all the multifaceted, broad-spectrum program offerings of the Syracuse-based Family Development Program, the only ones for parents described as "very popular" by Lally (1982) were the workshops where "mothers made clothing for themselves and their infants, created play materials for children, and made seasonal decorations for their homes" (Appendix A). While these activities would not be considered trivial by child development theorists, many would regard them as considerably lower in the pantheon of developmental values than other FDRP offerings — weekly home visits, meetings to discuss family and developmental issues, open houses, and other social activities designed to enhance social networks.

Another illustration of the possible clash between the needs, values, and intentions of program designers of putative program utilizers is provided by the Young Employment Training Program (Fetterman, 1982) which lost participants because of delays in federal funding after the program was announced. The immediate need for some form of income became more important, and the modalities of self-support provided by street-culture were more salient than the unaccustomed and future-oriented training program that might come through "some day."

It may of course be argued that low levels of effect or participation in programs does not prove that programs are off-target or *unneeded* but rather that enough has simply not been done. Thus, Head Start has shown some significant though not overwhelming long-term effects, and Zigler (1979) has raised the plausible argument that larger effects will result from long-term supportive efforts rather than those lasting a year or two. This implies, of course, that need has *not* been genuinely satisfied in full but only in small measure. On the other hand, Lally's program, which produced less than spectacular intermediate effects, lasted six years, and by his statement was adequately funded. Thus until there is better evidence for Zigler's assertions about long-term efforts, and cost-benefit justifications for such efforts are provided, questions of values, needs, and congruence between programs and recipients will remain.

Indeed it is likely that need for some social programs may exist in some generic sense. But this may not diminish the problem of receptivity to the specific programs proposed by social engineers not fully in touch with the cultural orientation and immediate life circumstances of those for whom the programs are intended. This means that public relations, recruitment, and participation issues will persist, to say nothing of the paucity of outcomes demonstrating progress.

THE MAGNITUDE OF EFFECTS PROBLEM

Having reviewed the successes and failures of social programs and how our theses fit the evidence, we now conclude with a few cautionary notes, observations, and recommendations. In judging the effects of many social programs, some, especially social scientists, have pronounced them of little value because statistical tests showing differences between program and control groups have proved to be nonsignificant. This is the "magnitude of effects" problem, one that is worthy of consideration here.

Head Start, as discussed earlier, did at first show sufficiently strong outcomes to withstand the rigors of statistical testing. Later, these effects seemed to "wash out" as the children involved in the project grew older. Still later, the work of Lazar and Darlington (1982) showed that where project activities were well implemented and evaluation designs were well carried out, one could show long-term gains for project children, especially if one pooled the variances from several (in this case 12) separate Head Start components.

Others, however, have informally criticized these findings because they claim that with such variance pooling procedures, one can show statistically significant program effects, but, individually, such effects are trivial in the policy sense. It is said that such small magnitude effects will also wash out in the still longer term because they are not substantial to begin with. Furthermore, by comparison with the grandeur generally promised by many program designers (cf. Nicol, 1976) — the exaggerated promises of I.Q. change to be achieved by Head Start, and the superpotent intervention that was the object of Bronfenbrenner's search — the gradualism, the very modest cognitive gains, and the only episodically potent interventions that have resulted are by no means heartening.

Finally, though formal cost-benefit analyses have been too infrequently carried out on interventions, those that are cited are frequently very discouraging. For example, the Oakland Project, designed to create jobs in the San Francisco bay area, produced only a very small number of jobs for the money spent. In one segment of the project, the cost was about 80,000 dollars per job gained (Pressman and Wildavsky, 1979).

The problem of small effects relative to costs and efforts expended is a serious one, and one that must be dealt with before concluding this volume on aspirations for social versus the actual gains we have recently achieved. We believe that future expectations for the magnitude of effects to be demonstrated by social programs of the future will need to be predicated on more realistic assessments of two factors discussed in earlier chapters — (1) the size and complexity of the problems we seek to remedy; and (2) the status of the informational and technological resources we bring to attempts to progress.

Problem Magnitude and Complexity

We have discussed at length in Chapter 7 the inadequacy of our scientific and technical knowledge about human nature, knowledge that in some respects does not transcend and may be inferior to what Heider (1958) has called "naive psychology." We apparently know even less about how to change human behavior. The psycho- and behavior therapy literature show that even intensive efforts to change the behavior of highly motivated and intelligent clients (seeing the same client three to five times a week for several years), do not assure positive outcomes or any sort of meaningful change. And while we know too little about human functioning (both individual and social), and less about creating change, we continue to have unrealistic expectations for effect size whether in the research laboratory or in the home or community.

Unfortunately, social scientists like Mischel (1968) have muddied the waters by repeatedly characterizing as "trivial" determinants of human behavior that account for only 10 percent of statistical variance, citing Bandura and Mischel (1965) as an example of what good research can achieve. On the other hand, Bowers (1973), Cronbach (1975), and a whole host of interactionist psychologists have demonstrated the multidetermined, complex, and interactive nature of human behavior, attempting to influence their colleagues to adopt a more realistic view of the amount of variance that can be explained with any specific conceptual orientation.

Mindick (1979), calculating from the tabled means-squares of the Bandura and Mischel (1965) paper, determined that the highly touted "model effect" accounted for less than 5 percent of the variance in one condition, less than 2 percent of the variance in the other, and essentially 0 percent of the variance in either condition in a delayed posttest one month later. It is important to remember that Mischel himself had selected this study as exemplary, and that this research is the kind of work that has earned both Bandura and Mischel the highest awards for scientific merit given by the American Psychological Association.

Using procedures comparable to Mindick's, Jamieson, Gallo, and Christian (1977) have shown more broadly that two-thirds of the univariate research published in our most prestigious psychological journals explains no more than 11 percent of the variance in dependent measures. Thus, the best of our researchers, generally working under the controlled conditions of laboratory experimentation are (roughly speaking) producing a 10 percent change in behavior by manipulating one independent variable.

Social programs, working with limited resources in the real world against problems of the magnitude we have delineated earlier, ought not to be held to a higher standard in trying to achieve long-range effects than social scientists working under "ideal conditions." Indeed, perhaps, at this point in time, the standard ought to be lower, or at least more realistic than it is currently. Especially when we consider that the problem of cities, the issues of *gemeinschaft vs. gesellschaft*, and the atomization of the family from its extended configuration to its current split-nucleus state have all evolved over the course of three or four centuries, it seems unrealistic to expect reversals of the powerful processes that brought about these circumstances in the course of a few months or even a few years.

Also, the subject of change suggests the need for another effort of hard-headed appraisal of the capacities of social programs — the realization that with the rapidity of change in Western society (cf. Toffler, 1970; 1980; Naisbitt, 1982), social problems present a shifting target. What may have worked in the past, may well be presently off-the-mark, and what may not have worked previously, may not necessarily be excludable as a future intervention.

The Experimenting Society

Campbell (1971) has written a classic paper in the area of program evaluation dealing with social reforms as experiments, arguing forcefully that despite the limits of social programs of the past, we must remain an *experimenting society*. Conservative, neo-conservative, and neo-Spencerians may argue that laissez-faire, small government, and not "imposing an unrealistic perfection" on what already exists are our best course vis-à-vis social engineering. But while due attention should be given to the concerns they raise and the critiques they level, the *nonexperimenting society* would seem bound to become the stultified society, where want and inequity are institutionalized. We would argue that strict experimental method probably ought not to be applied to all interventions, though empirical research methods should. And although our inquiry into social programs and other such examinations (e.g., Sieber 1981) are far from rosy as they review implementation and its outcomes, this does not lead us to a view that social experimentation ought not to be done. Rather, our view is that programs do need to be carried forward, but carried forward more carefully, more incrementally, more circumspectly, and with more humility — in short, better. Why? Perhaps a historical example, so rare in social scientific writing, may be instructive.

In the book of Deuteronomy, several "social programs" for the benefit of the disadvantaged are outlined. One of these was the sabbatical year, a concept in its latter day permutation that is so dear to the hearts of academics and others. Originally, however, one of the the main functions of the sabbatical year was to cancel all debts owed to creditors. Septads were observed by the society at large, and if a note was still due after the close of a year that was a multiple of six, there was no longer any obligation to pay. The intent of the law was to prevent the poor from falling ever deeper into debt.

But as time went on and societal change occurred, the intervention became one of those that boomeranged. Poor farmers were unable to borrow funds to buy seeds during years late in the cycle. Few individuals were altruistic enough to lend out money, especially since interest-taking was also forbidden, at a time when a debt might be cancelled in a year or two. Thus Hillel, the great Rabbinic legislator, instituted a legal formula to allow for the non-cancellation of notes by the sabbatical years "so as not to lock the doors of opportunity in the faces of poverty-stricken borrowers."

Observers in Hillel's day 2,000 years ago might have argued then about the social legislation that had caused the problem to begin with, or with Hillel's attempt to tinker with social reform in his own day. But if humanity had not tinkered with the social order since that time, we might still be living with a theocratic government under monarchical rule. It is our passion for progress that has brought us to what are on balance the beneficial changes in government, economy and production, and lifestyle that most of us enjoy today. Thus, like most passions, the one that impels us to make progress must be trammeled by restraint and by suitable form in its expression, but it is one that we cannot do without. In terms of social programs, we must be circumspect but still remain an experimenting society.

APPENDIX

The reader, especially the technical reader or the social scientist, may have questions about the methodological basis for our analysis of the "passion for progress," the Family Matters case study in that analysis, and our comparison with recent childhood-oriented interventions as well as with other social programs. This question is particularly important with regard to the description of the *implementation* of the Family Matters Program. How do we know what we purport to know about Family Matters, Syracuse and like urban areas, and social programs generally? Such concerns are especially salient because of the dearth of quantitative data and statistical analyses in our presentation. Thus, we will conclude this exposition in such a way as to provide an answer that will focus on our research methodology. This methodological treatment has been written as an appendix to allow the more general reader to proceed from the introductory chapter directly to the main analysis and its argument.

A STUDY OF PROCESS – ITS GUIDING PURPOSE

As indicated above, our research took as its chief focus the implementation *processes* inherent in the Family Matters Program component of the Comparative Ecology of Human Development Project (Bronfenbrenner and Cochran, 1976), in addition to processes at work in the urban environment that affected program families. The original proposal to the Carnegie Corporation enlisting support to conduct this study of process in October 1977 stated that the research was designed to satisfy an important need and to provide an opportunity for ". . . the systematic examination of . . . those factors associated with program success or failure." (Bronfenbrenner and Cochran, 1977, p. 2). Bronfenbrenner and Cochran continue:

> A review of existing programs in the United States indicates that they often founder not because of what they have to offer, but because of the particular ways in which they are carried out.

Further, our ecological perspective directs attention to the possibility that our experimental programs may have important effects other than those anticipated in the original research design (1977, p. 2).

As noted in Chapter 1, in this respect, Bronfenbrenner and Cochran have joined the growing number of prominent social scientists and others who are beginning to address program implementation alongside theory-related questions as variables of importance in the research endeavor (see Pressman and Wildavsky, 1979; Rossi, 1981; Gordon, 1979).

TRIANGULATION AND VALIDITY

Because the research on the outcomes of the intervention was heavily (though not exclusively) oriented toward quantitative analysis, our study of process was designed to complement that quantitative analysis of program products with an ethnographic analysis of program processes. This decision was also influenced by the recent calls from a number of scholars especially in the area of evaluation for the greater depth and breadth that can be provided by ethnographic analysis (McClintock, Brannon, and Maynard-Moody, 1979; Rist, 1981). And indeed, after 30 months of such data collection and as many more of analysis, our numerous over-stuffed file cabinets attest mutely but eloquently to the breadth and depth of this kind of research methodology.

Another reason for our voluminous data collection lies in our recognition of the need for breadth and depth to *strengthen the validity* of our findings. In recent years, methodologists have stressed the idea that credibility in demonstrating any research proposition is enhanced by a multi-method investigative approach. Quantitatively oriented social scientists often refer to this approach as that of showing "convergent validity," while qualitatively oriented colleagues usually call this "triangulation."

DATA SOURCES

It was this kind of triangulation or convergent validity that we sought to achieve in our multi-method, multi-source investigation of the translation of the conceptual model of Bronfenbrenner, Cochran, and Cross into the Family Matters Program. We examined relevant data from six different perspectives (Mindick and Cross, 1979):

(1) The original and evolving conceptualization of the project's principal investigators.
(2) Family perceptions of program services.
(3) Program and liaison staff perceptions of their own efforts and of the reactions of the families served.
(4) Views of community leaders about the program and the milieu in which it operated.
(5) Data gathered from archival sources that delineate the program's social, economic, demographic, and geographic context.
(6) Information supplied by the project's outcome-oriented field research staff and other project staff as well.

These perspectives along with examples of the data gathering methods used to study each perspective are shown in schematic representation in Figure 1.

THE PRINCIPAL INVESTIGATORS

The first perspective to be analyzed was that provided by the principal investigators, especially their view of the theoretical underpinnings of the research outlined in the conceptual model. The most frequently used data gathering techniques employed in studying principal investigator perspectives were interviews, observations, and the study of written documents.

Interview

All three principal investigators were interviewed formally in some depth, primarily by graduate students specially trained for their task under the aegis of the Process Study. The author believes that on many points these interviews reflected remarkable candor and frankness by the designers of the Family Matters Program.

FIGURE 1
An Illustration of the Multi-perspective, Multi-method Research Strategy.

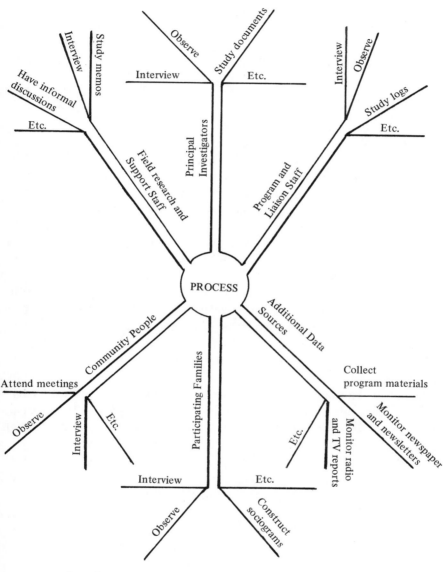

Legend:

= Perspective sought

= Examples of data gathering methods to be used to study a given perspective.

In addition to these formal interviews, the author obtained much more information about principal investigator thinking in the course of our routine interactions, such as the normal round of activities at the Cornell home base, executive staff meetings, site visits by reviewers for research sponsors, and chiefly during the shared round-trip, by car, between Ithaca and Syracuse.

Observation

In addition to the formal interviews and informal conversations, process analysts had full access to meetings held both within the project context and often outside it as well, at which the principal investigators presented their viewpoints about the Family Matters Program as well as related issues. An important example of within project meetings observed by the process staff was a retreat held on December 15, 1980 by Cochran, Bronfenbrenner, and Cross with Program Director Woolever to chart the course of program activity for the last seven months of the intervention.

Sometimes the intraprogram observation permitted comparative analysis of principal investigator perspectives through reports from operations and procedures of other early childhood intervention programs. Of course, much of this analysis was carried out by familiarizing ourselves with the appropriate research literature. At other times, contact was more direct, for example when the Ecology of Human Development Project invited colloquium speakers such as Deborah Belle from the Stress and Families Project. Although this particular project was not an intervention, its work was of importance in understanding families with young children.

Process staff observations also included "extramural" principal investigator expressions relevant to our research — both those associated with the Ecology of Human Development Project as well as those in charge of other comparable interventions. One example of such coverage occurred during the Society for Research in Child Development (SRCD) convention in Boston during April 1981. Process analysts Cox and Serkland were assigned to report on principal investigator presentations about the program and to compare these perspectives with those of other researchers in the area of human development presented at the SRCD conference. Special attention was given to the papers and discussions concerned with interventions aimed at children and young families. The author repeated like observations and data gathering at a similar SRCD in Detroit during April 1983 and during several comparable recent meetings of the American Psychological Association.

Our extramural comparative analysis of principal investigator perspectives was also carried out through firsthand contact with other similar programs. Direct contact with comparable programs included a visit by the process analysts in 1981 to the site of the Brookline Early Education Project (BEEP). The interviews with BEEP's historian and its director as well as the program materials obtained proved invaluable in helping to find similarities and contrasts in interventive style. Still other contacts with important comparison studies came more adventitiously, largely as a result of the growing awareness of our process study in the scholarly community and a desire for an informal exchange of ideas.

We have conferred with representatives from the Smithsonian Family Education Project and the Family Development Resource Program (FDRP). This last intervention was carried out in Syracuse under the leadership of Ronald Lally and Alice Honig during 1968-75. The FDRP was a far more intensive intervention, and examination of program intensity is a pivotal component of the analysis of program implementation. Such comparisons enhanced our longitudinal case study of the Family Matters Program as it was measured against other similar programs and research projects. Also enhanced by such comparative material was our ability to discuss early childhood intervention as a specific genre of social programming. Our research sometimes ranged far afield for the sake of comparison and breadth of coverage. This was necessary, however, because, as Gray and Wandersman (1980) point out, it is relatively rare that reports of the results of such projects find their way into peer-reviewed journals. However, the vast majority of our data, especially our information on the program designers' views, came from the routine of intraprogram activity.

Document Analysis

The chief source of data dealing with the Ecology of Human Development principal investigator perspectives, however, lay in their own writings. To gather the required data, we carefully examined books, research papers, progress, and final reports to sponsoring agencies, magazine articles, meeting minutes, and interoffice memos. We have also attempted over the years to collect similar written material from the designers and administrators of comparable programs for comparison's sake and to add breadth to our analysis. Detailed description of the salient content examined, and implications of the resulting data analyses, are presented in Chapter 7.

Topics Analyzed

The fundamental questions asked during examination of the program designers regardless of the data source, were: What were the views of Bronfenbrenner, Cochran, and Cross (and other comparable program designers) that were implicit in their original plan for program activity? How were these views communicated to the program staff? What modifications occurred in the basic program blueprint as a result of: (1) communication with program workers; (2) actual program implementation; (3) self-initiated changes by the principal program architects over time; and (4) pressures by funding sources. Here again the results of these analyses are found in Chapter 7.

PROGRAM AND CONTROL FAMILIES

The second major perspective examined by our research was that of families participating in the Family Matters Program. We also devoted some effort to studying control families as will be described later in this section and in another segment devoted to the perspectives of research and liaison staff members. Our major emphasis, however, was on program families. The two chief data collection methods employed in documenting their perspectives were observation and interview.

Observation

Observations were carried out during both the home visits and neighborhood group meetings that constituted the program's two-pronged intervention strategy. In the course of these observations, process analysts assumed two divergent roles. One of these roles was that of a participating onlooker watching as program workers, families, and children carried on regular program activity. In general, the process analyst spoke or interacted with others present in the situation only enough to avoid the awkwardness of simply sitting by, staring, and recording. As a matter of fact, process analysts were instructed to refrain from any data recording at home visits (and generally at group meetings as well). According to recommendations made by Rist (1979), field notes were made away from the observation site as soon as the session was over.

The second role assumed by at least one process staff member in observing program families in actual program activity was that of full participation as a program family. Process analyst Serkland was a single parent living in a program neighborhood. Her older child was well within the age parameters established for the program's "target children," and she and her children, Laura, then age 6, and Andrew, age 2, took part regularly as a program family in the Westcott-Thornden neighborhood group. Consequently, Serkland had the opportunity to observe the dynamics of the Family Matters Group Program from within.

Also, in order to simulate the elements experienced by other program families, she was contacted by the liaison staff in a manner comparable to that used for other participants. That contact later led to administration of the standard baseline research interviews utilized by the project. She took part in the outcome interviews at program's end as well, to enable her to give a full account of her perceptions of both research and program processes from the standpoint of an actual participant. The data she provided relative to *outcome measurement* could not be utilized, of course, because Serkland was far from being a naive subject. But her accounts related to *process variables* have proven to be extremely valuable.

Interview

In addition to observations, process study interviews were also an important source of information on program family perceptions. In the fall of 1980, a random 50 percent sample of the approximately 180 families in the pilot and main study neighborhoods was drawn, and interviews were obtained with 72 percent of these families. The remaining 28 percent of the families were unavailable for interview either because they had moved out of the county or had dropped out of the program and were unwilling to participate in any further study activities. However, those program dropouts or inactive families who did display a willingness to be part of this aspect of process study research were interviewed despite their nonparticipatory status in the program itself.

Interviews with each family lasted from one to three hours. The main thrust of our inquiries was to learn which elements of the program might or might not have been effective in achieving the program's two major goals, increasing parent-child activities and providing social support for parenting. The results of analyses carried out on these interviews were made available to Principal Investigators Cochran, Bronfenbrenner, and Cross as well as to Program Director Woolever so as to furnish them with general information about family perceptions of program implementation and also to provide specific recommendations as background for their December 15, 1980 senior staff retreat to plan the last months of program activity.

A second round of interviews was conducted at the end of the program and outcome data collection during the late spring and early summer of 1981. At this time, the remaining 50 percent of the families not interviewed previously (both those who had been active and inactive) were surveyed. This data collection yielded responses from 62 families to in-depth interviews quite similar in form and content to those in the earlier round of interviews described above. When these 62 were added to the 66 interviews with the other half of the random sample of families, the result was a total of 128 usable interviews. This number represented virtually all the accessible program families, and compared favorably with the 123 usable interviews obtained at program's end in Wave II of the *outcome* data collection.

Interview of Control Families

At program's end we also interviewed 31 control families. Unanticipated in our original plan, these process study interviews were undertaken when it became apparent from our discussion with program families that the outcome research data collection which involved both program and control groups had a very real impact on participants. In at least some cases, it was clear that the outcome data collection rivaled the program in sensitizing families to the need for both parent-child and social network activities so as to enhance child and family development. Answering the research questionnaires was itself an intervention independent of the planned program. In order to separate program processes and effects from outcome research processes and effects, it became necessary to examine the interview experience of both the program and control groups and to sort out its likely effects. Thus, a 25 percent random sample of control families was interviewed briefly by process analysts concerning their experience in research participation.

Topics Analyzed

The most pertinent questions underlying our analysis of material on program family perceptions were: (1) How did families perceive Family Matters generally? (2) How did families react to specific program elements (home visits, groups, the integrated program, program materials, etc.)? (3) What changes in family life are likely to be attributable to program participation? (4) What program elements did families find to be the most positive and praiseworthy? (5) What criticisms or suggestions did families have concerning the intervention? (6) What implications did family perceptions have for future program implementation?

PROGRAM AND LIAISON STAFF

Of the six perspectives documented in our research, three were given highest priority in our plans for data collection, i.e., those of program families, of the principal investigators, and of the program and liaison staff. As mentioned earlier, the liaison staff consisted of one or two persons whose job it was to link both program and control families to the project generally through mail, personal visits, or phone calls. Data collection strategies designed to document program and liaison worker perspectives produced the largest volume of data and emphasized participant observation, interviews, and the study of program worker logs as well as other written materials.

Participant Observation

The Family Matters Program and the Carnegie sponsored Process Study operations were both housed in the same office space. Staff members from both project components had continuous and frequent contact with one another. Some of the most fundamental criteria for selection of process analysts included their social skills and general affability. Even though factionalism grew up within the program staff itself, process analysts were able to move freely between the various elements and enjoyed a large measure of confidence by all. There was a fair amount of social mixing among program workers and process analysts outside office hours, and rapport between the two groups could hardly have been better. In addition to observing program workers in external program delivery activities as well as in internal full-staff and committee meetings, process analysts occasionally took an active role in the committee work inherent in program planning.

This kind of involvement is not ideal in terms of the sort of unobtrusive measurement that is most desirable methodologically, but *participant observation* which entails some active involvement in events being recorded by the ethnographer is frequently a part of traditional ethnographic methodology (see Glazer, 1972; Schatzmand and Strauss, 1973). Furthermore, this participatory role was required of the process staff members by Program Director Woolever, who felt that limiting the process analyst role strictly to observation would be awkward. He was concerned about giving program workers the same kind of feeling of being placed under a microscope that was a consideration in the above-discussed research techniques used in observing families.

As a result of these and other factors, we may sum up participant observation by the process analysts in the following way. The two staff groups worked together, lived together in the same office space, celebrated and sorrowed together. Program and liaison staff members shared confidences with the process staff members, and they learned that, as promised, the privacy of these confidences was maintained until program's end when each worker had gone off to seek his or her fortune elsewhere. Indeed, the frequency with which program workers shared confidences with the process staff that they did not share with each other provides evidence that workers usually placed more trust in the process analysts as confidantes than they did in one another or in other professional persons outside the project staff. This trust, daily observation of internal program operations, participation in program planning activity, and observation of the program in actual operation with families, all gave process analysts a voluminous store of data on program worker perspectives.

Interviews

In addition to participant observation and informal conversations, program and liaison workers were interviewed in detailed fashion by the process staff. An intensive interview program was conducted by process study personnel in the winter and spring of 1980. Process analysts obtained three or four interviews lasting two to four hours with each program worker. In addition to this systematic interview substudy conducted over a relatively brief period of time, interviews with program workers and liaison staff personnel continued episodically for the duration of the intervention. The occasions for these interviews were conditional upon special events in the history of program development, personal inclinations of program and liaison workers, or specific research tasks assigned to process staff members or assumed by them on their own initiative. In short, process analysts were given considerable discretion in planning data gathering as is traditional in ethnographic research.

Systematic interviewing of program workers, however, was again carried out in spring and early summer of 1981 in preparation for the end of program activity on July 31 of that year. This round of interviews was quite crucial in debriefing the program staff of their accumulated knowledge, wisdom, and opinion before they left to pursue their new career paths. Debriefing of program workers involved a fourfold emphasis: (1) individual worker perceptions of individual families and the progress of each family over time; (2) individual worker perceptions of program processes more broadly; (3) group perceptions by neighborhood worker team members of program and other relevant processes within program neighborhoods;

and (4) group perceptions by the program staff as a whole of program processes and historical evolution.

Throughout the whole debriefing process, candor, cooperation, and rapport between program and process staff members remained outstanding, especially considering the "lame duck" status of program workers at the time.

Logs and Other Program Documents

In addition to the material derived from observation and interview, a third source for staff perspectives was the written matter produced by workers in recording their own observations of program activity. These observations were found primarily in logs required of all program workers. The logs contained information about the place and timing of program activities, their frequency, the number and kind of persons present, the level of participation, and the nature of activity carried out. Comparable, though much less detailed information was contained in a card-file called "the recordex," which was to catalogue *all* contacts by *all* project members (i.e., program, liaison, and research staff) made with both program and control families according to their date, time, and/or medium of communication (mail, phone, personal visit, or group meeting).

Unfortunately (but not unexpectedly in such an intervention) we found that both the logs and the recordex were too often in error, incomplete, improperly maintained, and sometimes downright mutually contradictory and/or falsified. In such cases of inaccuracy or dishonesty, our multi-method convergent research strategy proved invaluable. For example, if a program family told us that they rarely saw their worker, and if, as happened with at least one staff member, the same worker recorded many, many visits with that very family, each occurring exactly two weeks after the previous one, we considered this grounds for suspecting the genuineness of worker records. In at least some instances, our comparisons of data sources were also able to set the record straight, especially with regard to contacts recorded in one source but not the other.

In addition to the logs and recordex data, which documented, among other things, family participation in the program, other written matter was also collected and has been analyzed. These documents include memos, policy statements and guidelines, manuals, and other training materials, program materials distributed to families, and especially the program modules developed late in the program dealing with schools and with other topics that are important to families.

Topics Analyzed

The fundamental questions asked by the process study during its analyses of all sources bearing on program and liaison staff perspectives were: (1) What were the perceptions of program means and ends that were held by those involved in the implementation process? (2) How were these perceptions formed in the early training of staff by the principal investigators and the program director? (3) How did staff thinking evolve over time and what effect did this have on the program? (4) As the end of the program activity approached, what recommendations did staff members have for change or constancy in program design? (5) What implications do such recommendations have for comparable interventions of the future? And of course the most basic implementation-centered questions of all, (6) in what ways did the program as implemented by workers resemble the core conceptualization of the principal investigators? and (7) in what ways did it differ?

ADDITIONAL DATA SOURCES

The perspectives we have discussed until now, those of the principal investigators, program families, and Family Matters staff, were largely those derived directly from contact with people. Two exceptions to this rule were the above mentioned program worker logs and recordex as well as certain important documents, articles, and books, chiefly those produced by the study's principal investigators. In assessing our utilization of what we simply term "additional data sources" in the present study, we turn to a perspective that is derived not from any recognizable individual or set of individuals, but rather a potpourri of evidentiary material.

Monitoring Radio and Television

This material was derived, for example, from monitoring relevant radio and television reports. The process analysts in Syracuse as well as the process study director in Ithaca received all the Syracuse television channels. Both commercial and publicly sponsored broadcasts provided important background for process study observations of program and general community activity. For example, in October of 1979, process analyst Eulas Boyd predicted that when unemployment rose a bit more, county agencies would make it more difficult for recipients to obtain benefits. Within a month of his prophecy, the NBC television affiliate in Syracuse, WSTM, announced that the County Department of Social Services offices in the city would be open only one hour a day (between 8 and 9 a.m.) to receive new applications for welfare. The television channel noted a great deal of protest and possible litigation over this tactic. The expressions of consternation were covered by only one television channel and not at all by the city's print media, giving us our only opportunity to confirm Boyd's prediction about the planned contraction of social services and its potential effects on Family Matters participants and other families. This attempt to "control the flow" of benefit seekers was not a concern for all program families, but it certainly was a source of stress for some. Our monitoring of TV and radio allowed us to uncover the dramatic but not always highly publicized pressures and counter-pressures exerted by both social service agencies and their clients.

Monitoring Newsletters and Newspapers

In addition to monitoring Syracuse radio and television outlets, more systematic coverage of the broader context of the Family Matters intervention was provided by culling relevant materials from the city's two daily newspapers, the Syracuse Herald American and the Syracuse Daily Journal. Process analysts subscribed to both of these papers, and articles were selected and clipped from each day's newspaper for interpretation concurrently with program activity during a period from about January 1, 1980 through July 31, 1981. Topics that guided selection included the city's: economy and employment, taxes, housing and construction, crime and crime prevention, education, politics and government, and demographic trends, as well as organizations and activities that were of even more immediate concern in family life.

Newspaper accounts were utilized because they seemed to meet two important tests: (1) they provided a focus for systematically reporting and analyzing major macro-level events observed by the process staff members over the duration of the program (and more episodically afterwards as well); (2) though they cannot be considered inherently impartial or objective either in their selection or interpretation of events, newspaper accounts are more overt and susceptible to scrutiny (cf. Ziman's 1968 definition of science as "public knowledge") than completely covert selection and interpretive processes by field observers. In addition, besides reporting occurrences, newspaper stories themselves often influence later events.

The chapter on Syracuse illustrates the importance of newspaper accounts in helping to document the context of the Family Matters Program, of its families, and to provide examples of the problems confronted by urban families more generally. Additional printed material was also culled from *newsletters*, although on a less systematic basis. Newsletter material was especially important in gaining information about special interest groups within the city as well as about some of the particular concerns of black families.

Collection of Other Program Materials

Supplementing these media sources were program materials generally available within the community that were relevant to families with preschool children. It should be noted that the program materials referred to here were not those offered by Family Matters. These have been treated above since they helped document Family Matters Program workers perspectives. Here we refer to program materials put out by such organizations as Child and Family Services of Onondaga County, the Public and Private School Systems, New York State Cooperative Extension, Head Start, and similar groups.

Also, two of the three process analysts (Serkland and Boyd) were themselves parents of young children, and Serkland had recently served as vice-president of the Child and Family Services Committee of Onondaga County. She thus had good connections within the city's network of persons interested in children and their parents. Process Analysts Cox and Serkland were both former teachers and were "tied in" with people associated with elementary education in Syracuse. Process Analyst Boyd had been a highly visible leader of adults, and especially of youth, in the black community. Thus the contacts of all three process analysts allowed them to be exposed episodically to relevant materials which shed light on offerings by programs other than Family Matters to the city's families. We will have more to say on this score in describing documentation of our next perspective, that of key figures in the community.

Archival Data Sources

In addition to monitoring the communications media and collecting non-Family Matters Program material relevant to parenting concerns, archival data sources were extremely important in dealing with specific questions and topics of interest to the process study. Institutions and agencies consulted include: the Syracuse Historical Society, the U.S. Bureau of the Census, the U.S. Weather Bureau, the Syracuse University Library, the Mayor's office, and several other sources as well.

Other archival sources on Syracuse have been consulted, some dealing with city history, others providing background on the growth of the black community. One important data source of this kind is the "Places Rated Almanac" (Boyer and Savageau, 1981) which compares the "livability" of 277 major U.S. cities. As mentioned in Chapter 4, because of its cultural amenities, Syracuse was rated the seventh best place to live in the country. But as noted earlier, its economy was the fifth worst in the nation, an ominous statistic that explains many of the stresses encountered by program families.

Topics Analyzed

The questions we were trying to answer in referring to these archival materials as well as the other "additional data sources" described above were: (1) What was the history of the environment in which program families lived? (2) What was its current status in terms of quality of life? (3) What were the major social, economic, demographic, and political trends then operating; (4) How were such trends likely to have affected program families? And most fundamentally, (5) what was the relationship (auxilliary, antagonistic, or neutral) between processes within the urban context and processes set in motion by the Family Matters Program in influencing the program's basic aim, enhancing the development of preschool children?

COMMUNITY PEOPLE

Of the two remaining perspectives we set ourselves to document, those of prominent persons in the community and of the field research and support staff, the former is one that we had greater success in delineating than we had anticipated in our original planning. The perspective of community persons was next to last in priority in our early thinking, but as we began increasingly to notice the very profound impact on program implementation by its urban context, the views of community leadership assumed greater and greater importance. Consequently, we sought and gained considerable information on two basic points: (1) how community leaders saw the needs and resources of families with preschool children residing in the community, and (2) how they saw the Family Matters Program and its effects on participating families.

Attendance at Meetings and Informal Observation

As indicated in the previous section, process analysts Boyd, Cox, and Serkland were selected for their unique qualifications and their connections with key figures and organizations in the community that were closely associated with process study concerns. Reaching out to groups involved with parents and children, youth more broadly, education, social and health services, and the black ethnic community, the three process analysts not only succeeded in collecting relevant non-Family Matters Program material described above, they also obtained much information through informal contacts and through attendance at meetings (e.g., the School Committee, Child and Family Services, a city-sponsored neighborhood group meeting with the mayor, etc.). The author was also able to meet and cultivate an acquaintanceship with the mayor's special assistant for neighborhoods.

Interviews

In addition to these more episodic aspects of data collection related to community persons' perspectives, systematic study was conducted as well. Process analyst Boyd, a prominent member of the Syracuse leadership community and a former employee of Onondaga County government, spearheaded this dimension of our research which was essentially an analysis of community leaders' perceptions of the Syracuse environment as a developmental context and the Family Matters Program. Using a format patterned after the "Stresses and Supports Interview" designed by the project's outcome research component, Boyd structured a Community Perceptions Interview to probe the views of key figures in the city to determine which factors they saw as facilitating the task of child rearing and those that made it more difficult.

Fifty-seven completed interviews were obtained from policy makers, high-level management in human service agencies, service deliverers themselves, and community "gatekeepers." The policy makers interviewed included several county legislators, the director of the metropolitan development association, several members of the city's common council, and the chief of police.

Upper echelon human service management personnel interviewed were the deputy director of the Department of Social Social Services, the deputy commissioner for Probation, the research director for Health System Agencies for Central New York, and the administrators of three local hospitals. Other top management in social and related services were queried; for example, the directors of the Jewish Welfare Federation, Catholic Charities, Child and Family Services, Project Head Start, and the NAACP. Also interviewed were various service deliverers who were staff members of various human service agencies, as well as social workers functioning under both public and private auspices.

The community gatekeepers questioned included several local clergymen from both the black and the white communities, local organizers of both of these races, and the vice president of a Syracuse community college and other persons associated with the educational system.

Topics Analyzed

In the interviews with community persons and in other data gathering from these sources as well, we were concerned with answering the following questions: (1) How was the Family Matters Program perceived in the community? (2) Which, if any, of its effects were not noticeable to community leaders? (3) Generally what were the needs of families with young children? (4) Which external forces made their task more difficult and which facilitated parenting activities? And most fundamentally, (5) what was the result of forces among program efforts, and facilitating or hindering factors in the urban environment?

FIELD RESEARCH AND SUPPORT STAFF

The last perspective to be documented was that provided by project support staff and by the field research staff assigned to collect baseline and outcome data related to program effects. Our priority scheme assigned the lowest rung to this perspective, although our data collection suggested that especially with regard to the field research staff, the information they provided was far from trivial. Field research staff members in general spent approximately ten hours in the homes of both program and control group families in each of the two waves of data collection. The formal interviews, their observations in the homes and neighborhoods, and the informal conversations constituted a treasure-trove of data. This was true for four reasons: (1) the 20 or so hours spent by research staff members was for some families more time than they ever spent with their program worker (sometimes this lack was the responsibility of the worker, sometimes the decision of the family); (2) for control families, the research contacts were their sole experience with the project; (3) some of the highly idealistic research staff members befriended some of the families, and, in at least a few cases, assumed a role as pseudo-home-visitors (even though this was against project policy and sometimes defeated the carefully drawn distinction between program and control families); and (4) families sometimes felt comfortable enough to confide to research staff members their feelings about the program or the project that they might not have divulged to program or liaison workers.

Since we had regular contact with both the field research and support staff in both Syracuse and Ithaca, participant observation, informal discussion, and access to project memos all allowed us a good deal of exposure to the views of these staff members. Also, periodic interviews, especially those conducted as employees left the project, gave us a large amount of information. The number of interviews ranged from one, for some support persons, to as many as three or four, for research staff or for the administrative-aide who had served the program staff since the project's inception. Although somewhat less effort went into documenting this last perspective, much valuable material did emerge and this phase of the research has received its due attention.

Topics Analyzed

In debriefing the field research staff, we aimed at shedding light on such questions as: (1) What was it like to be the parents of young children in the environment studied? (2) How did these parents react to the research component of the project? (3) What influences did research participation have on program participation? And a very important question, (4) what, if any, changes would be observed in program families between baseline measurement and outcome assessment approximately three years later? Of the support staff we asked the fundamental question: What was it like to be on the inside (structurally and organizationally) of the day-to-day processes of program and project operations?

QUALITATIVE ANALYSES

Qualitative analyses were carried out on the ethnographic data discussed above. Most interviews were recorded on audio-tape, and content analytic techniques were utilized including verbatim transcription of interviews and field notes. These transcriptions were typed on special protocol forms with numbered lines and a very wide left-hand margin. Protocols also contained information on the time, place, and subject of each observation, the name of the recording process analyst, and a number unique to each protocol. In these protocols, factual material was explicitly distinguished from observer comment. Analysis and content coding were done by the original recording process analyst in a manner that permitted easy retrieval of subject matter by protocols and lines within each protocol through cataloguing, indexing, "densification," and cross-referencing, according to techniques developed by Schatzman and Strauss (1973) and Rist (1979). This approach to analysis allowed for the preservation of the ethnographic flavor, breadth, and depth, while at the same time helping us to avoid impressionistic interpretation of the data and excessive anecdotalism in aggregating material for the interpretative process.

Far more data were collected on the Family Matters Programs than can be reported in this volume. The original intent of the ethnographic data collection was simply the delineation of a case study, with far less emphasis by way of comparative material. The winds of *zeitgeist* about childhood intervention and other social programs have shifted considerably since the inception of the process study. This and other factors have mandated less emphasis on the case study, and more on the comparative material. The author hopes that the approach ultimately decided upon will be found to be valuable to the reader but he cannot help but bewail the limitations that the breadth sought here has placed on the presentation of detail supporting the inferences drawn. Most of our conclusions are put forward without the dozens of citations, quotations, and "proof-texts" that stand behind the inferences. The interested reader is invited to write to the author for study reports that provide more detail in specific topic areas than much of the material presented here, or to monitor the relevant research literature areas for past and future papers.

BIBLIOGRAPHY

Abbott, D. (1979, December 2). "Zone Patrol New City Police Strategy." *Syracuse Herald-American*, p. 18

Abt Associates, Inc. (1981, April 4). *Child and Family Resource Program.* Presentation at the 1981 Society for Research in Child Development.

Advisory Committee on Child Development, National Research Council. (1976). *Toward a National Policy for Children and Families.* Washington, D.C.: National Academy of Sciences, p. 92.

Andrews, R.W. (1981, March 25). "Steam Plant Hearings Offer Projection of Pollutants." *The Syracuse Post-Standard*, p. C-1.

Auerbach, M.M. (1974). "On Burke," *International Encyclopedia of the Social Sciences.* New York: Macmillan, The Free Press, p. 222.

Ausubel, D.P. (1964). "How Reversible are the Cognitive and Motivational Effects of Cultural Deprivation? Implications for Teaching the Culturally Deprived Child." *Urban Education, 1,* 16-38.

Bandura, A., and Mischel, W. (1965). "Modification of Self-Imposed Delay of Reward Through Exposure to Live and Symbolic Models." *Journal of Personality and Social Psychology, 2,* 698-705.

Banfield, E.C. (1974). *The Unheavenly City.* Boston: Little, Brown.

Barker, R.G., and Schoggen, P. (1973). *Qualities of Community Life.* San Francisco: Jossey-Bass.

Baumrind, D. (1972). "An Exploratory Study of Socialization Effects on Black Children: Some Black-White Comparison." *Child Development, 43,* 261-67.

Beach, F.A. (1950). "The Snark was a Boojum." *American Psychologist, 5,* 115-24.

Beller, E.K. (1979). "Early Intervention Programs." In *Handbook of Infant Development,* edited by J.D. Osofsky, pp. 852-96. New York: Wiley.

Bennis, W. (1969). *Organization Development: Its Nature, Origins, and Prospects.* Reading: Addison-Wesley.

Berger, J. (1984, September 19). "Study Reports Exodus of Affluent and Educated New Yorkers in Late 70's." *The New York Times,* B-1.

Berk, R.A. (1983, June). "An Introduction to Sample Selection Bias in Sociological Data." *American Sociological Review, 48,* 386-98.

Berman, P., and McLaughlin, M.W. (1978). "Federal Support for Improved Educational Practice." In *The Federal Interest in Financing Schooling,* edited by M. Timpane, pp. 209-28. Cambridge: Ballinger.

Blatt, B., and Garfunkel, F. (1969). *The Educability of Intelligence: Preschool Intervention with Disadvantaged Children.* Washington, D.C.: The Council for Exceptional Children, Inc.

Bliven, L.F. (1980, March 19). "Carey Budget Cuts Not Likely to Pass." *The Syracuse Post-Standard.*

Bloom, B.S. (1964). *Stability and Change in Human Characteristics.* New York: Wiley.

Bo, I. (1979, June 30). *In Support of Families: The Pilot Testing of Two Experimental Programs.* Paper prepared for the Carnegie Corporation of New York.

Boswell, J. (1973). *The Rise and Decline of Small Firms.* London: Allen & Unwin.

Bowers, K.S. (1973). "Situationism in Psychology: An Analysis and a Critique." *Psychological Review, 30,* 307-36.

Boyer, R., and Savageau, D. (1981). *Places Rated Almanac: Your Guide to Finding the Best Places to Live in America.* Chicago: Rand McNally.

Bronfenbrenner, U. (1974). "A Report on Longitudinal Evaluations of Preschool Programs." In *Is Early Intervention Effective?* (Vol. 2). Washington, D.C.: Department of Health, Education and Welfare.

Bronfenbrenner, U. (1977, February, 7). Memo on Treatment I. Memo to M. Cochran, Cornell University.

Bronfenbrenner, U. (1979a). "Head Start, A Retrospective View: The Founders." In *Project Head Start: A Legacy of the War on Poverty*, edited by E. Zigler and J. Valentine, pp. 77-88. New York: The Free Press.

Bronfenbrenner, U. (1979b). *The Ecology of Human Development*. Cambridge, Mass.: Harvard University Press.

Bronfenbrenner, U. (1980, February). Paper delivered to the Executive Staff of the National Institute of Education. Bethesda, Maryland.

Bronfenbrenner, U., and Cochran, M. (1976, January 1). *The Comparative Ecology of Human Development: A Research Proposal*. Cornell University.

Bronfenbrenner, U., and Cochran, M. (1977, February). Memo to staff and consultants. Cornell University.

Cain, G.G., and Goldberger, A.S. (1983, October). "Public and Private Schools Revisited." *Sociology of Education, 56*, 208-16.

Campbell, D.T. (1971, September). Methods for the experimenting society. Paper presented at the meeting of the American Psychological Association, Washington, D.C.

Campbell, D.T. (1975, December). "On the Conflicts Between Biological and Social Evolution and Between Psychology and Moral Tradition." *American Psychologist*, 1103-23.

Carnegie Corporation Quarterly (1978, Summer).

Chen, H., and Rossi, P.H. (1980, September). "The Multi-Goal, Theory-Driven Approach to Evaluation: A Model Linking Basic and Applied Social Science." *Social Forces, 59*, 106-122.

Cicirelli, V., et al. (1969, June). The impact of Head Start: An evaluation of Head Start on children's cognitive and affective development. Report presented to the Office of Economic Opportunity, pursuant to Contract B89-4536. (Report No. 184 328). Westinghouse Learning Corporation for Federal Scientific and Technical Information, U.S. Institute for Applied Technology.

Cochran, M. (1977, January 24). The inclusion of the parent-child specialist intervention in the Ecology of Human Development Project. Memo to U. Bronfenbrenner, Cornell University.

Cochran, M.M., and Brassard, J.A. (1979). "Child Development and Personal Social Networks." *Child Development, 50*, 601-16.

Cochran, M., and Woolever, F. (1978, February). Program II: The neighborhood worker. Internal Document. Cornell University.

Cochran, M. and Woolever, F. (1980, April). *A Family Support Strategy: Fusing Family and Neighborhood Components*. Progress report submitted to the National Institute of Education.

Cole, M. (1979). Forward. In *The Ecology of Human Development: Experiments by Nature and Design*, by U. Bronfenbrenner, pp. vii-x. Cambridge, Mass.: Harvard University Press.

Coleman, J. (1972). [Introductory quote]. "On The Utility of Ethnographic Research for the Policy Process." In *Urban Education*, 15(4), by R.C. Rist (1981, January), 485-94.

Coleman, J.S., Campbell, E.Q., Hobson, C.J., McPartland, J., Mood, A.M., Weinfeld, F.D., and York, R.L. (1966). *Equality of Educational Opportunity*. Washington, D.C.: Government Printing Office.

Coleman, J.S., and Hoffer, T. (1983, October). "Response to Taeuber-James, Cain-Goldberger and Morgan." *Sociology of Education, 56*, 219-34.

Coleman, J.S., Hoffer, T., and Kilgore, S. (1981). Public and private schools. Draft Report submitted to the National Center for Education Statistics, Washington, D.C.

Coleman, J.S., Hoffer, T., and Kilgore, S. (1982). "Cognitive Outcomes in Public and Private Schools." *Sociology of Education, 55*, 65-76.

Connor, M. (1979, December 12). "Alexander's Style Altered City's Local, National Image." *The Syracuse Post-Journal*.

Cook, S.W. (1983, April 14). "Experimenting on Social Issues: The Case of School. Desegregation." Lecture in the Psychology Lectureship Series. New York: New York University.

Costello, J. (1983, April 24). Variations in the Effectiveness of Parent-Child Support Programs. Discussant for the symposium presented at the annual meeting of the Society for Research on Child Development, Detroit, Mich.

Cox, K.R. (Ed.). (1978). *Urbanization and Conflict in Market Societies.* Chicago: Maaroufa Press.

Crain, R.L., and Mahard, R.E. (1983). "The Effect of Research Methodology on Desegregation-Achievement Studies: A Meta-Analysis." *American Journal of Sociology, 88*(5), 839-53.

Cronbach, L.J. (1975). "Beyond the Two Disciplines of Scientific Psychology." *American Psychologist, 30,* 116-27.

Cross, W., Bronfenbrenner, U., and Cochran, M. (1977, August). *Black Families and Socialization of Black Children: An Ecological Approach.* Proposal submitted to the Administration for Children, Youth, and Families, DHEW.

Dahl, R.A., and Lindblom, C.A. (1953). *Politics, Economics, and Welfare: Planning Politico-Economic Systems Resolved into Basic Social Processes.* New York: Harper & Row.

Datta, L. (1979). Another Spring and Other Hopes: "Some Findings from National Evaluations of Project Head Start." In *Project Head Start: A Legacy of the War on Poverty,* edited by E.F. Zigler and J. Valentine, pp. 405-32. New York: The Free Press.

Dawson, P., and van Doorninck, W.J. (1979, March 17). *Increasing the Effectiveness of Parent-Infant Support Program: Lessons from the Parent-Infant Project.* University of Colorado Health Sciences Center.

Deutsch, C.P. (1973). "Social Class and Child Development." In *Review of Child Development Research* (Vol. 3), edited by B.M. Caldwell and H.R. Ricciuti. Chicago: University of Chicago Press.

Donzelot, J. (1979). *The Policing of Families.* New York: Random House.

Driscoll, N. (1979, December 2). "City Tax Assessment Blasted." *Syracuse Herald-American,* p. 17.

Dunn, E.P. (1980, April 14). "Neighborhood Watch: Crime Early Warning System?" *Syracuse Post-Standard,* p. C-1.

Elmore, E.F. (1978, Spring). "Organizational Models of Social Program Implementation." *Public Policy, 26*(2), 185-228.

Epstein, E.J. (1977). *Agency of Fear.* New York: Putnam.

Eysenck, H.J. (1952). "The Effects of Psychotherapy: An Evaluation." *Journal of Consulting Psychology, 16*, 319-24.

Fabian, D., and Pitkin, A. (1979, November 1). *Early History and Organizational Development of the Family Matters Project.* Internal document, Cornell University.

Family Matters. (1977). Draft of Program I guidelines for families. Cornell University.

Family Matters. (1978, July 26). Minutes of project meeting. Internal document. Ithaca. Cornell University.

Farrar, E., DeSanctis, J.E., and Cohen, D.K. (1980, Fall). "Views From Below: Implementation Research in Education." *Teachers College Record, 82*(1), 77-100.

Fetterman, D.M. (1982). "Blaming the Victim: The Problem of Evaluation Design and Federal Involvement, and Reinforcing World Views in Education." In *Evaluation Studies Review Annual*, edited by E.R. House, S. Mathison, J.A. Pearsol, and H. Preskill, pp. 65-76. Beverly Hills: Sage Publications, Inc.

Fienberg, S.E. (1977). "The Collection of Analysis of Ethnographic Data in Educational Research." *Anthropology and Education Quarterly, 8*(2), 50-57.

Forrester, J.W. (1971). "Counterintuitive Behavior of Social Systems." *Theory and Decision, 2*, 109-40.

Fredericksen, L.W. (1984, Spring). "Editorial: Marketing OBM." *Journal of Organizational Behavior Management, 6*(1), 1-3.

Freire, P. (1971). *Pedagogy of the Oppressed.* New York: Herder & Herder.

Gale, S., and Moore, E.G. (Eds.). (1975). *The Manipulated City.* Chicago: Maaroufa Press.

Glazer, M. (1972). *The Research Adventure: Promise and Problems of Field Work.* New York: Random House.

Gordon, E.W. (1979). "Evaluation During the Early Years of Head Start." In *Project Head Start: A Legacy of the War on Poverty*, edited by E.F. Zigler and J. Valentine, pp. 399-404. New York: The Free Press.

Grace, J.P. (1984a). *War on Waste: President's Private Sector Survey on Cost Control.* New York: Macmillan.

Grace, J.P. (1984b). *Burning Money: The Waste of Your Tax Dollars.* New York: Macmillan.

Gray, S.W., and Wandersman, L.P. (1980). "The Methodology of Home-based Intervention Studies: Problems and Promising Strategies." *Child Development, 51,* 993-1009.

Groeneveld, L.P., Tuma, N.B., and Hannan, M.T. (1980). The effects of negative income tax programs on marital dissolution. *Journal of Human Resources, 15,* 654-74.

"Group Wants City Plan Audited." (1980, March 27). *The Syracuse Post-Standard.*

Guba, E.G. (1969). "The Failure of Educational Evaluation." *Educational Technology, 9*(5), 29-38.

Hall, S. (1980, October). Syracuse. Internal document of the Ecology of Human Development Project. Ithaca, N.Y. Cornell University, Department of Human Development and Family Studies.

Halpern. R. (1984, January). "Lack of Effects for Home-Based Early Interventions? Some Possible Explanations." *American Journal of Orthopsychiatry, 54*(1), 33-42.

Harrington, M. (1974). "The Welfare State and Its Neoconservative Critics." In *The New Conservatives: A Critique From the Left,* edited by L.A. Coser and I. Howe, pp. 29-63. New York: Quadrangle/The New York Times Book Co.

Harvey, D. (1978). "Labor, Capital, and Class Struggle Around the Built Environment in Advanced Capitalist Societies." In *Urbanization and Conflict in Market Societies,* edited by K.R. Cox. Chicago: Maaroufa Press.

Heider, F. (1958). *The Psychology of Interpersonal Relations.* New York: Wiley.

Heller, T. (1980). The effects of involuntary relocation: A review. Chicago, Ill.: Illinois Institute for Developmental Disabilities. Unpublished report.

Henig, J.R. (1982). *Neighborhood Mobilization: Redevelopment and Response.* New Brunswick, NJ: Rutgers University Press.

Henshel, R.L. (1976). *Reacting to Social Problems.* Don Mills, Ontario: Longman Canada.

Hess, R.D., and Shipman, V. (1965). "Early Experience and the Socialization of Cognitive Modes in Children." *Child Development, 34,* 869-86.

Horowitz, D., and Erlich, R. (1974). "Proving Poverty Pays: Big Brother as a Holding Company." In *The Poverty Establishment,* edited by P. Roby, pp. 141-56. Englewood Cliffs: Prentice-Hall.

Hunt, J.M. (1961). *Intelligence and Experience.* New York: Ronald Press.

Ilich, I. (1976). *Medical Nemesis.* New York: Bantam.

Jamieson, K., Gallo, P.S., Jr., and Christian, K. (1977, April). *The strength of experimental effects in the psychological literature — How well are we doing?* Paper presented at the Western Psychological Association Meeting, Seattle, Wash.

Kahn, A.H., and Kamerman, S.B. (1982). *Helping America's Families.* Philadelphia: Temple University Press.

Kaplan, S. (1976, September 6). *On the Fear of Cognitive Chaos.* Paper presented at the annual meeting of the American Psychological Association. Washington, D.C.

Karnes, M.B. (1969). *Research and development program on preschool disadvantaged children: Final report.* Washington, D.C.: U.S. Office of Education.

Katz, D., and Kahn, R. (1978). *The Social Psychology of Organizations* (2nd ed.). New York: Wiley.

Keniston, K. (1977). *All Our Children: The American Family Under Pressure.* (1st ed.). New York: Carnegie Council on Children.

Kertzer, M.N. (1976). *Tel Me, Rabbi.* New York: Collier Books.

Kimberly, J.R. (1979). Issues in the Creation of Organizations: Initiation, Innovations, and Institutionalization. *Academy of Management Journal, 22,* 437-57.

Kimberly, J.R., Miles, R.H., and Associates. (1980). *The organizational life cycle: Issues in the creation, transformation, and decline of organizations.* San Francisco: Jossey-Bass.

Kirschner Associates, Albuquerque, N.M. (1970, May). *A National Survey of the Impacts of Head Start Centers on Community Institutions.* Washington, D.C.: OEO (ED045195).

Knudsen, J.H., Scott, R.A. and Shore, A.R. (1977). "Household Composition." In *The New Jersey Income-Maintenance Experiment: Vol. III. Expenditures, Health, and Social Behavior; and the Quality of the Evidence,* edited by H.W. Watts and A. Rees. New York: Academic Press.

Kozol, J. (1967). *Death at an Early Age.* Boston: Houghton Mifflin.

Kuhn, T.S. (1962). *The Structure of Scientific Revolutions.* Chicago: University of Chicago Press.

Lally, J.R. and Honig, A.S. (1977, April). The Family Development Research Program: A Program for Prenatal, Infant, and Early Childhood Enrichment. Syracuse, N.Y.: Family Development Research Program.

Lally, J.R., Mindick, B., Darlington, R., Honig, A., Barnett, W.S., and Haiman, P.E. (1982, July 27). *The Effects of the Family Development Research Program on Families, Children, and Staff: A follow up study of low income/low education families whose children received continuous health, social, psychological and cognitive services from birth to five years of age.* San Francisco: Far West Laboratory for Educational Research and Development.

Lambie, D.Z., Bond, J.T., and Weikart, D.P. (1974). *Home teaching with mothers and infants: the Ypsilanti-Carnegie Infant Education Project — an experiment.* (Monograph Series, No. 2). Ypsilanti, Mich.: High/Scope Educational Research Foundation.

Lambro, D. (1980). *Fat City: How Washington Wastes Your Taxes.* South Bend: Regnery/Gateway.

Lazar, I. (1979). "Social Services in Head Start." In *Project Head Start: A Legacy of the War on Poverty,* edited by E.F. Zigler and J. Valentine. pp. 283-90. New York: The Free Press.

Lazar, I., and Darlington, R. (1982). "Lasting Effects of Early Education: A Report From the Consortium for Longitudinal Studies." *Monographs of the Society for Research in Child Development, 47*(2-3, Serial No. 195).

Leamer, E.E. (1983, March). "Let's Take the Con out of Econometrics." *The American Economic Review, 73*(1), 31-43.

Lerman, P. (1968). "Evaluative Studies of Institutions for Delinquents: Implications for Research and Social Policy." *Social Work, XII*(4), 55-64.

Levenstein, P. (1972). *Verbal Interaction Project*. Mineola: Family Service Association of Nassau County, Inc.

Levitan, S., and Taggart, R. (1976). *The Promise of Greatness*. Cambridge, Mass.: Harvard University Press.

Lipsett, J. (1979, June). Parent Education from 1925-1979: Family-Centered Programs in N.Y.S. Cooperative Extension and the College of Human Ecology. Unpublished manuscript. Ithaca, N.Y.: Cornell University, Department of Human Development and Family Studies.

Lyman, P. (1982, January). "Syracuse Ranks Seventh in 'Livability'." *Syracuse Herald Journal*, pp. A1, A2.

Lynn, L.E., and Salasin, S. (Eds). (1974, Spring). *Evaluation. Special Issue: The Human Services Shortfall*, 4-5.

Lyon, D.W. (1976, December). *Welfare Policy Research for New York City: The Record of a Five-Year Project* (R-2119-RC). Santa Monica: The Rand Corporation.

Maccoby, E.E. (1983, April). Presidential address at the Annual Meeting of the Society for Research in Child Development, Detroit, Mich.

Maddaus, J. (1978, October). The role of the neighborhood worker: An assessment and alternative proposal. Internal document, Family Matters.

Majone, G., and Wildavsky, A. (1978). "Implementation as Evolution." In *Policy Studies Review Annual* (Vol. 2), H.E. Freeman (Ed.). Beverly Hills: Sage Publications.

McClelland, D.C. (1961). *The Achieving Society*. Princeton: D. Van Nostrand Reinhold.

McClelland, D.D., Atkinson, J.W., Clark, R.A., and Lowell, E.L. (1953). *The Achievement Motive*. New York: Appleton-Century-Crofts.

McClintock, C.C., Brannon, D., and Maynard-Moody, S. (1979). "Applying the Logic of Sample Surveys to Qualitative Case Studies: The Case Cluster Method." *Administrative Science Quarterly, 24*, 612-29.

Mills, E.S., and McKinnon, J. (1973). "Notes on the New Urban Economics." *Bell Journal of Economics and Management Science, 4*, 593-601.

Miles, R.H., and Randolph, W.A. (1980). "Influence of Organizational Learning Styles on Early Development." In *The Organizational Life Cycle: Issues in the Creation, Transformation, and Decline of Organizations*, edited by R.H. Miles and W.A. Randolph, pp. 44-82. San Francisco: Jossey-Bass.

Mindick, B. (1979, September 1). Personality characteristics as Transsituational Predictors of Contraceptive Behavior. Paper presented at the meeting of the American Psychological Association, Toronto, Ontario, Canada.

Mindick, B. (1980a, May). *Salt City and family matters: Supporting families in the urban environment*. Report prepared for the Carnegie Corporation of New York, Cornell University.

Mindick, B. (1980b, June 5). Confidential Memorandum to the Principal Investigators on Programs. Internal document of the Ecology of Human Development Project. Ithaca, N.Y.: Cornell University, Department of Human Development and Family Studies.

Mindick, B. (1980c, December 15). Preliminary Process Study Report on Family Feedback Study. Internal Document of the Ecology of Human Development Project. Ithaca, N.Y.: Cornell University, Department of Human Development and Family Studies.

Mindick, B., and Boyd, E. (1982). A Multi-Level, Bipolar View of the Urban Residential Environment: Local Community vs. Mass Societal Forces. *Population and Environment: Behavioral and Social Issues, 5*, 221-41.

Mindick, B., and Cross, W.E., Jr. (1979, December). *A Report on Projected Plans for Ecology of Human Development Progress Study*. Prepared for the Carnegie Foundation.

Mindick, B., and Maples, M. (1980). Differences in Response Rates Associated with the Cross Identity Study. Internal Document of the Ecology of Human Development Project. Ithaca, N.Y.: Cornell University, Department of Human Development and Family Studies.

Mintz, M., and Cohen, J.S. (1976). *Power, Inc.*. New York: Viking.

Mischel, W. (1968). *Personality and Assessment*. New York: Wiley.

Mitford, J. (1974). *Kind and Usual Punishment*. New York: Random House.

Molnar, J. (1979, September). *On Working with Families and Children: An Account of the Syracuse "Family Matters" Training Program*. Paper prepared for the Carnegie Corporation of New York. Ithaca, N.Y.: Cornell University.

Moynihan, D.P. (1969). *Maximum Feasible Misunderstanding*. New York: The Free Press.

Moynihan, D.P. (1973). *The Politics of a Guaranteed Income*. New York: Random House.

Naisbitt, J. (1982). *Megatrends: Ten New Directions Transforming Our Lives*. New York: Warner Books.

Newer, D. (1979, December 17). Mortgage woes impede transfers. *The Syracuse Post-Standard*.

Nicol, E.H. (1976, October). *The History of the Brookline Early Education Project: The Planning Year*. Brookline: Brookline Early Education Project.

Nisbet, R. (1980). *History of the Idea of Progress*. New York: Basic Books.

Olson, M., Jr. (1965). *The Logic of Collective Action: Public Goods and the Theory of Groups* (Harvard Economic Studies, Vol. CXXIV). Cambridge, Mass.: Harvard University Press.

Orbell, J.M., and Uno, T. (1972). "A Theory of Neighborhood Problem Solving: Political Actions vs. Residential Mobility." *American Political Science Review, 66,* 471-89.

Orne, M.T. (1969). "Demand Characteristics and the Concept of Quasi-Controls." In *Artifact in Behavioral Research*, edited by R. Rosenthal and R.L. Rosnow, pp. 143-79. New York: Academic Press.

Orton, R.E. (1979). "Head Start: The Early Administrators." In *Project Head Start: A Legacy of the War on Poverty*, edited by E. Zigler and J. Valentine, pp. 129-134. New York: The Free Press.

Pells, R.H. (1973). *Radical Visions and American Dreams: Culture and Social Thought in the Depression*. New York: Harper & Row.

Perrow, C. (1978). "Demystifying Organizations." In *The Management of Human Services*, edited by R.C. Sarri and Y. Hasenfeld, pp. 105-20. New York: Columbia University Press.

Peters, K. (1979, December 27). "Bernardi Takes Office." *The Syracuse Post-Standard*.

Pierce, A. (1980, April 16). Interview with Mon Cochran.

Pierce, A. (1980, April 23). Interview with Urie Bronfenbrenner.

Pilisuk, M., and Pilisuk, P. (1973). *How We Lost the War on Poverty*. New Brunswick: Transaction Books.

Piven, F.F., and Cloward, R.A. (1971). *Regulating the Poor: The Functions of Public Welfare*. New York: Vintage, Random House.

Poirer, D. (1977). "The Determinants of Home Buying." In *New Jersey Income Maintenance*, edited by H.W. Watts, pp. 73-91. New York: Academic.

Powell, D.R. (1981, April). Creating and Sustaining Parent Groups: Critical Program Process Dimensions. Paper presented at the meeting of the Society for Research in Child Development, Boston, Mass.

Powell, D.R. (1982, May). "From Child to Parent: Changing Conceptions of Early Childhood Intervention." *Annals of the American Academy of Psychological and Social Sciences, 461*, 135-44.

Powell, D.R. (1984, January). "Social Network and Demographic Predictors of Length of Participation in a Parent Education Program." *Journal of Community Psychology, 12*, 13-20.

Pressman, J.L., and Wildavsky, A. (1979). *Implementation: How Great Expectations in Washington Are Dashed in Oakland; Or, Why It's Amazing that Federal Programs Work at All, this Being a Saga of the Economic Development Administration as Told by Two Sympathetic Observers Who Seek to Build Morals on a Foundation of Ruined Hopes*. (2nd ed.). Berkeley: University of California Press.

Ramey, C.T. (1982). Commentary on lasting effects of early education: A report from the Consortium for Longitudinal Studies. *Monographs of the Society for Research in Child Development, 47,* (2-3, Serial No. 195).

Ramey, C., Collier, A., Sparling, J., Loda, F., Campbell, F., Ingram, D., and Finkelstein, N. (1976). "The Carolina Abecedarian Project: A Longitudinal and Multi-Disciplinary Approach to the Prevention of Developmental Retardation." In *Interion Strategies for High Risk Infants and Young Children,* edited by T. Tjossem. Baltimore: University Park Press.

Rand Corporation. (1975, April). *Federal Programs Supporting Educational Change: The Findings in Review* (R-1589/4-HEW). Santa Monica, Calif.: Rand.

Raspberry, W. (1984, October 8). "Do Unto Others." *Washington Post.*

Richardson, H.W. (1977). *The New Urban Economics.* London: Pion.

Rist, R.C. (1981, January). "On the Utility of Ethnographic Research for the Policy Process." *Urban Education, 15*(4), 485-94.

Rist, R. (1979, November). Personal communication regarding qualitative research methodology and data management.

Rist, R. (1977). "On the Relations Among Educational Research Paradigms: From Disdain to Detente." *Anthropology and Education, 8,* 42-49.

Robinson, J.L., and Choper, W.B. (1979). "Another Perspective on Program Evaluation: The Parents Speak." In *Project Head Start: A Legacy of the War on Poverty,* edited by E. Zigler and J. Valentine, pp. 467-76. New York: The Free Press.

Rogers, C.R. (1954). *Psychotherapy and Personality Change.* Chicago: University of Chicago Press.

Rosenthal, R., and Rosnow, R.L. (1974). *The Volunteer Subject.* New York: Wiley.

Ross, C.J. (1979). "Early Skirmishes with Poverty: The Historical Roots of Head Start." In *Project Head Start: A Legacy of the War on Poverty,* edited by E. Zigler and J. Valentine, pp. 21-42. New York: The Free Press.

Rossi, P.H. (1966). "Boobytraps and Pitfalls in the Evaluation of Social Action Programs." In *Evaluating Action Programs: Readings in Social Action and Education*, edited by C.H. Weiss, pp. 224-235. Boston: Allyn & Bacon.

Rossi, P.H. (1981). *Think Before You Randomize: The Role of Theory in Social Experiments*. Paper presented at a collopuium at Cornell University, Ithaca, N.Y.

Rossi, P.H., Wright, J.D., and Wright, S.R. (1978, May). The Theory and Practice of Applied Social Research. *Evaluation Quarterly, 2*(2), 171-191.

Roweis, S., and Scott, A.J. (1978). "The Urban Land Question." In *Urbanization and Conflict in Market Societies*, edited by K.R. Cox, pp. 38-75. Chicago: Maaroufa Press, Inc.

Sacks, S., and Andrews, R. (1974). *The Syracuse black community, 1970.* Occasional paper #41. Syracuse: Syracuse University.

Schatzman, L., and Strauss, A.L. (1973). *Field Research: Strategies for a Natural Sociology*. Englewood Cliffs: Prentice-Hall.

Schlossman, S.L. (1976, August). "Before Home Start: Notes Toward a History of Parent Education in America, 1897-1929." *Harvard Educational Review, 46*(3), 436-67.

Shadish, W.R., Jr. (1982, Spring). "A Review and Critique of Controlled Studies of the Effectiveness of Preventive Child Health Care." *Health Policy Quarterly, 2*(1), 24-52.

Sharabany, R. (1978, March). Proposal for Experimental Intervention I. Parent-Child Specialist. Project document, Haifa University.

Sieber, S. (1981). *Fatal Remedies*. New York: Plenum Press.

Sowell, T. (1984). *Civil Rights: Rhetoric or Reality?* New York: William Monoward Co.

Stember, C.H. (1968). "Evaluating Effects of an Integrated Classroom." *Urban Review, II*(7), 3-4, 30-31.

Suttles, G.D. (1972). *The Social Construction of Communities*. Chicago: The University of Chicago Press.

Thunen, J.H. von. (1966). *Der Isolierte Staat in Beziehung auf Nationalo-konomie und Landwirschaft.* Stuttgart: Gustav Fischer. (Reprint of 1826)

Titch, S. (1980, March 28). "As Population Shifts, So Must Urban Policy." *The Syracuse Post-Standard*, p. B-8.

Toffler, A. (1970). *Future Shock.* New York: Bantam.

Toffler, A. (1980). *The Third Wave.* New York: Bantam.

Travers, J. (1979, November). Letter to O. Moles. Unpublished Document, National Institute of Education.

Travers, J.R., and Light, R.J. (1982). *Learning From Experience: Evaluating Early Childhood Demonstration Programs.* Washington, D.C.: National Academy Press.

Trimble, J.E. (1980). "Forced Migration: Its Impact on Shaping Coping Strategies." In *Uprooting and Development: Dilemmas of Coping with Modernization*, edited by G.V. Coelho and P.I. Ahmed. New York: Plenum Press.

Truman, D.B. (1958). *The Governmental Process.* New York: Knopf.

Tuckman, B.W. (1965). "Developmental Sequence in Small Groups." *Psychological Bulletin, 63*, 384-99.

Twain, D. (1983). *Creating Change in Social Settings.* New York: Praeger.

U.S. Bureau of Census in Onondaga County, New York. Preliminary census figures. Undated printed material obtained May, 1981.

Valentine, J., and Stark, E. (1979). "The Social Context of Parent Involvement." In *Project Head Start: A Legacy of the War on Poverty*, edited by E. Zigler and J. Valentine, pp. 291-314. New York: The Free Press.

Weeks, E.C. (1979). *Factors affecting the utilization of evaluation findings in administrative decision making.* Unpublished doctoral dissertation, University of California at Irvine.

Weiss, C.H. (1972). *Evaluation Research: Methods of Assessing Program Effectiveness.* Englewood Cliffs: Prentice-Hall.

White, B. (1975). Reassessing Our Educational Priorities. *Report of the National Conference on Parent/Early Childhood Education* (pp. 37-41). Washington, D.C.: U.S. Office of Education.

White, K.R. (1982, May). "The Relation Between Socioeconomic Status and Academic Achievement." *Psychological Bulletin, 91*(3), 461-81.

Wilson, J.Q. (1973). *Varieties of Police Behavior.* New York: Atheneum.

Woolever, F. (1978, January). Working Paper: General principles for program components. Internal document.

Woolever, F. (1979, November). *Ecology of Human Development.* Progress Report on the Program Component, prepared for the Mott and Kellogg Foundations and the National Institute of Education.

Working Committee on Program I. (1977a, November 2). Defining Program I. Memo to project staff. Internal document.

Working Committee on Program I. (1977b, November 7). The activities home visitor. Memo to project staff. Internal document.

Zelnik, M. and Kantner, J. (1980, March). Untitled presentation made by Melvin Zelnik at the Center for Population Research Workshop for researchers in the area of adolescent fertility.

Zigler, E. (1979). "Head Start: Not a Program but an Evolving Concept." In *Project Head Start: A Legacy of the War on Poverty*, edited by E.F. Zigler and J. Valentine, pp. 367-98. New York: The Free Press.

Zigler, E.F., and Valentine, J. (Eds.). (1979). *Project Head Start: A Legacy of the War on Poverty.* New York: The Free Press.

Ziman, J.M. (1968). *Public Knowledge.* London: Cambridge University.

INDEX

ABOUT THE AUTHOR

BURTON MINDICK is a Senior Research Associate in the department of sociology at Cornell University. Also an associate of the Cornell International Population Program, he has published in such diverse areas as: population psychology, urban affairs, program evaluation, and personality development.

Dr. Mindick is co-editor of the journal, *Population and Environment: Behavioral and Social Issues*. Family life has been an important focus of his research for more than a decade now. It has involved him in both ethnographic and quantitative studies, evaluation, and substantive subject areas in various field sites stretching from California, to New York state, to Costa Rica. Similarly broad is his academic training which includes six degrees in science, education, and theology. His interest in the contemporary social issues in the urban context is not strictly a theoretical one, since Dr. Mindick has also served as a member of the Planning Commission for the city of Irvine, California.